PLOWING THE SEA

PLOWING THE SEA

Nurturing the Hidden Sources of Growth in the Developing World

MICHAEL FAIRBANKS & STACE LINDSAY

MONITOR COMPANY

Foreword by Michael E. Porter

Harvard Business School Press
Boston, Massachusetts

Copyright © 1997 by Michael Fairbanks, Stace Lindsay, and Monitor Company

Printed in the United States of America

01 00 99 98 97   5 4 3 2 1

Library of Congress Cataloging-in-Publication Data

Fairbanks, Michael.
    Plowing the sea : nurturing the hidden sources of growth in the
developing world / Michael Fairbanks and Stace Lindsay.
       p.   cm.
    Includes bibliographical references and index.
    ISBN 0-87584-761-7 (alk. paper)
    1. Industries—Andes Region—Case studies. 2. Industrial policy—Andes
Region—Case studies. 3. Andes Region—Economic conditions—Case studies. 4. Andes Region—Economic policy—Case studies. 5. Economic development—Case studies. I. Lindsay, Stace. II. Title
HC 167.A5F35 1997
    338.098—dc21   96-35391
                                                                                                    CIP

The paper used in this publication meets the requirements of the American National
Standard for Permanence of Paper for Printed Library Materials Z39.49-1984

Whomsoever has worked for a revolution has plowed the sea.

—*Simón Bolívar's epitaph*

Contents

Foreword

Michael E. Porter

In my book *The Competitive Advantage of Nations* (1990), I undertook to explain the sources of sustained national prosperity in the modern global economy. I argued that wealth is governed by productivity, or the value created per day of work, dollar of capital invested, and unit of the nation's physical resources employed. Improving national productivity depends on simultaneously upgrading the sophistication of company strategies and the quality of the national business environment. My research in ten industrial nations and subsequently in many others established the conditions governing the process of national (and regional) economic upgrading and the role of business and government in the process. Progress depends on improving and specializing the local factors of production, making a nation's home demand more sophisticated to help local producers anticipate and respond to international needs, unleashing local rivalry on increasingly advanced competitive dimensions, and building clusters of related and supporting firms and industries.

The heartening attention my book has received stems from at least two reasons. First, the book came at a good time, when nations were refocusing, turning away from the cold war and toward improving prosperity for their citizens. Yet coping with the global economy has proved difficult. In many parts of the world, the rich have been getting richer and the poor have been getting poorer, especially in Latin America. The quality of relationships between the governments and the private sector has often been strained. National leaders, still prone to overvalue the importance of natural endowments, have been puzzled that oil, minerals, and other natural assets no longer create the wealth they once did. My book provided a systematic framework for addressing these problems.

Second, while much progress has been made in understanding the macroeconomic side of development, there has been an increasing recognition that macroeconomic reform is necessary but not sufficient. As, or more, important are the microeconomic foundations of development, rooted in the nature of firm strategies and in the institutions, resources, and policies that constitute the environment in which firms compete. My book filled a gap in its focus on the microeconomic side of competitiveness.

Michael Fairbanks and Stace Lindsay have experienced the process and problems of economic development firsthand. Unlike many academically trained development specialists, they started their respective careers as a Peace Corps teacher in Africa and a grass roots community activist in Central America. They have come to advise scores of companies and many heads of state on how to think about firm-level competitiveness and national economic development in some of the world's most challenging business environments. Much of what they have learned is captured in the pages that follow.

This book builds on my work in three important ways. First, while I am a scholar and concentrate on ideas, Fairbanks and Lindsay are practitioners. They have built on my work and also on that of others such as James Austin and Chris Argyris, and have shown how these ideas apply in practice. The book is brimming with rich case studies that will inform both theory and practice for years to come. Most importantly, however, the book is based not just on ideas but on the results Fairbanks and Lindsay have achieved during projects set in many countries.

Second, while my work sought to articulate an overarching framework that applied to any country, Fairbanks and Lindsay focus their attention on developing nations with very difficult business environments. They have worked in such countries as Haiti, the Russian Federation, Peru, Bolivia, and South Africa, and are frequent contributors to the dialogue on early-stage economic development at the World Bank, the United Nations, and other development and educational institutions.

Third, while my work set out a normative framework, Fairbanks and

Lindsay break important new ground in their focus on the change process. Understanding what to do to advance the economy in a developing nation is not enough, an observation my own experiences confirm over and over again. Equally, if not more, challenging is getting change to happen, because of disagreements over the appropriate competitiveness paradigm, deep-seated suspicions between business and government, overlapping and conflicting roles and responsibilities in government itself, and other causes. Fairbanks and Lindsay offer a wealth of valuable insight into the barriers to change in countries and how to overcome them.

The ultimate purpose of this book is to establish and contribute to, in developing nations, a more constructive dialogue about the role of firms and governments in wealth creation and distribution. Many of the examples in the book are drawn from the Andes, a recent focus of the work of Fairbanks and Lindsay. But the lessons here are applicable in many locations: Africa, Asia, and even less developed parts of advanced countries, including the United States.

I titled my own book *The Competitive Advantage of Nations* to highlight the important distinction between comparative advantage and competitive advantage as sources of wealth. Fairbanks and Lindsay show that failure to understand this distinction is one of the root causes of the problem of economic development. *Plowing the Sea* is a vivid and eloquent statement of why developing nations must embrace the new competitiveness paradigm.

If, as I have contended, the macroeconomic agenda of the developing world is becoming well understood, then it is time that leaders in both the public and private sectors in developing countries begin to work together to tackle the shared microeconomic agenda. This book represents an important and timely resource for doing so.

Michael E. Porter
Professor
Harvard Business School

Preface: The Hope of Nations

> You can fall asleep to dream or you can dream to change the world.
> —*Frantz Fanon (1925–1961), Martinican psychiatrist, philosopher, political activist*

A great many developing nations are in economic crisis today, but not exactly because they are doing the wrong things. Rather, they are doing the right things for times they no longer live in. That may seem a subtle distinction and little consolation, especially in the countries of the Andes—Colombia, Venezuela, Peru, Bolivia, and Ecuador—whose businesses, and whose children, seem to be falling further and further behind the leading industrial democracies every year. But we have worked extensively in that region, have learned from and advised virtually all of its leaders in the arena of competitiveness, and we have found reason to hope.

Hope is not only for the Andean countries but also for poor countries all over Latin America, the Middle East, the former Soviet Union, and Africa, where we have also worked. It is a hope grounded in a framework for change, which we believe has helped our clients to take action, a framework in which the competitive advantages of knowledge supersede the advantages of nature. Moreover, hope is kept alive by a growing conviction that the leaders of developing nations are open to change as never before and are willing to commit themselves to the new fundamentals of economic development without really having made a success of the old ones. Countries do not have to follow outdated assumptions to the bitter end.

What is less certain is whether those new principles of economic development will actually be put into practice soon enough to make a difference to the people of our own generation. The situation is urgent, and yet the solutions cannot be rushed. Andean leaders will have to work their way through layer upon layer of inherited polemic, cynicism, and bureaucratic rigidity. The most determined among them will struggle to keep to their work and can expect little to show for their efforts for many years to come. Nor will they be able to achieve much on their own. Some novel experiments in public and private sector partnership will have to be tried to prepare citizens for the often unprecedented, long-term investments in business infrastructure, market development, and public education. These investments will have to be made under increasingly desperate conditions, which tend to drive government and business leaders into a defensive and mutually suspicious frame of mind: not the best conditions for learning and cooperation.

Nevertheless, it is to advance the prospects for just such partnerships that we have decided to write this book. We will argue for a new approach to economic development and try to justify our claims with in-depth studies of Andean industry, advantage, attitudes, and opportunity. But just as important, we will map out what we think is a humane process through which government leaders and business managers can engage in productive reasoning. People who want to make a difference in developing nations have an obligation not only to say what needs to be done but also to explore the most effective ways to say it.

THE ANDES: A LABORATORY OF DEVELOPMENT

To most educated people in the United States and Europe, people old enough to remember John F. Kennedy's Alliance for Progress, the name "Bolivia" or "Colombia" still conjures military dictatorship and burlap sacks of cheap coffee. Younger people hear "Cali" or "Medellín" and think "cartel," their images of the Andes inextricably linked with helicopters flying low over coca fields, with Uzis at the house gates of drug lords. In either case, the Andean countries have continued to seem exotic, struggling, and curiously lost places. We tend to imagine the squalor of the countryside, rates of inflation higher than rates of literacy, intractable guerrilla activity led by swashbuckling (and, by now, rather exhausted) Marxists. We also think of foreign businesses in danger of expropriation, businesses there to appropriate tin or timber or to buy up crops, with precious little going to the workers—businesses we are not sure do not deserve to be in danger.

Some of these stereotypes will die hard, rooted as all stereotypes are in a grain of truth. But the facts are more complex and, in a way, more promising. The Andean countries are home to approximately 95 million people, about half of whom live in cities—cities nested in lush mountains, people hardened by thick traffic and thin air. The collective gross domestic product of the Andean countries is approaching $200 billion. If this were a more primitive industrial age, we would have said that the economies of these countries have much to recommend them. They have famously abundant natural resources: timber reserves in the rain forests and unimaginable stores of minerals in the mountains. They have the remnants of a fascinating native history, a potential magnet for adventure tourists. Their plains are mostly fertile and enjoy an equatorial growing season. Their high-elevation cities offer a surprisingly temperate climate.

National, hence economic, cohesion has become more practically possible in the Andean countries, especially during the last twenty years, with the coming of more advanced telecommunications and national broadcast television. For people doing business, commuter air routes have become much more important than the serpentine roads that used to isolate Andean cities from one another as much as connect them. Global links are newly real, too. International telecommunications are good in Colombia and acceptable elsewhere. Bogotá, a city of nearly 7 million, is about as long a plane ride from Miami as Miami is from Boston. In all major cities—Lima, La Paz, but especially Bogotá and Caracas—there is a growing upper-middle class of (often U.S.-educated) owners, managers, and professionals who are hungry for progress.

These nations are now all recognizably democratic, each with a president who assumed power in a peaceful election, an active though somewhat aggressive press, and an elected legislature. Actual political conditions, however, continue to vary widely from country to country, administration to administration. Most political leaders came to power promising economic advance and then found themselves caught between the pressure of violent insurgency—coming, indeed, from drug cartels and old-left guerrillas—and the temptation of resorting to military despotism. (For example, in 1994 some 4,000 Colombians were kidnapped and usually released for ransom.) Political leaders have also had to preside over government bureaucracies not immune to bribes. One Bolivian leader put it to us this way: "This country is ruled by 100 sons-of-bitches; I should know, they are all my best friends."

The Andes has been a fantastic laboratory for us, sharing as it does so many characteristics of so many other nations in the developing world. The Andean countries span virtually the entire span of the world's lower-middle income countries.[1] The World Bank lists Bolivia, with a per capita income at USD 760 ($760, 1996 U.S. dollars), as the forty-ninth poorest country in the world and very near to some of the richer countries of Africa such as Senegal and Cameroon. Venezuela is the eighty-seventh poorest country with per capita income of USD 2,840. It resides in the same per capita neighborhood as the Czech Republic, Turkey, South Africa, and Estonia.

These countries have experienced the entire scope of macroeconomic adjustment experiences. Bolivia, with its annual rate of inflation peaking at 20,000 percent in 1985, got the close attention of the multilateral institutions, as did many African nations in the 1980s. Yet Colombia's monetary and fiscal conservatism makes it the only South American nation that never even had to reschedule its debt.

Businesses in these countries vary widely in size and type. In Peru and Bolivia, estimates of the size of their respective informal sectors (businesses not registered with the government or chamber of commerce) range up to two-thirds of their economies, with companies that often have only five or ten employees. This is no different from Zaire, parts of the Russian Federation, Mexico, or even Asian countries not so long ago. The Andes also have some massive state-owned enterprises that employ thousands. Most people in Bogotá who are formally employed work for the Colombian government, and 80 percent of Venezuela's exports are owned by the government—a situation similar to those in Eastern Europe and Africa.

Every type of national strategy that has been tried in developing countries has been looked at in the Andes. We have seen import substitution, monetarism, open trade, redistribution, agricultural-led, and even flirtations with socialism in the Andes over the past three decades. The breadth and scope of experimentation with these various national strategies—let alone the rapidity of the changes—has amazed us, but it is not confined to this part of the world.

In Mike Fairbanks' years as a banker in Africa and Stace Lindsay's time as a development worker in Central America and the Caribbean, we have seen patterns that repeat themselves over and over at the micro or firm level: leaders of countries who overrely on the abundance of their natural advantages to compete in world markets and create prosperity for their citizens; little or no learning about end-users, competitors, or cost structures; little forward integration into sophisticated markets; an overreliance on government support; and, by and large, poor relationships between government and private sector. We have made the Andes the laboratory in which we can explore these patterns of underdevelopment of the business sector—and their hidden opportunities—in detail.

A NEW WILL TO CHANGE

Have Andean political leaders come to power with a clear idea of how to advance the competitiveness of their economies? Actually, the question helps to frame the governing principle of our work and what we like to think is most original about it.

From our conversations with them, it is clear that Andean leaders have had a much clearer idea of what confounds economic development than what advances it. They are now, for the most part, committed to macroeconomic stability and reform—to open markets, to fiscal responsibility—and are keenly aware that the absence of a healthy macroeconomic environment in the past has led to stagnation and hyperinflation.

They have come by that commitment honestly. Take Peru. Between 1968 and 1990, from President Velasco to President García, the Peruvian government changed its stance with respect to foreign ownership of domestic companies no less than five times. The result was devastating. Between 1968 and 1992, Peru's share of world exports fell about 6 percent. Productivity fell dramatically between 1980 and 1990, and the "informal" sector, the black market, grew to accommodate workers displaced from increasingly uncompetitive firms. Fiscal deficits created a tremendous foreign debt that increasingly isolated the nation from international assistance and left the government with no alternative but to print money. By the time President Fujimori took office in 1990, inflation was 7,000 percent. The stock market was in shambles.

Leave aside for the moment the policies President Fujimori has enacted since taking office. Stability in the macroeconomy is only table-stakes today. A more predictable and business-friendly economic climate can get a developing country into the game, but it cannot ensure success in the game—except maybe for a few elite who are able to play it well. Macroeconomic stability, without a corresponding shift in the way developing economies compete, will not alter the social crisis inherited by many of the current leaders in the region.

What has been most difficult for Andean leaders—indeed, for most leaders of developing economies—to grasp is that to advance the prospects of domestic businesses, their governments must master the details of how successful global businesses make competitive choices, strategic choices, in an age of global markets and networked information technologies. Government leaders have always been absorbed by the macrotheories of an old wealth creation paradigm, in which companies' strategic goals were assumed to be nearly self-evident: exploit economies of scale, get cheaper labor, or limit competitive pressures. They have now to learn the complex theories of firm-level strategy and choice, new microeconomic theories that are fit for the new economy; they have to learn how chains of value creation are really formed and how global businesses choose to participate in them.

Governments that fail to understand these details will be unable to create the conditions to help domestic companies to compete globally, they also will be unlikely to incubate the conditions that would make global companies want to invest in their countries. The investments of global competitors, whether domestic or foreign, are important for the people they employ and the wealth they create. But they are even more important for the learning they impart to other rising domestic entrepreneurs.

THE ORGANIZATION OF PLOWING THE SEA

Part 1 of this book is a chapter-by-chapter summary of the seven patterns of uncompetitive behavior that have become so familiar to us (and that may sound familiar to the reader as well). We will spend time discussing them in detail because we believe they represent both the problems with the way things have been done as well as the opportunities to nurture growth in what are often fragile economies.

Part 2 is about root causes: the systemic reasons we believe it is so difficult for countries to take advantage of opportunities that present themselves. This part of the book is about strategy, institutional structures and mental models, and the challenges ahead for those who would move beyond the old patterns and ways of doing business.

Part 3 is what we consider the integration section of the book. Soon it will not be sufficient to talk about what changes need to be made. Those leaders who are able only to talk about change will disappear. Change creation is a mystery, and yet we have seen some very observable patterns in that as well. We set forth here a vision of change creation that has grown primarily (and ironically) out of our frustration with our own inability to make change happen. It is a model in the spirit of Paul Krugman, who wrote: "If a model is a good one, it is an improved insight into why the vastly more complex real system behaves the way that it does."[2]

What follows in this book is a glimpse into a remarkable journey we have had the opportunity to live in the Andean region during the years 1990 to 1997. But it is not limited to that time. Stace has worked in chaotic environments since 1984, including time spent working in rural development in the Dominican Republic and working with refugees and studying the politics of humanitarian aid in Central America during the height of the Sandinista/Contra conflicts in Nicaragua and the Salvadoran government/FMLN conflicts in El Salvador. He has spent the past five years in Latin America, directing national projects in almost twenty industries. Mike has worked in these uncertain places since 1979, including as a Peace Corps volunteer in Kenya, a diplomat in West Africa, and a merchant banker in southern Africa. For the past seven years he has worked in the Middle East, the Russian Federation, Latin America, and the Caribbean as an adviser to business and government leaders.

We began our journey working at a very grass-roots level of development and migrated through our graduate work and professional experience. Along the way we have observed that certain patterns repeated themselves. It occurred to us that there might be some theme or themes that united these patterns and, in fact, made some sense of them. And so we decided to give up our biases as best we could and began searching.

ABOUT THIS BOOK

The title of our book, *Plowing the Sea*, is taken from the epitaph on the tomb of South American revolutionary Simón Bolívar, which quotes him: "America is ungovernable. Whomsoever has worked for a revolution has plowed the sea." Bolívar, who led the fight for the independence of the Andean nations from Spain in the early nineteenth century and died a dispirited and somewhat controversial figure, is a hero today to every school child throughout the five Andean countries. Paintings of his image reside in the offices and homes of many Andean leaders. We have taken up his epitaph, which he meant to express the seemingly impossible task of the revolutionary, as a challenge—to be relentless, to never stop; to work in the countries with the most dire conditions, countries that are "in transition;" to work and learn—in a way, with the most demanding and critical consumers of our ideas. We decided some time ago that changing the minds of leaders was its own revolution, one in which we would strive to play a role. And if changing the mind of a nation is the task, changing our own mind is the means. This book has facilitated our own learning and change. Ultimately, it is dedicated to the reorientation of those who read it, on the chance that of all the ideas we cast in the form of seeds on a sea that mostly churns and swallows them whole, one or two will find themselves landed on some fertile ground.

People often ask us what we think we've helped the nations we work with to achieve. We believe there are three areas of change by which to judge our work.

The first, which is the easiest to achieve and in which we have been most successful, is the change in *language* systems. Most leaders in the countries where we worked now talk about "competitiveness"; they have the language for "upgrading" down cold, and they claim to understand the importance of social capital in global competition. Countless radio and television shows have been receptive to this new model of competitiveness and have broadcast our messages to places as far and remote as the Amazon jungle, inner city barrios of Bogotá, the altiplano of Bolivia, the villages of southern Africa, and the historic cities of Eastern Europe. Linguistic change is occurring.

The second level of change is the capacity of nations to put into *practice* new learning. On that score, our results are mixed. In some places a great deal has been accomplished. The example that comes most to mind is Christine Ternent in Bogotá. Christine is the vice president for competitiveness at the Chamber of Commerce in Bogotá and has been a key person in keeping strategy and competitiveness at the forefront of the discussion among business and public leaders in Colombia.

The third and highest level of change is *generative*. This is the capacity of leaders to create new integrated technologies of their own, based on principles of competitiveness and social capital. On this level, there remains much to be accomplished. We are optimistic, though, because we believe that these three changes are sequential; that linguistic change comes before change in practice, which comes before generative change.

We believe that these changes will take a long time, not months in a country, not years in a region, but probably decades around the world in some of its toughest places. They will require relentless work and an immense amount of learning on the part of everyone involved—both those helping to implement the change and those undergoing it.

We hope this book will not be a testament to lives partially ill-spent but to the learning and reframing process. We hope it is not viewed as an end, insofar as it displays much learning, but a beginning to a style of learning and a quality of discourse that edifies those whom it touches. If it inspires people to change their language system, and then to practice those changes, and then to generate new and better processes of learning and reframing, we will have accomplished more, perhaps, than we have a right to expect. And in that spirit we invite the reader to join our own intellectual community of those who choose not "to fall asleep to dream."

Acknowledgments

Monitor Company cofounder and CEO Mark Fuller has urged and supported our group of about fifty consultants and researchers to put ourselves on "the firing line," believing that most learning and innovation occurs under conditions of dramatic demands, often far away from our headquarters—"on the frontier," he would say. Most who know us would say that we take him seriously. We did this first by choosing to work in countries in dire circumstances: Colombia during the reign of terror of drug lord Pablo Escobar; Peru, which was harassed by the Shining Path guerrillas during its transition to stability; South Africa in the year leading up to universal suffrage and Nelson Mandela's election to the presidency; the Russian Federation as republics fought for autonomy; and the West Bank and Gaza Strip during their on-again, off-again peace process. Our consultants have been involved in a bomb attack in Bogotá, stoned by Trotskiite students, and then gassed by the *policia* in La Paz; they have crawled into the safety of a doorway to escape a hail of bullets in Cali and been threatened by street crime in Moscow, Port au Prince, and Johannesburg. In all of these places the economies have been in transition; transitioning to what, we do not know. But we do know that we tend to learn the most in the midst of the chaos and confusion.

This book represents the cumulative knowledge of a very remarkable group of people, beginning with our colleagues at Monitor Company who challenged us to put ourselves on the firing line and created the conditions that made this book possible: Joe Fuller, Roger Martin, Tom Craig, and Alan Kantrow.

We appreciate the support of Michael Porter, Chris Argyris, and James Austin at the Harvard Business School, whose intellectual contributions laid the groundwork for our own research and whose encouragement and support throughout the publication process has been invaluable. Also, we are grateful to Diana Smith, whose work with Monitor Company leaders on creating change was an inspiration for our own work with leaders in developing nations.

We are particularly grateful for the close collaboration and honest dialogue we have been able to have with the following leaders in Colombia: Luis Alberto Moreno, the demanding and insightful former Minister of Development, who started our work in Colombia; Guillermo Fernandez, Fabio Rodriguez, Francisco Piedrahita, Augusto Martinez, and Christine Ternent, leaders in their Chambers of Commerce; Mauricio Rodriguez in the business press; Jimmy Mayer, our first private sector champion; Orlando Cabrales, a leader in both the public and private sectors; Raul Sanabria in business academia; former Minister of Trade Juan Manual Santos; Ministers of Finance Juan Antonio O'Campo and Guillermo Perry; Minister of Defense Rafael Pardo; Juana Maria Unda in the industry associations; Luis Jorge Garay, the scholar and former trade negotiator; Gabriel Mesa; and Enrique Lucque. We need to especially mention former President of the Republic, Cesar Gaviria, for allowing us to interview him numerous times on his views of Colombian history, economic reform, and leadership.

In Bolivia we thank the President of the Republic, Gonzalez Sanchez de Losada, for allowing us to test our ideas with him; Douglas Ascarrunz, the Minister of Industry and Trade, who has been the most courageous leader of the competitiveness movement in his country; and the business leader Marcos Iberclyde, whose company is an example for all companies that export from developing nations. Also Bern Abendroth, Peter Weiss, Juan Carlos Cremer, Ricardo Rojas, Juan Luzio, Gerardo Velasco, Carlos Meave, and Gonzalo Miranda.

In Peru we wish to thank President Alberto Fujimori for the tremendous opportunity to travel with him up into the mountain villages and into the shanties of Lima; our main client, Liliana Canale, the former Minister of Industry, Tourism, and Trade, for her gentle leadership and openness to change; and former Prime Minister Alfonso Bustamante, who brought us to Peru. Thanks also to Pablo de la Flor, Gabriela Ruiz, Luis Chang, Joey Koechlin, Samuel Gleiser, Richard Custer, Patricio Barclay, Andres Von Viedermeyer, Jan Mulder, and Derek Mitchell.

In Venezuela we thank former Minister of Trade Gabriela Febres Cordero, who has been a champion of this work for many years throughout the Andean region, and Ministers Werner Corrales, Freddy Rojas Parra, and Teodoro Petkoff. And Jose Luis Cordeiro, one of the leading opinion makers in the country, for his constant enthusiasm. And Jonathan Coles and Leonardo Vivas of Venezuela Competitiva, Pedro Carmona and Juan Francisco Mejía of Conindustria, Henrique Machado of Sivensa, Elba de Mago of CVG, Nelson Quintero of FONCREI, former Vice Minister Rafael Pena, and Francisco Peleato, who was the administrator of our project there.

It was through countless late nights, seminars, breakfast, lunch, and dinner meetings, and long plane rides that we had the opportunity to learn and test our ideas with these world class decision makers. Their insights forced us to rethink many of our beliefs about development. And many of them we have come to consider good friends.

We would like to acknowledge in particular the Corporation for Andean Development (CAF) for its support of the learning that these pages show. Without the vision of CEO Enrique García and José Luis Lupo, head of strategy, this book might not exist. They are of the most unique kind of bankers, the type that is comfortable, even aggressive, in investing in knowledge—one of a nation's intangible assets. García and Lupo's actions will be increasingly imitated by other leaders around the world. Also special thanks to Judith Rojas for her able administration of our projects at the CAF.

Many of the stories in this book come from our work in the field. The following Monitor consultants contributed significantly to the shape of the book itself, and the quality of its insights: Matthew Eyring on the Colombian flower industry, Jeffrey Glueck on the Peruvian tourism and Alpaca industries, Joseph Babiec on the analysis of Bolivian and Peruvian politics and economics, and Kaia Miller and Jonathan Donner on mental models.

The first project team that worked with us in Colombia deserves special mention. Dubbed "The Macondo Team," after Gabriel García Márquez's mythic land, it consisted of Ben Powell, Gabriela Alvarez, Ethan Berg, Amy Birtel, David Coppins, Phil Cooper, Matthew Eyring, Ralph Judah, Jennifer Kelly, Randall Kempner, Claudia Levy, Susan Mayer, Meredith Moss, Moses Muthini, Rob Price, and Michael Sagan.

These projects are extremely labor intensive. We would be remiss if we did not take this opportunity to thank our Monitor colleagues and team members who have helped us to create such a stimulating intellectual community over the last five years. They include Bill McClements and David Kaplan, whose patience and forbearance created the conditions for our projects' success. And to Juan Solé, Phil Cunningham, Ignacio Masias, Ignacio Giraldo, Alejandro Salazar, Laura Reyes, Eduardo Gomez, Josh Green, Jim Vesterman, Heidi Ellemberg, Veronica Gil, Rafael Araque, Andres Hernandes, Anne Lufkin, Carmen Helena Marin, Mauricio Anaya, Joanna Sieh, Wendy Gutierrez, Neal Donahue, Carlos Diaz, Juan Carlos Pascual, Herman Olade, Alejandra Guerra, Mariana Merech, Carola Blohm, Mellina Del Vechhio, Carlos Segovia, Tony Perez, Felipe Bedoya, Michael Brennan, Pato Guerra, Christina Pero, Sandra Martinez, Charlie McMaster, Dawn Sylvester, Carolyn Volpe, John Warner, Brendan Kiernan, Giovanna Sardi, Herman Hererra, Jennifer Jones, Sabine Charpentier, Jackie Cleere, Arlene Guerrera, Denise Oates, Janice Bertwell, James Costa, Romney Resney, Claire Cronin, Karen Buholski, Judy Freeman, Cynthia Mastroianni, Kevin Grund, Paul Grund, Joe Balis, Tim Shaughnessy, Tim Sayers, Wendy Falcigno, Anthony Chiccuarelli, and Lizette Figueredo. And to Whit Porter, and then Neil Lieberman's team in information resources—Rosemarie Alongi, Eric Smith, Gatumba Abu, Freddy Yaitanes, Sean Walter, Jonathan Duce, Michael Moore, Larry Tosi, and Pat DeVoe—whose constant attention provided us with a competitive advantage in remote environments.

Mike wishes to thank Kirk Lovenbury, Steve Mossholder, Mike Cannon, Melanie May Thompson, Marty Brenner, and Tom Millsop—and the rest of his Peace Corps friends in Kenya, 1979–81, whose original ideals and openness to learning continue to inspire him, all these years later. And to his mom Jeanne Fairbanks, and to Regis Dale, Peter Henriques, Kelly Fealy, Hannah Blomgren, Zoe Stein, Dan Donahue, Mike Brennan, Ken Buntz, Ray Miller, Amy Davidsen, Lisa Ceremsak, Nigel Jagernauth, and Jeanine Bourcier, whose friendship and enthusiasm for his work sustained him throughout the research and writing of this book. And his father Matt Fairbanks, Edward Gannon, Ed Jarvis, Stephan Ryan, Len Gougeon, Jack Earl, Mike Didoha, and Tom Garrett, all writers and professors, who provided different and important life lessons that contributed to the development of our practice and this book. And to Kenya's Minister of Technology—Zachary Onyonka.

Stace would like to thank Lisa for her patience and good humor throughout this process, and Abigail and Cameron, who sat on his knee during many hours of edits—he hopes they like it when they are able to read it. And he thanks his family, Diane and Tim Jerhoff, Myke and Pat Lindsay, and Robbe and Jay Lindsay, whose almost always unwaning support enabled him to visit his first uncertain countries. Thanks to Dave Hagstrom and Scott Lynch, who first inspired him to think about Latin America, and César Lopez and César Torres, who taught him an appreciation for the beauty and complexity of its culture. Thanks also to Gary Buchanan, who impressed on him the importance of public and private sector partnerships, and to Bill Kunnath, who has been a constant source of inspiration and a challenge to both mind and spirit. And finally to Father Timothy Healy, S.J., whose early guidance was fundamental to Stace's growth, and is now sorely missed.

We would never have been able to shepherd this book through to the end without the tireless commitment and friendship of both Liz Caldas and Nancy Nichols.

We wish to especially thank our editors: Nick Phillipson at Harvard Business School Press, who invested in us when the book was only an idea and whose advice was always right; and Lucy McCauley, whose good taste in writing and gentle persuasiveness helped to make us better writers. A special word of thanks to Bernard Avishai, the first author to whom we spoke, who helped us with the introduction and during that process began to teach us about the medium of a book.

Michael Fairbanks   Michael_Fairbanks@Monitor.com
Stace Lindsay   Stace_Lindsay@Monitor.com
Cambridge, Massachusetts
April 1997

PLOWING THE SEA

Introduction

The Cautionary Tale of Colombian Flowers

Why has the developing world had such a difficult time creating wealth for the majority of its citizens? The reason, we have come to conclude, is that the traditional way of competing is flawed; leaders in the developing world must find new ways to compete in a global economy. But before we can hope to pursue these new ways, we need to clearly understand the limits of the old. An instructive exploration of those limits can be found in the story of what has become perhaps the most respected industry of the Andes: Colombian flowers. Its fate reveals particular patterns in assumptions made and actions taken; patterns that have been repeated in many once-thriving export industries, now failing. The assumptions were plausible enough in the old economy but are self-defeating in the new. They have led to missed opportunities for growth and helped create patterns of competition that must be broken if we are to realize the tremendous hidden potential of so many countries in the developing world.

FINDING EL DORADO

Señor Edgar Wells was a man with an idea. A floricultural hobbyist turned entrepreneur, he returned to Colombia with his family after twenty years abroad, intent on turning his homeland into the source of the best flowers in the Americas.

At the time, the only growers of high-quality flowers in the hemisphere were in the United States. In 1950, American growers sold almost $220 million of cut flowers, 68 percent to consumers in the

Northeast, especially Boston, Philadelphia, and New York. Seventy percent of all flower producers, mostly small, family-owned operations, were located in the Northeast as well. The limitations of transportation at that time, and the perishable quality of the product, meant that those growers competed largely with each other, oblivious to the producers or consumers in other parts of the country or elsewhere in the world.

But changes were coming, and they would be dramatic. The 1960s saw the development of new, large-scale farms and innovations in transportation that could reshape the lucrative North American market. Because of the relative freshness of their flowers, northeastern producers had commanded premium prices over producers from the South and West for years. But this was the heyday of new jet fleets; the development of regularly scheduled commercial flights all but eliminated the eastern growers' ability to charge a premium for freshness. Air transportation and refrigerated ground transport made it possible for flowers to be cut and then transported to any location in the United States within hours.

That was the opening for new players. Producers could choose to relocate to rural areas in the American West where they could enjoy lower production costs, in particular lower wage rates, and beat northeastern growers, even though transportation costs from the West would be higher. By 1968, in fact, more than two-thirds of American-grown flowers were produced in California and Colorado. By 1975, the U.S. Department of Agriculture reported that 25 percent of American growers accounted for nearly 75 percent of total U.S. cut-flower production. Low-cost, scaled-up farms in the West, employing inexpensive workers to pick flowers, had driven many higher-cost eastern operators out of business.

The lessons from those changes in the U.S. market were not lost on Edgar Wells. Although not an expert in the mass production of flowers, Wells knew that Colombia could offer a flower wholesaler all of the advantages of the American West and more. The Savannah of Bogotá, the plateau surrounding Colombia's capital city, was indeed one of the Western Hemisphere's best climates for growing flowers. The Savannah offered year-round moderate and unvarying temperatures, twelve-hour days of bright sunlight, and an abundance of rich soil. The conditions were so favorable that many years later growers would recount: "In the early days, you could stick a pole in the ground, drop seeds around it, spit on the ground, and cover them with a plastic sheet. Up came the flowers."

That is pretty much what Wells and other early Colombian flower entrepreneurs did. High-quality flowers grew year-round on the Savannah de Bogotá in simple wood and plastic structures. Not only were the flowers relatively easy to grow, they also proved inexpensive to harvest: the daily wage for Colombian agricultural workers was slightly more than half a U.S. dollar; by 1966, those wages had risen only to eighty-two cents—still minimal compared with American workers' daily wage. After struggling for several years to implement the growing techniques developed in the United States, Wells and his associates managed to convince a U.S. wholesaler to accept a trial shipment of flowers. They sent their first shipment to the United States on October 18, 1965.

By then, however, Wells was not the only one to perceive Colombia's potential in the cut-flower industry. In the same year his first shipment went to the United States, a series of University of Chicago studies noted the perfect match between the climatological requirements for growing carnations and the conditions in the Savannah de Bogotá. Then, in 1969, a team of four Americans, including a California flower grower, each invested $25,000 and formed a company that would pioneer Colombian cut-flower exports. Called Floramerica, the company began with exports of carnations and chrysanthemums, flowers that are sturdy and technically less demanding to produce, handle, and transport. They quickly added roses, which are more fragile and more complex to produce, handle, and transport.

Floramerica exported almost $400,000 worth of carnations to the United States in 1970 and almost $2 million in 1972. By 1986, the company had $50 million in annual sales (33 percent of the total) and had become one of the world's major cut-flower exporters. Soon, other Colombian companies began to copy Floramerica's production and marketing methods and hired away members of Floramerica's staff. The growing companies were able to take full advantage of Colombia's longer growing season and much lower wage costs, giving them a 31 percent cost advantage over U.S. producers, even after accounting for higher shipping costs.

Between 1966 and 1978, Colombian exports rose from less than 1 percent to 89.6 percent of total U.S. cut-flower imports. A 1971 Colombian government study estimated that local producers exporting to the U.S. market and selling their products at U.S. prices could expect to earn a profit amounting to 57 percent of revenues. That type of profitability offered early investors an attention-getting 600 percent return per year on their initial investment. Edgar Wells compared the flower industry with the legendary gold source sought by the Spanish in Colombia: "After 400 years, the true riches of *El Dorado* have been discovered . . . a permanent source of riches for all Colombians, for all time."[1]

Pattern: Overreliance on Basic Factors

Domestic producers assume that advantages in natural resources and cheap labor will gain them leading positions in export markets, and they therefore fail to create the conditions for innovation.

THE MIAMI HUB:
COMPLETING THE EXPORT VALUE CHAIN

Buoyed by startlingly good results, Colombian producers looked for ways to build on their early successes. They quickly came to see that in spite of their tremendous cost advantages, if exports to America were to grow to their potential, the producers would have to pass two tests: find a way to efficiently distribute their flowers, and find out how to expand their customer base. In time, they would find innovative ways of doing those things. Their solutions set the stage for explosive growth, but they simultaneously sowed the seeds of the industry's future problems.

The first test the Colombians faced—speedy and efficient distribution of their flowers to the United States—would be difficult. Colombia's internal transportation infrastructure was weak, with no prospect of being significantly improved. Roads were of poor quality, no independent trucking companies provided refrigerated transport, and the airport holding facilities moved product inefficiently and were overheated, which hurt freshness. Moreover, up until the early 1990s, the airport in Bogotá had only one runway, which had led, on at least one occasion, to major delays and flower losses during the critical Valentine's Day holiday season.

Pattern: Poor Interfirm Cooperation

A weak grouping of related and supporting industries, for example, in transportation, seriously disadvantages firms in developing countries.

What the flower industry did was convince Avianca, the national carrier, and several Colombian transportation companies to provide special handling, so that flowers might be shipped to America with care and reliability, first in the baggage holds of passenger planes and later in dedicated cargo planes. At the same time, poor telecommunications and lack of direct marketing presence in the United States limited the Colombian's ability to coordinate from Bogotá the routing of flowers to destinations around the United States. If they could not surmount that difficulty, they would never have staying power in the U.S. market.

The Colombian producers responded to that challenge by pioneering a sophisticated system of receiving and distribution facilities in Miami. Through the industry association, Asocolflores, Colombian growers formed a common handling company called Transcold. The handling company unloaded flowers into refrigerated storage areas and prepared them for customs inspection and shipment by truck to wholesalers, who, in turn, sold the flowers to retailers. Over time, a complex system of brokerage houses evolved to match supply arriving from Colombia with demand from wholesalers around the country.

The distribution center in Miami provided the Colombians with the beachhead they needed to penetrate deeply into the American market. The very existence of the Miami hub created many more new and demanding customers along shipping routes. That greater scale allowed transportation costs for Colombian flowers in eastern markets to fall below that of flowers shipped from the West Coast. Several Colombian growers, including Floramerica, established wholly owned importer/distributor companies in Miami, which permitted them to eliminate third-party brokerage houses and gain greater control over the marketing of their products. Having overcome their distribution impediments, Colombian exports grew dramatically and established the producers of Bogotá as serious competitors with the Americans in their own market.

New Markets

Having increased the efficiency of the existing distribution channels, Colombian producers turned to their second challenge, which was to expand their customer base through new distribution channels. Up to this point, small florists accounted for nearly all of the retail sales of flowers in the United States. Long accustomed to the high prices of U.S. producers, and significant seasonal fluctuations in flower supply and quality, florists generally charged high prices for their carefully husbanded inventories. American consumers had come to perceive flowers to be a luxury good, available only in specialty stores. From the perspective of the Colombian producers, that consumer belief had held down the growth of overall flower consumption.

Limits like that are overcome by targeting customers through new distribution channels, and that is precisely what the Colombians did. The low price, good quality, and year-round availability of Colombian flowers transformed the ways cut flowers could be marketed and distributed in the United States. Consistent supply and low price reduced the retailer's costs and risks associated with holding large inventories of flowers. That meant nontraditional flower retail outlets, like supermarkets, might be targeted, while reliance on florists could be diminished. And the scale of production in Colombia, combined with growers' willingness to create bouquets of flowers on their farms or in Miami, meant that supermarkets were willing to give the Colombians a chance.

The Colombians did precisely what they should have done, increasing demand through new channels through which American consumers could purchase flowers. By making inexpensive flowers more readily available through different distribution channels, Colombians dramatically increased U.S. demand for cut flowers; and using mass advertising, they kept demand growing, transforming cut flowers from luxury products into goods within the means of almost anyone. Flowers became a staple of many supermarkets, street vendors, and malls. For example, in 1977, only 13 percent of supermarkets handled flowers, while in 1986 that number had risen to 86 percent. Consumers responded warmly. Between 1976 and 1988, total U.S. flower consumption grew more than 300 percent, from $227.5 million to $713.6 million. Imports of Colombian flowers rose an average 21 percent per year, from $22.6 million to $175.6 million.

The Colombians had discovered a segment that was attractive, based on low prices and reasonable quality for the impulse buyers that frequented the U.S. grocery markets. They were responding to the latent demand that had been there for some time and quickly learned to align their natural advantages with what the customers appeared to be demanding. As we will demonstrate, however, the producers at that point began to underestimate two things: how low were the barriers to entry in their segment, and how dynamic was the producer-customer relationship. The flower producers were *responders* and *seekers* of demand, but they were not learning how to *create* sophisticated demand in customers by educating them about the value of their flowers.

Pattern: Poor Understanding of Customers

Firms tend to produce goods, then look for markets in which to sell them. Little homework is done on understanding buyers' needs before pushing products to new buyers. In addition, there is little understanding of the long-term strategic implications of choosing to serve certain segments of buyers.

THE GOVERNMENT

For the most part, the early successes of the Colombian flower industry belonged to the entrepreneurs in the Savannah de Bogotá and to their innovative counterparts in Miami. The pioneers of the flower industry did, however, benefit from changes in government policy affecting exports, which happened to coincide with the growers' most ambitious period of growth. Between 1967 and 1973, the government specifically acted to counter the anti-export bias of the Colombian business climate, devaluing the chronically overvalued peso, relaxing import restrictions that had put deflationary pressure on the currency, and establishing a crawling peg to prevent a recurrence of overvaluation. The result was a real exchange rate that remained reasonably constant through 1972.

In addition to changes in exchange rate policy, the government established several general export promotion measures. First, a new exporting certificate, the *Certificado de Abono Tributario* (CAT), provided more generous tax credits than had previously been offered to nontraditional exporters, including cut-flower producers.[2] Second, a new export promotion agency and fund, PROEXPO, provided promotional services, such as trade fairs and market studies, and subsidized short-term "working capital" loans (and, to a lesser extent, longer-term loans for capital assets). Third, the Plan Vallejo allowed the duty-free import of inputs used in exported products.

Those policies led to a dramatic surge in nontraditional exports. During the export boom of 1967–74, nontraditional exports grew by more than 500 percent, compared with an increase of only 86 percent in traditional exports. Not coincidentally, cut-flower exports grew in the same years from less than $100,000 to $16.5 million.

UNFAMILIAR PRESSURES

And yet at the same time that flower exports were reaching record levels, flower growers on the Savannah de Bogotá began to feel new kinds of pressures. Indeed, like tragic heroes in a Greek play, the Colombian growers found that their very success was becoming the source of their undoing. Today, Colombians feel they are a long way from the days when it was easy to make money: "Now we are fighting to survive," as one grower said.

How could that change have come about so dramatically? The first problem was with the increasing power of the people controlling the distribution channels. Success meant tremendous wealth for the growers in the Savannah de Bogotá, but it also meant increasing profits for brokerage operations in Miami. In fact, those vertically integrated growers who had bought into the brokerage operations came to recognize their Miami hub as crucial for building relationships with customers and gathering market data. They eventually sought to consolidate their power by bargaining hard with (some would say taking advantage of) the increasing number of small, nonvertically integrated Colombian growers who needed brokerage services.[3] They also sought to hedge their risks in a market prone to heavy seasonal demand and accompanying price fluctuations.

Brokers accomplished both goals. First, they accepted third-party flowers on consignment only. That meant there would be no fixed-price orders from third-party growers: brokers would buy from other farms only when their own flowers were in short supply, and they would then receive 15 percent on the sale of third-party flowers, with no responsibility for unsold product. Moreover, as a hedge against declining prices, brokers instituted a "box charge" system. They would receive $12 per box, irrespective of the price at which the flowers were sold. The system would work to the benefit of both growers and brokers in an environment of growing production and strong prices. But it would benefit only brokers in an environment of high volume and *falling* prices. And, given the strategic focus of the Colombian growers on a limited variety of cut flowers, oversupply was increasingly likely. This would suppress the price of flowers and hurt the industry structure of the flower growers—but it would not hurt the brokers in the short term.

Pattern: Failure to Forward Integrate

Many firms are typically at the mercy of distribution intermediaries, who have a great deal of bargaining power over them and shield them from critical market learning. The firms that do forward integrate tend to set up mechanisms that promote short-term profits and fail to reexamine and reinvent their sources of competitive advantage.

U.S. Producers Prompt an Important Change

The growing tide of Colombian imports during the 1970s provoked a defensive response. In 1977, U.S. growers filed a petition to reduce all cut-flower imports, no matter whether or not the originating country could be proven guilty of dumping. That petition was followed in 1979 by another, limited to imports of roses. Although the petitions did not target specific countries, it was clear that the actions were aimed at Colombian exports, which by then comprised 89 percent of total U.S. rose imports.

Both petitions ultimately failed. The American government concluded that the difficulties of U.S. growers were largely the result of the recession following on the oil price shock of 1973-74; that the flower industry was essentially healthy; and that imports were not causing it serious or unfair injury. But the petitions of U.S. growers did cause Colombian growers and their brokerage partners in Miami to produce a united front, and that would prompt an important change in the role of the Colombian industry association Asocolflores.

The flower industry association was originally chartered to provide its members with assistance through initiatives such as U.S. market studies, supply consolidation, and agricultural and biological research. Starting with the trade duel in the late 1970s, however, Asocolflores increasingly functioned as a coordinator of the human and financial resources required to battle U.S. grower protectionist efforts.

One of its efforts was the creation of the Colombian Flower Council, which assumed a leadership role in coordinating U.S. lobbying and advertising efforts on behalf of Colombian growers. Asocolflores then focused more on the challenges facing growers within Colombia.[4] The decision of the industry association to remove itself from the battle of the marketplace and to focus its efforts exclusively on affairs within Colombia was a subtle, but in our view, critical, turning point in the history of Colombian cut flowers. In the choice between new market-driven competitive advantages or government protection and lobbying, the Colombian growers chose protection and lobbying.

A pattern begins to develop, therefore, in which the industrial association views its role as lobbying the government to wage battles against the U.S. government, which advocates the interests of the U.S.-based growers. The association also lobbies its government for benefits like cheaper cost of inputs, such as labor and imported machinery, and for advantageous economic structures, such as a devalued currency that makes the flowers cheap for U.S. consumers.

Pattern: Paternalism

Government feels overresponsible for the success of industry, but historically has not been effective in helping create sustainable advantages; business becomes underresponsible for its future, and having grown accustomed to a lack of real competitive pressure and help from the government, it begins to rely on easily imitated advantages.

INEVITABLE OVERSUPPLY

Although American growers failed to find a satisfactory protectionist response to Colombian exports, Colombian growers began to recognize an enemy closer to home: themselves. Capitalizing on the excellent growing conditions and cheap labor in neighboring Ecuador, Colombian investment fueled Ecuadorian production growth from 50 hectares in the early 1980s to more than 500 hectares (one hectare equals 2.47 acres) in the early 1990s to a reported 800 hectares by 1996. In addition, the relatively low capital requirements and easy access to necessary technology continued to entice many more Colombian growers to establish operations in Ecuador.

U.S. demand did not keep pace with the tremendous production growth. As a result, prices began to drop. The real average price for a basket of flowers dropped from $18.88 to $15.96 between 1980 and 1990. Supermarkets, a low-price channel that represented an increasing portion of flower sales, contributed to the problem. In addition, the very mechanisms designed to protect the interests of the Miami brokers began to contribute to the price decline. Brokers became concerned about unwanted flowers wilting in inventory and were forced to price according to market demand, which in some cases amounted to the cost of production or less. While that meant that both brokers and Colombian growers earned almost nothing on the sale of the flowers, the brokers still earned the box charges on the flowers they moved. The brokers' net margins fell below 10 percent in the early 1990s, but the Colombian growers' margins evaporated. While that was troublesome for farms that had vertically integrated operations in Miami, it was deadly for independent Colombian growers.

Lack of information regarding the relative cost position of firms in Colombia and abroad became increasingly problematic. Besides Ecuador, countries like Mexico had increased their greenhouse production from 100 hectares in 1982 to 750 hectares in 1992. Although traditionally viewed as competitors with a lower-quality flower that served different geographical markets, the Mexican firms had increased product quality and had plans to make direct truck shipments to the United States. What was their cost position now, and what would be their cost position and plans for expansion in the future? Questions like that became deadly serious.

Pattern: Poor Knowledge of Relative Position

Companies and governments neither understand nor appreciate their position relative to competitor companies or countries. Operating without that knowledge inhibits firms' abilities to shape the future of their industry.

THE OPENING OF THE ECONOMY

And so the Colombian growers and brokers were in trouble, entrenched in a system that had gained too much momentum. With an oversupplied U.S. market, and a relatively narrow range of increasingly commodity-like flower products, their margins threatened to turn negative in the early 1990s. Could the growers, at that point, turn to the Colombian government for any kind of relief?

The government, it must be said, had not given the Bogotá growers much reason to hope that it was either willing or able to help. The history of its relations with the industry was mixed. Between 1973 and 1982, the government had taken several actions that practically reversed the pro-export orientation of Colombia's business environment. To stem rising inflation, the government reduced the rate at which it devalued the peso, so that its real exchange rate appreciated continuously from 1975 to 1981. By 1978, it had actually fallen below its level in 1967. Subsidies in the CAT program were reduced, and in 1982 import restraints were tightened to address continuing macroeconomic imbalances.

The growers were nonetheless able to accelerate export growth during that period. While nontraditional exports as a group grew at an average rate of only 2 percent per year, cut-flower exports averaged 17 percent growth, boosted by the power of the Miami distribution and marketing operations. And in 1984, when the government reversed itself yet again by devaluing the peso sharply and relaxing import restrictions, the flower industry boosted export revenues, averaging more than 20 percent growth per year. On the whole, then, the flower industry had gotten off the ground without targeted government help and had begun to thrive more in spite of government policy than because of it. After the government determined to support exports, however, it was not clear that anything the government could do for the Bogotá growers would be enough to mitigate the strategic difficulties the flower industry was facing.

The Colombian government certainly proved ineffectual in countering the increasingly protectionist demands of U.S. growers.[5] Beginning in May 1986, American growers began filing masses of petitions for protection in segments of the flower industry in which import competition was most intense. Naming ten countries, including Colombia, Ecuador, and Holland, U.S. producers, in effect, sought to defend themselves from 98 percent of all American imports. These demands were rather blatant, and similar ones had failed in the 1970s. But in the new atmosphere of managed trade in the 1980s, many of the American petitions were granted. The Colombian government's protests did nothing to block the U.S. government from imposing retroactive penalty duties and enacting trade restrictions against Colombian and other imports. True, those penalty fees and restrictions proved slight (although the costs of management attention and legal fees were significant), but Asocolflores and the Bogotá growers were certain that their government had failed them in a time of need.

And that feeling of abandonment was only to grow worse. In 1989, President Barco initiated the *apertura* program, the transition of the Colombian economy to free trade, which aimed to restore macroeconomic stability to Colombia and lead to sustainable growth. His government slowed the rate of devaluation of the peso. This, combined with inflation rates, meant an effective *revaluation* of the currency, resulting in an effective cost increase for Colombian growers in a market overwhelmed by surplus flowers. That was the last straw.

Tension Rising

Banding together and voicing its opinions through its industry association, Asocolflores, the Bogotá growers began pointing an increasingly desperate finger at the government. In the flower growers' opinion, the government had not only been apathetic toward their cause but had actually tried to hurt it with reckless management of the peso. Using the press liberally, Asocolflores began to accuse the government of "anticompetitive behavior." The war was on.

Stung by the accusations from Asocolflores, the Colombian Minister of Foreign Trade publicly lambasted the flower sector for its "laziness" in the face of world competition. It is worth quoting some of his charges, which he made during a large public conference on U.S.-Andean free trade that we attended in June 1993:

> In a world that is each day more competitive, he who sleeps is carried by the current. Although the flower sector has benefited from ATPA [Andean Trade Preferences Agreement[6]] more than any other, if the Colombian flower growers don't "get it in gear," they will disappear in five years. The flower sector has developed upon a base of comparative natural advantages, such as light, geographic location, and cheap labor. With those advantages they have achieved second place in world exports. But as occurs in every dynamic process, those advantages are not sufficient anymore, and if the flower people think they are, they run the risk of being very surprised. . . . We should follow the example of the Dutch, who without any of those natural advantages maintain their first place in the world market. How have they done it? With commercial strategies: segmenting the market, improving distribution, and innovating technologically.
>
> Meanwhile, although it pains me to say it, the Colombian flower growers are resting on their laurels. For example, today they have only one point of access to the U.S. market: Miami. They are concentrated in Florida, which consumes only 10.2 percent of the flowers in the United States. . . .

I am conscious that the government should make a greater effort to better the airport infrastructure, roads, and telecommunications, and that a greater monetary revaluation must be avoided. We're working on this. But meanwhile, the flower growers have to take action to avoid being converted into victims of their own success.[7]

The president of Asocolflores replied in an open letter a few days later in the newspaper:

Dear Minister,

Respectfully, but emphatically, I reject your attribution made during the Free Trade Seminar that the flower sector is sitting on its laurels, and that we should be more aggressive—attending to new niches of the market and following the example of the Dutch, who according to your statements have maintained their world leader status by merely developing commercial strategies.

First, permit me to remind you that the position Colombia has gained in the international market is not the consequence of the mere coincidence of advantageous natural factors; those are certainly present in many parts of the world. The success of Colombia is also due to the development of our own production technology (flowers used to be commercially produced only in countries with seasons). It is also due to the development of important and dynamic channels of distribution, combined with serious, orderly, and futuristic firm export strategies. That effort is supported by more than 70,000 Colombians that work efficiently and arduously every day to bring flowers of the highest quality to the world.

In analyzing the development of Dutch flower exports, Minister, it is surprising to note the coincidence of the revaluation of the guilder with the loss of share in the North American market. In the case of the chrysanthemum, for example, Holland today has only 3 percent of the North American market, after having more than 30 percent in 1985.

Without doubt, Holland continues today to be the leading exporter of flowers in the world. That it has accomplished by serving markets on its own continent, whose high per capita incomes make its people the best flower customers in the world. In addition, their close geographic proximity and communications infrastructure permits a rapid delivery of the product, which is a transcendental advantage in the marketing of perishables.

Revaluation, without any doubt, caused the Dutch to lose competitiveness in North America. Because of that, I also share your attribution today, in the sense that if we don't "get it in gear," the Colombians will exit the

North American flower market. That is, Minister, if the government does not decide to give favorable internal treatment to exports, eliminating the differential between domestic inflation and devaluation that this year amounts to more than 25 percent.

It is indeed surprising that flower exporters still maintain their position in the international market, despite all of the internal obstacles they face. These include revaluation, serious deficiencies in the telecommunication and airport infrastructure, and high costs of energy, not to mention our recent energy crisis.

As you mentioned, other countries are developing the flower sector as a result of the assistance of their governments, who understand that in the international arena, it is not only the private sector that competes, but also the country.[8]

And the following is the Minister's reply:

I read with interest, and I will confess, some surprise, the open letter that you had the kindness to send me. I say something of surprise, because apparently the industry associations are untouchable. The government cannot make reference to them, nor suggest that they adopt a more aggressive attitude or change their way of doing things, because they become annoyed. Within a spirit of partnership, I believe that must change.

As I said in my speech, I used the example of flowers among many I could have chosen to illustrate a point: Colombia should orient its production, its marketing, and its distribution toward the consumer. It should vertically integrate, improve its efficiency in each link of the chain, and, most important, change its frame of mind.

I in no moment refuted that we have to work harder to improve infrastructure, and I believe I have been the Minister who has most battled revaluation. But that does not mean that exporters should not make greater strides in becoming more efficient in a world where productivity and innovation are every day more important.

The situation in the flower sector has ebbed and flowed over time. It is an industry with a great history in Colombia, and in the end it may be that it will not live up to its promise. One reason will be that the public and private sector never had a shared view of its possibilities, its strengths, and its weaknesses; and it caused them to carp at one another, with each side holding only a piece of the truth.

Pattern: Defensiveness

As the competitiveness of the export industry becomes more desperate, public and private sector divide into opposing sides, and each side assumes that the other is to blame for the failure at hand: the public sector accuses the private sector of strategic mismanagement, the private accuses the public of failing to create a supportive macroeconomic climate. Both sides seem right.

SUMMARY

The purpose of recounting the Colombian flower story was to introduce seven patterns prevalent in many firms and industries throughout the developing world. The *overarching* pattern is that firms develop business propositions that, when tested in the marketplace, prove successful. That success, in the developing world, is based on some combination of abundant resources, government favor, cheap labor, or some other basic advantage. In the short run, the success is a tremendous boon to the economy, the pride of the politicians, and the paragon of "competitiveness" virtue for the business community.

Over time, however, things change. The initial success formula no longer works. It is the great misfortune of the developing world that this cycle of finding successful ways to compete, and then not being able to adapt to changing competitive realities, is continually repeated. We will argue in this book that the tremendous advantages developing nations have in natural resources, inexpensive labor, and fertile soil have ultimately sustained their poverty rather than created economic growth.[9] The comparative advantages they have are not sufficient to create high and rising standards of living for the average citizen. And efforts to convert their sources of easily imitated comparative advantage to more complex and sustainable sources of competitive advantage are not working.[10] No one seems able to break the cycle: not the governments, not the private sector, not the multilateral organizations trying to help. Billions of dollars have been spent in Africa and Latin America to eradicate poverty and to improve economic growth. Yet these regions remain as dependent on volatile natural resource exports and foreign aid as ever before. The seven patterns underlie—and contribute to the seemingly unchanging nature of—the larger problem.

Consider the following: that the flower sector is a "fractal" of Colombia—the seven patterns we discuss repeat themselves in individual firms in the flower industry, in other industries in Colombia, and in Colombia's performance as a nation, as well as in other developing nations.[11] A useful metaphor would be that the seven patterns reside at the levels of the firm, industry, nation, and developing world much the way that a twig looks like a branch, which in turn resembles a tree.

PART ONE

Breaking with the Past: Patterns of Uncompetitive Behavior

This book is subtitled *Nurturing the Hidden Sources of Growth in the Developing World* because we do not wish to point out only what is wrong with things as they have been. We would also like to suggest what could be right. The seven patterns identified in the introduction are the result of certain paradigms of competition and wealth creation. Understanding and changing these patterns is our goal. Consequently, we prefer to look at these patterns more as opportunities for growth than as symptoms of failure:

1. *Pattern:* Overreliance on basic factors of advantage. *Opportunity:* Develop more complex sources of advantage.

2. *Pattern:* Poor understanding of customers. *Opportunity:* Invest in knowledge about more demanding and sophisticated customers.

3. *Pattern:* Ignorance of relative competitive position. *Opportunity:* Understand and improve relative competitive position.

4. *Pattern:* Failure to forward integrate. *Opportunity:* Study the opportunities for forward integration.

5. *Pattern:* Poor interfirm cooperation. *Opportunity:* Improve interfirm cooperation.

6. *Pattern:* Defensiveness. *Opportunity:* Engage in productive reasoning.

7. *Pattern:* Paternalism. *Opportunity:* Control the strategic levers in your business.

In the next seven chapters, we take each of the patterns of uncompetitive behavior just listed and explore them in detail. We then build a framework designed to facilitate the practice of new concepts and to turn the seven patterns into opportunities for growth.

CHAPTER ONE

Avoid Overreliance on Basic Factors of Advantage

Sure, we can sell soybeans. The problem is that no one will pay us anything for them. How can trade be a good thing when I am worse off after I sell to you?

—*Bolivian Soy Industry Official*

A Central Bank governor of an Andean country once told us he believed very strongly that his country was well positioned to be a low-cost competitor in many global industries. As proof, he cited the low wage rates in his country versus those of Europe and North America. He went on to argue passionately that low wages gave his nation a competitive advantage.

While there was no denying that U.S. wages were indeed much higher, something about his logic was fundamentally wrong. If his country's firms were competing directly with U.S. firms, his statement would be true. The problem was that they were competing not against U.S. firms but against firms in the poorest parts of Asia, where wage rates were even cheaper. This is a critical distinction, because it raises the question of relativity: when it comes to highly imitable sources of competitive advantage, such as cheap labor or abundant natural resources, there will always be others who can do it cheaper, making this type of "comparative" advantage highly unsustainable.

As the story of the Colombian flower industry illustrates, the growers' advantages of rich soil and year-round sunlight did not translate automatically into wealth. We believe that countries whose export strategies are based solely on comparative advantages—be they raw materials, location, climate, or cheap labor, will in the long run make themselves poorer rather than richer.[1] In fact, our research reveals that in nations that are highly dependent on exporting natural resources, the citizens are poorer, as measured by their ability to buy goods and services in their country (their "purchasing power parity," or PPP).[2] Figure 1-1 illustrates that correlation using a sample of 26 nations.[3]

Figure 1-1 Relationship between Natural Resource Exports and Wealth

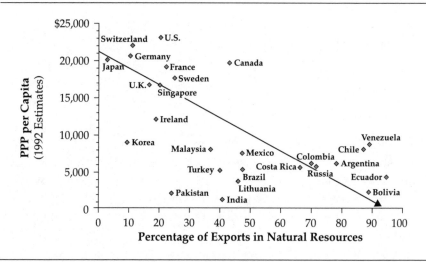

Source: UN SITC Trade Statistics Data Revision 2, World Bank, World Tables 1994.
Notes:
1. Countries unable to reduce natural resource dependency have lower standards of living.
2. Purchasing power parity is standard in this presentation as opposed to GNP because it is an estimation of exchange-rate changes based on keeping prices of goods in different countries fairly similar by offsetting inflation differentials with changes in the currency exchange rates.
3. Correlation coefficient determines the relationship between two properties; coefficients closer to 1 indicate that variations in one variable are perfectly explained by variations in the other.
4. Arrow illustrates the −.66 correlation between purchasing power parity and exports in natural resources.

There are three problems with using a factor-driven approach to wealth creation and competition:

1. It's all relative: there will always be some other country that has better natural resources or that can do things more cheaply.

2. Cost competition from other resource-rich countries creates pressure to keep costs low, which creates an incentive for producers to keep wages low; the average worker, therefore, does not reap the benefits of growth.

3. If countries export their natural resources at devalued exchange rates, there is a double loss: those resources become depleted, and wealthy foreign consumers, who can afford to buy those products at competitive prices, are able to buy them at subsidized, artificially reduced rates instead.

The use of comparative advantages as an approach to wealth creation is one of the most fundamental problems facing both business and political leaders throughout the developing world. As economies become increasingly global and competition more fierce, those who choose to participate in such easily imitated approaches to doing business are dooming themselves to continued poverty.

Government and private sector leaders in the developing world, multilateral organizations, and nonprofit development agencies must create the needed changes. While the strategies to avoid overdependence on natural endowments can be relatively straightforward, few countries have pursued them, for two basic reasons—lack of awareness and politics:

- Few leaders realize how damaging this type of competition is to their economies.

- The pain of continuing to use past behaviors is less than the pain required to fundamentally restructure the way firms in developing countries compete.

KEY TENETS OF COMPARATIVE ADVANTAGE THINKING

In some ways, the belief in comparative advantage originated with David Ricardo. In 1817, he published his influential treatise *Principles of Political Economy*, in which he explored the question of whether international trade was helpful or harmful to the wealth of a nation. As he mused about the potential for the exchange of goods between England and Portugal, Ricardo laid out an argument that, more than 175 years later, remains at the core of modern debates on international trade. His theory of comparative advantage, which promises benefit from trade for all participants, helped Great Britain lead a prosperous era of free trade in the nineteenth century and inspired the victorious Allies after World War II to enshrine free trade as the cornerstone of the postwar international political economy. But in today's world, where the old rules of trade no longer apply, Ricardo's theory falls short: many formerly protected economies in the developing world are relying on comparative advantages—their wealth of oil or sunshine or cheap labor—to engage the international economy in ways that will keep them poor.

In the story of the flower industry, the Colombians became trapped by their model of wealth creation. Relying on the country's factor advantages in rich soil, proximity to markets, favorable climate, and low-cost labor, Bogotá growers succeeded in driving U.S. flower producers out of their own markets and forced the Dutch out of such important markets as roses and carnations. Yet the Dutch, who initially left the low end of the flower market to the Colombians, continue to dominate the most attractive and profitable segments of the flower industry in the United States. Clearly Colombia's comparative advantages—though a critical starting point for trade—were not sufficient to build sustainable competitive advantages. How is it that the Dutch, for whom the sun never shines, the cost of labor is among the highest in the world, and land must be reclaimed from a jealous sea, remain the most successful exporters of cut flowers in the world?

In this chapter, we would like to examine some key tenets of the theory of comparative advantage that govern the behavior of business and government leaders throughout the developing world. We've already introduced them, but we will state them again here:

1. Abundance of raw materials: the trap of raw material and commodity exports.
2. Abundance of inexpensive labor: the relativity of labor rates.
3. Strategic geographic location: competing on the basis of location.

In chapter 7, where the concept of paternalism is discussed, we will cover a fourth type of comparative or factor advantage that includes certain economic and political programs that provide abundant but unsustainable advantages.

All of these advantages have one thing in common: they are easily imitated and therefore impossible to sustain, especially as technological advances shrink the distances between countries. As long as companies continue to rely on comparative advantages as a source of competitive advantage, we believe that they will continue to find themselves in increasingly unattractive positions.

The Trap of Raw Materials and Commodity Exports: The Bolivian Soy Industry

There are many examples throughout the Andean region of the deceptive wealth created by exporting raw materials such as oil, gas, or minerals. To assess the real viability of commodity export-driven strategies, we would like to consider an industry not commonly associated with more traditional export products: the Bolivian soy industry. Bolivia began producing soy in the 1970s, and the World Bank began to support soy production in Bolivia in the mid-1980s to help offset the collapse of the tin and cotton industries. Soy had been touted as the "miracle crop" to help Bolivia break its dependence on coca and to drive economic development in the eastern half of the country. Exports of soy have risen from essentially nothing twenty years ago to one of Bolivia's leading nontraditional exports, its leading legal agricultural export, and a valuable source of employment and foreign exchange.

Despite political turmoil, macroeconomic instability, and tremendous logistical challenges, the soy producers of the Santa Cruz region have made tremendous achievements. The soy industry has grown by an average of 26 percent per year since 1972. Bolivian producers have displaced world leaders Brazil, Argentina, and the United States in the markets of Andean Pact countries. These achievements have helped fuel Santa Cruz's growth and given it an identity as an agricultural exporting region.

While the soy producers have managed to build an export industry worth $60 million per year in the hemisphere's second poorest country,[4] there are signals that should cause the industry and the country to pause and reflect.

In 1993, 92.5 percent of Bolivia's soy exports were soybeans, soy meal, or crude soy oil. The problem is that these exports are all commodity products, sold solely on the basis of price rather than on elements of quality or service that a soy producer could leverage to earn a higher price from customers. Moreover, end-users do not care where a soy product comes from: they are buying protein, not Bolivian or Brazilian soybeans. To make matters worse, since 1973, the first full year of soy production in Santa Cruz, the world price for soy has fallen each year by an average of 5.8 percent.

What choices do the Bolivian soy producers have as they respond to these price pressures? As with any question of profit, they could try to increase price or lower cost. If the Bolivians provided a large portion of the world's production of soy, they might withhold some amount of their usual production and let the law of supply and demand drive the price back up. This strategy has worked well in the past for Saudi Arabia in oil, for example, and might work for the Brazilians, who produce 22 percent of the world's soybeans. Because Bolivian soy comprises only 0.26 percent of the world market, however, restricting production would not have much influence on soybean prices worldwide and would only cause export earnings to fall.

Since altering the world soybean price is beyond the Bolivians' control, it seems their only option is to improve profitability by lowering costs. At first glance, it looks like they have succeeded with this approach. We analyzed the average costs of soy production and transport in Bolivia and in Brazil, Bolivia's primary competitor, located just across the Paraguay River from Santa Cruz. To make the analyses comparable, we estimated the costs for producers in both nations to export soy to one of Bolivia's primary markets, Colombia. If we look at total costs, Bolivian producers appear to be doing quite well. See figure 1-2.

Despite the smaller scale of their operations, the Bolivians have a slight cost advantage over the Brazilians in production and transportation of $6 per metric ton of soy shipped to Colombia. So have the Bolivians won the soy battle?

Before declaring Bolivia the winner, let's break down these costs a bit more. First, consider only the costs associated with the farm that produces soy: fertilizer, seeds, pesticides, and other materials and labor associated with growing soy. For this category, the Bolivians' cost advantage is $1 per metric ton. See figure 1-3.

Figure 1-2 Costs of Soy Production and Transportation to Colombia from Bolivia and Brazil, 1994

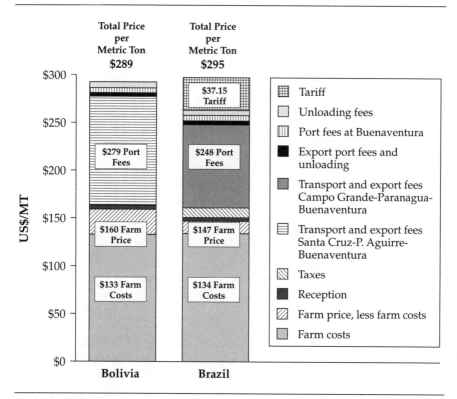

Sources: ANAPO; SAFRAS & Mercado (March, October, 1994); Parana State Department of Agriculture; Oilseeds and Products (Report Code: BR9406A); Monitor interviews.

Note: Costs above based on averages in the Santa Cruz region, and the Centro-Sul region of Brazil and do not include cost of land. Costs will vary based on individual yields, location, equipment ownership, land use, market price, and farm level strategy choices.

But when we compare the components of the total farm costs, an interesting pattern emerges. Out of the twelve components of costs, the Bolivians have an advantage in only four: fertilizer, land depreciation and improvement expenses, financing costs, and the per-ton cost of contracted labor. The soil of Santa Cruz is among the richest in the soy-producing world, yielding a full 2.2 metric tons per hectare compared with Brazil's 1.7 metric tons per hectare. Taking advantage of this

Figure 1-3 Average Farm Cost of Soy Production in Bolivia and Brazil, 1994

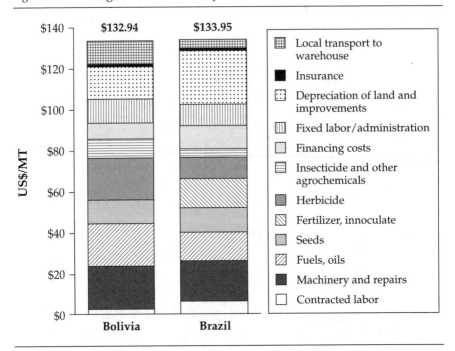

Sources: ANAPO; SAFRAS & Mercado (March, October, 1994); Parana State
Department of Agriculture; Oilseeds and Products (Report Code: BR9406A);
Monitor interviews.

Note: Based on Santa Cruz and Centro-Sul averages and do not include cost of land.
Individual costs will vary based on yields, equipment, ownership, and farm level
strategy choices.

greater yield, the Bolivians have grown soy for years without using
fertilizer, and their other land-related expenses are low. The cost of
unskilled labor in Bolivia is also lower than in Brazil.

While the Bolivians' costs are lower in four categories, they are higher
in seven of the other eight (insurance costs were minimal in both
countries). These categories include the costs of machinery and repairs,
fuels and oils, seeds, herbicides, insecticides, administrative labor (su-
pervisors, accountants, and the like), and transport of soy harvests from
the fields to local warehouses for storage. There are few Bolivian suppliers of specialty products to the soy industry, so producers must
import technology and agricultural inputs from abroad—usually at
high prices—as well as all the chemicals and machinery they use.

Agricultural chemicals, for example, cost 95 percent more in Bolivia than in Brazil. Often Bolivians buy used machinery from the Brazilians (machinery the Brazilians consider nearly obsolete), but while buying second-hand machinery saves money in the short run, over time it is much costlier to maintain. Moreover, making investments in capital improvements or technology is difficult because agricultural loans are expensive, short-term, and require very strong guarantees, and because banks will not accept land as collateral.

While farm costs alone represent almost half of the total cost of producing soy, more dramatic patterns emerge in the remaining categories of costs. Both Brazilians and Bolivians transport soy by sea to Colombia. This involves transferring the soy from storage warehouses onto trucks, unloading the trucks at a port on the Paraguay River, and then shipping the soy to the Colombian port of Buenaventura. One would think, by looking at a map, that the transportation processes for Bolivia and Brazil would be roughly the same, but when we tally up the associated costs we see a dramatic $31 per metric ton *disadvantage* for Bolivian producers. See figure 1-4.

Inefficient railroad and road services account for much of the difference. There are no paved roads connecting the soy-growing regions of Bolivia to the Paraguay River. An inefficient government monopoly runs the single railroad line connecting the producers to the port at Puerto Aguirre. By contrast, the Brazilians have built paved roads leading from their soy-producing regions to their river port at Rosario. To their credit, the Cruzeño soy producers are working hard to improve railroad service and acquire needed trucks, however they are not always successful.

Clearly, the slight advantage the Bolivians have in farm costs is negated by their transportation cost disadvantage. But there are two additional costs to consider—taxes and tariffs—and that is where Bolivians have an advantage. Bolivians pay almost $21 less per ton in taxes than their Brazilian counterparts. Even more significantly, Bolivians pay no tariffs when exporting to Colombia since both countries are members of the Andean Pact; the nonmember Brazilians must pay $37 per ton. The combination of lower taxes and no tariffs allows the Bolivians to draw ahead of the Brazilians at the end of the race for the lowest costs.

Interestingly, the soy producers and processors have no control over three out of the four cost categories—transportation, taxes, and the

Figure 1-4 Transportation Costs to Colombia from Bolivia and Brazil, 1994

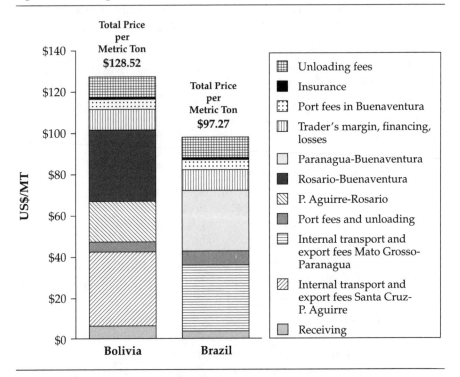

Sources: ANAPO; SAFRAS & Mercado (March, October, 1994); Parana State
  Department of Agriculture; Oilseeds and Products (Report Code: BR9406A);
  Monitor interviews.
Note: Based on Bolivian (Santa Cruz-Aguirre-Buenaventura) and Brazilian
  (Centro-Sul-Paranagua-Buenaventura) averages. Individual costs will vary based
  on location, market price, and other factors.

Andean Pact—and those are precisely the ones that make up the largest
cost differential with Brazil (since Bolivian and Brazilian producers'
farm costs are essentially equal). About 45 percent of the Bolivians' total
cost is determined by the policies of government trade negotiators,
railroad company managers, or road engineers. If average soy prices
continue to fall by 5.8 percent each year, as they have since 1973, this
leaves soy producers with little room to maneuver.

Suppose Bolivia's trade preferences were to disappear, for example
if members of the Andean Pact joined Mercosur to create a Latin American free trade area. (Mercosur is the trade agreement of the nations of

the southern cone of South America: Chile, Argentina, Brazil, Paraguay, and Uruguay.) Given the Bolivian producers' approach to competitiveness, they probably would not be able to compete in commodity segments. This vulnerability is a primary source of our disagreement with the comparative advantage approach to competitiveness: it gives away all of the power to exogenous variables or actors.

There are many other complex dimensions to the soy story, and we will revisit the industry in subsequent chapters to address some of them, such as dependence on government-provided sources of advantage and the need to think strategically about questions of integration. The point for now should be clear: it is perilous, at best, to compete in price-sensitive segments in competitive environments, especially if one's advantages are beyond one's control.

The Relativity of Labor Rates

As we indicated in recalling the faulty logic of the Central Bank governor on wages at the beginning of the chapter, cheap labor and favorable exchange rates are not compelling sources of advantage for firms. In fact, they represent only half of the question; the other half is about the competition. Figure 1-5 shows just how *relative* advantages that are based on labor rates can actually be.

Having labor rate advantages is not in and of itself bad. Having cheap labor as the principal source of advantage, however, is: it is not sustainable, and in fact it is not desirable to sustain. As mentioned above, if one's principal source of advantage comes from cheap labor rates, inherent pressures keep wages low. While large-scale, low-paying employment may appear to be good for a nation, choosing to compete in industry segments on the basis of labor rate advantages is a very poor strategic choice. Wealth creation is the object of economic growth; to grow in a manner that actually impoverishes people should not be the objective. Better to develop capacities that enable companies to pay workers well. Economic growth and social equity, as we will argue later in this book, are no longer inherently contradictory objectives. They are, however, impossible to achieve simultaneously if the growth strategy is based on cheap labor.

Firms do need to begin competing where they have real advantages. And in the developing world, the only real advantages to begin with often appear to be cheap labor or natural resources. Any strategy that

Figure 1-5 Relative Wage Rates in the Textile Industry, 1990–1993

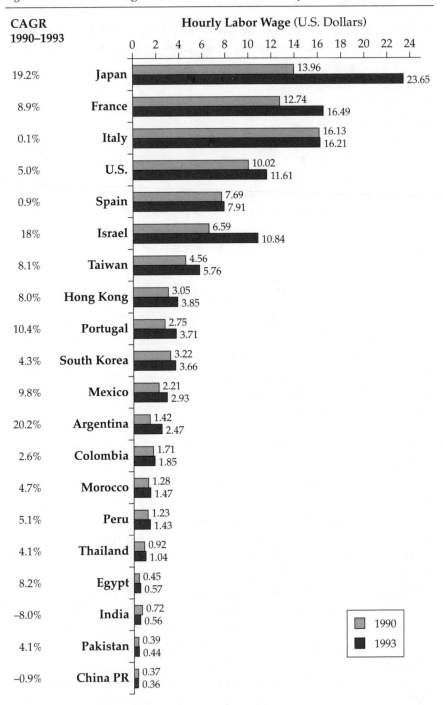

CAGR 1990–1993	Country	Hourly Labor Wage (U.S. Dollars) 1990	1993
19.2%	Japan	13.96	23.65
8.9%	France	12.74	16.49
0.1%	Italy	16.13	16.21
5.0%	U.S.	10.02	11.61
0.9%	Spain	7.69	7.91
18%	Israel	6.59	10.84
8.1%	Taiwan	4.56	5.76
8.0%	Hong Kong	3.05	3.85
10.4%	Portugal	2.75	3.71
4.3%	South Korea	3.22	3.66
9.8%	Mexico	2.21	2.93
20.2%	Argentina	1.42	2.47
2.6%	Colombia	1.71	1.85
4.7%	Morocco	1.28	1.47
5.1%	Peru	1.23	1.43
4.1%	Thailand	0.92	1.04
8.2%	Egypt	0.45	0.57
–8.0%	India	0.72	0.56
4.1%	Pakistan	0.39	0.44
–0.9%	China PR	0.37	0.36

Sources: Gherzi Textile Organization; Monitor analysis.
Note: CAGR = compound annual growth rate.

begins that way, however, also should contain a clear plan for migrating away from those kinds of unsustainable advantages. Otherwise, once the short-term success occurs, business leaders and politicians will find it hard to argue for change and will begin a loop that only keeps people poorer longer.

Competing on the Basis of Geographic Location: Two Cases

Location isn't necessarily everything, as the stories of Barranquilla and the Peruvian fishing industry show.

The Story of Barranquilla, Colombia

Barranquilla, Colombia, was one of the country's leading cities from about the late nineteenth through the beginning of the twentieth century. It boasted the second airline ever established in the world and the longest dock in the world, and it was considered an intellectual and cultural center of Colombia. At the mouth of the Magdalena River, Barranquilla was a natural deep-water port and the commercial center for international trade. Many goods from the United States and Europe entered Colombia and the rest of South America through Barranquilla, and most of Colombia's coffee exports were shipped from it. In fact, the city's nickname at the time was the "Puerto del Oro," the port of gold.

Barranquilla's local leaders during that era were content with Barranquilla's development of its maritime advantages. With the opening of the Panama Canal in 1914, however, many things changed for the city. Suddenly Colombian growers could transport their coffee by train to the Colombian port of Buenaventura and then access their major markets via the Canal. Thus growers avoided transporting crops on the long and arduous journey down the Magdalena River, which often proved difficult because the river needed to be dredged continually. Buenaventura registered dramatic increases in coffee exports after the Panama Canal opened and created alternative shipping routes for the coffee producers. This, in addition to the fact that the Magdalena River had not been properly maintained, instigated a fierce competition in Colombia for commerce—a competition that Barranquilla eventually lost.

The poverty rate in Barranquilla is now among the highest of all Colombian cities. Yet to this day, the leaders in Barranquilla think of their city as blessed with geographic advantages, even though the city has not really benefited from those advantages in decades. The lesson of Barranquilla is the same as that for Bolivia's soy producers: basic sources of advantage, in this case location, may be enough to create competitive momentum, but not to sustain it.

The Story of Peruvian Fishmeal

Another country blessed by geographic location is Peru. However, like Barranquilla, Peru has not taken full advantage of its potential—in this case for becoming world-class producers of fresh fish.

Peru produces fishmeal, which is a high-protein flour made from ground fish used primarily for animal (and fish) feeds. Peruvians manufacture fishmeal almost entirely from anchovies and sardines, both of which the country has long enjoyed in abundance because of the Humboldt Current, a stream of cool water about 120 to 180 miles wide that runs along the coast of Peru and Northern Chile. Plankton thrive in these cool waters, attracting anchovies and sardines that in turn attract other fish, such as bonito, tuna, and corvina.

The fishmeal industry runs all along the coast of Peru, from the Chilean border up to Ecuador, with large centers of production in Chimbote and Callao. There are many fishmeal companies as well as one large state-run company that will soon be privatized, PescaPeru, which comprises the majority of national fishmeal production. The Peruvian fishmeal story is similar to that of Bolivian soy, only in this case Peru is globally competitive in its chosen industry segment.

The fishmeal industry in Peru began in earnest in the early 1950s and evolved in response to an export-led growth strategy. Viewed by most as a great success, the Peruvian industry was the world's leading producer and exporter of fishmeal in 1994. As a result, Peru has become a world leader in fish-catching and production methods; in fact, it is fourth in the world in fish production as measured in metric tons (though not in dollar value), and most of this—83 percent—is fishmeal. Moreover, the fish industry is a growing component of Peru's GNP, and fish production now comprises about 1.2 percent of the Peruvian GDP, almost double what it was twelve years ago. Overall, the fish industry makes up 18 percent of exports. Since 95 percent of that number is fishmeal exports, the industry plays a large role in the Peruvian economy.

Peru generally produces six types of fish products: fishmeal, fish oil (a byproduct created during fishmeal production), canned fish, frozen fish, cured fish, and fresh fish. While fishmeal makes up 83 percent of total fish production, fish oil makes up only 9 percent, frozen fish 6 percent, and all others 2 percent.[5] By concentrating on fishmeal, Peru has in fact focused on the least sophisticated portion of the fish business.

As with soy processors, the fishmeal producers' choice of scope has dictated their competitive advantage: competing in commodities means competing in a cost game. Although there are different grades of fishmeal, the price for each grade is essentially determined by the world market on the basis of protein and moisture content. There is a little room for differentiation in high-end "prime" fishmeal for special uses (such as aquaculture), but few Peruvian manufacturers have chosen to compete in this subsegment. Most choose to compete in a game where the primary variable is cost.

Unlike the Bolivian soy producers, the Peruvian fishmeal fleets command a substantial position in their industry. Could they raise the price of fishmeal by reducing world supply? Though they could attempt this strategy, another issue limits its appeal. Fishmeal is a substitute product for soy in many markets, livestock feed being one. This means that fishmeal prices cannot rise much above the price of soy without a significant number of buyers switching to soy. Therefore, even though Peruvians control a large share of the world's fishmeal supply, their ability to control the price is limited.

Like the Bolivian soy producers, the fishmeal fleets follow a factor-driven model. The ample supply of sardines and anchovies combined with the inexpensive labor available to harvest them have made competing in the Peruvian fishmeal business almost as easy as throwing a net over the side of the boat. Fuel, machinery, and other production costs are higher in Peru than in other countries, but those are easily offset by the strength of the country's natural resource advantages. The irony of the fishmeal industry is that the concept of value-added gets turned upside down: customers actually pay less for the more "processed" product of fishmeal than they would for fresh fish. But for the Peruvians, the sophisticated logistics and technology they would need to sell fresh fish are harder to achieve than those required for fishmeal production.

By concentrating so overwhelmingly on fishmeal, Peru's fishing industry is ignoring a potentially large market for species of fish that it could catch for canning or selling fresh to premium hotels and resorts in Latin America and the Caribbean. When we consider the Peruvian industry's focus relative to other fishing nations over time, an interesting picture emerges. (See figure 1-6.)

The strategy in Peru has been to direct all investment toward increasing fishmeal production. And in fact the country's production has increased significantly in the past ten years, despite a decreasing stock of anchovies and sardines and decreasing worldwide prices. Furthermore, Peru's contribution to increasing the world's fishmeal supply has only driven prices—and profit margins—down.

A decade ago, Chile's fishing industry started out in about the same position Peru's is in today: focused on fishmeal production. But as figure 1-6 indicates, Chile has since become a leading exporter of many higher-value fish, notably salmon and trout. Having begun in earnest

Figure 1-6 Strategic Choices: Positioning in the Fish Industry
(Fish and Fishmeal Exports for 1987, 1990, 1993 in $U.S.)

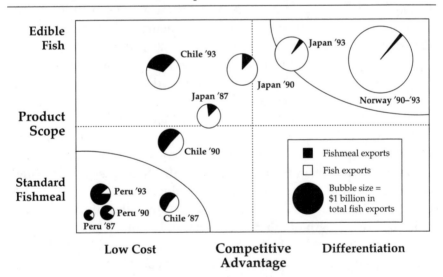

While Peruvian manufacturers are very competitive within the fishmeal segment, other producers have increased total fish export volume by adding edible fish production.

Sources: United Nations Trade Statistics; National Marine Fisheries Service;
Manedsstatitikk over Utenrikshandelen; Monitor analysis.

fewer than ten years ago with salmon breeding, Chile is now the second-largest producer of that fish in the world (producing 46,000 tons to earn $250 million in 1992). Chile's exports of other kinds of fresh, frozen, and canned fish also are rising rapidly.

Korea and Japan have also become leading suppliers of premium fish for restaurants and resorts. In fact, and perhaps most disturbing of all, Peru's own Ministry of Fisheries sells to fishermen from Asian countries the licenses to harvest fresh fish in Peru's deep-sea waters—for a mere $80 million per year. For that investment, the Asians export an estimated $800 million of fresh fish to Japan and Korea.

SUMMARY

The belief we examined first in the story of the Colombian flowers and have explored in greater detail here—that countries and companies can compete globally based on factor advantages such as natural resources, cheap wages, or geographic location—dominates economic activity throughout the developing world. The challenge that business and political leaders of those countries face is two-fold: (1) to develop more sophisticated sources of advantage that are not so easily imitated, and (2) to realize that depleting natural resources and suppressing wages will not lead to sustainable, long-term wealth creation. It is critical for leaders to develop the capacity to think about the future and to move out of such unattractive "factor-based" industries. That will require a fundamental reassessment of how competitiveness and wealth creation are understood. The sources of growth for developing nations are hidden behind the abundance of natural resources that so many of them possess.

CHAPTER TWO

Improve Understanding of Customers

It's a foreign idea that we can choose our customers. We always thought that customers chose us.

—*Peruvian tourist official*

When the Dutch won over the most lucrative part of the U.S. flower market, as discussed in chapter 1, Colombians lost it less because of the Dutch strategy than because of their own lack of a strategy. With the Dutch targeting a more discerning, high-end customer willing to pay a higher price for quality, the Colombians, by default, found themselves selling flowers that appealed to a less profitable customer segment. In the countries where we have worked, we have come across many similar stories in which companies "decide by not deciding" about who their customers are. The result is inevitably lost profits and lost competitiveness.

In Peru, for example, the two airlines that fly daily between Lima and Arequipa offer a limited choice of flight times. The Lima businessperson needing to get to Arequipa for the day has two equally unattractive choices: fly AeroPeru at 6 A.M. or its rival Faucett at 10 A.M. Leaving at 10 A.M. means losing the whole work morning, while for most Lima residents, who live far from the airport, leaving at 6 A.M. means getting out of bed at 4 A.M. to make the long drive. And on arriving in Arequipa at 7:15 A.M, barring delay, there is nowhere to go. It is too early to make office visits, and hotel rooms are usually unavailable since it is still many hours before checkout time.

When people at the airline ticket counter were asked why the hours were set that way, they responded: "*Así ha sido siempre.*" That's the way it has always been. It seems that 6 A.M. is the most convenient hour for the airline. It need use only one plane, servicing it in Lima overnight and sending it to Arequipa in time to return passengers by 8:30 A.M. for morning business meetings.

The Peruvian airlines' service decisions are not driven by customer preference, and as a result Arequipa undoubtedly suffers as a tourist attraction. In 1995, at the Annual Peruvian Tourism Convention, the key opportunity to introduce Peru to foreign tour operators, the showcase trip was to Arequipa. A British tour operator who had returned from the organized daytrip to Arequipa had this to say: "I don't remember much about Arequipa. They woke us up before 4 A.M. to go to the airport, and I kept falling asleep in the bus all through Arequipa. I recall a few nice sights, but I hardly feel like I saw the place, not enough to recommend it."

A new state hotel in the Colca Valley near Arequipa provides another example of the lack of customer focus that we often see in developing nations. The National Tourism Promotion Agency (FOPTUR in Spanish), proudly shows the new hotel to foreign visitors. But though the Colca Valley offers breathtaking scenery and daily condor-watching trips to the upper canyon, the hotel will never be a magnet for tourists. It was created from prefabricated metal housing that had been used years before to house irrigation project workers. Unlike the charming adobe guesthouse being built a few miles away by a local ecological activist, the state hotel feels like a sterile trailer park in middle America. Moreover, the radiators are turned off centrally at 11 P.M., and not a drop of hot water graces the showers. The dining room looks more like a high-school cafeteria than a restaurant, complete with folding chairs and tables. Waiters roam the restaurant, ignoring customers while they set other tables with plastic dishes; breakfast consists of bread and butter with instant coffee. Despite FOPTUR's best intentions, the hotel may have difficulty attracting the affluent tourist it hopes to target.

These examples illustrate an attitude toward customer service that we encountered in Arequipa and that we later confirmed through a survey we administered in the region. The survey identified two main problems: a lack of interest among private-sector employers to invest in training employees, and a lack of focus in the public sector on developing specialized institutes to train people for tourism-related jobs, like guide, waiter, and hotel administrator.

In the last chapter we discussed how overdependence on basic factor advantages, such as natural resources or geographic location, can impede competitiveness. Tourism is an industry whose initial success is most often driven by natural resources. The Colca Valley, deeper than the Grand Canyon in Arizona, is a marvel of nature. The ruins of Machu Picchu near Cusco are a wonderful and mysterious reminder of civilizations past. These are resources that no other country in the world has. Yet as the world's consumers become more demanding and as competing tourist destinations offer increasingly competitive services, products, and prices, the many comparative advantages that the Peruvians now have in tourism will fall away.

Customer service is important at a thousand separate points during a tourist's visit to a particular site. Consequently, each company that interacts with tourists should make itself aware of what is most important to the tourist in terms of quality and comfort as they relate to its products or services. That means making choices about which segments of potential customers to serve and investing in understanding how to ensure that those customers are satisfied. Failing to do so only perpetuates the pattern of overdependence on inherited factors.

Some might argue that the type of customer service we are talking about reflects a U.S. standard that visitors are wrong to expect in a developing country. We disagree. Visitors from the United States represent some of the most lucrative segments that Andean countries could attract, because of their proximity, interests, and large disposable income. In neglecting to make the effort to gain the know-how they need to attract and satisfy these lucrative customer segments, Andean countries are losing income they deserve to receive in exchange for the unique tourist experiences they have to offer.

Toward a Customer-Driven Model of Development

In Third World countries, development per se cannot occur apart from the mechanisms of a market economy. Accordingly, multilateral development agencies have traditionally espoused the following goal: rather than provide people with fish, teach people how to fish for themselves. The new model of development, however, may well not teach others how to fish but rather help them learn how to manufacture high-quality fishing rods to export to the most sophisticated fishermen in the world.

Understanding how to compete effectively in an open economy, especially for those whose economies have been long sheltered from the forces of competition, begins with the knowledge that it is critical to decide which customers to serve and how best to serve them. Contemporary management thinking abounds with approaches to strategy and competition. And implicit in all these approaches is the idea that in any business the customer is paramount. Next to the often-repeated phrase "location, location, location," there is perhaps no other piece of business advice so accepted as "the customer is always right." Obtaining and using customer knowledge effectively is the critical first step for the firm wishing to become competitive on a global scale. And in our experience throughout the developing world, customer knowledge is woefully inadequate for competition in the twenty-first century.

Business executives throughout Latin America regularly complain that they are unable to compete globally because they are "Third World" competitors. But in fact global consumers are increasingly blind as to the origin of products they buy. Whether a product originates from the "First World" or any other world is unimportant; what matters is that producers meet critical customer needs. Insofar as inadequate infrastructure, poorly trained workers, and high input costs inhibit a firm's ability to compete in its chosen industry segment, business owners should make a clear decision: Is this a good industry segment for me to be in, and will I be able to compete in this segment if I make the investments necessary to address critical customer needs?

Again, the question is not "First" or "Third World." The question is: What capabilities are needed to meet ever-changing customer needs? Development efforts should focus on creating an environment that enables firms to compete globally by providing real alternatives to traditional forms of competition. In other words, as we will demonstrate later in this book, countries will not create sustainable wealth by continuing to compete in basic factor-dependent industries. They will do it by gaining increasingly sophisticated knowledge of, and delivering service to, demanding customers.

As the world becomes increasingly small through improvements in transportation and communications technology, customers all over the globe are becoming more sophisticated. Opportunities abound for developing-world firms to insert themselves in this process. Yet despite those opportunities, companies in developing countries often opt for the path of least resistance: exporting simple products that require little investment in customer knowledge.

As the example of the FOPTUR hotel in Arequipa implies, customers have increasingly different purchasing criteria. What we have learned, however, is that these different criteria are knowable and statistically segmentable. The challenge for firms throughout the world, but especially in the developing world, is to get better at knowing their customers. What they will find is that some will be attractive to serve and some will not. Gabriel García Márquez, the Nobel laureate from Colombia, says that you can tell as much about a good author from what is in the wastepaper basket as you can from what is in the finished work. The same is true for world class companies: their success is as much a function of what they choose *not to do* as what they choose *to do*. And nowhere is this more important than in choosing which customers to serve.

Companies face a large potential market for their products or services and typically do not have enough resources to compete in the entire marketplace. As a result, whether explicitly or implicitly, companies target particular market segments. In factor-driven economies with legacies of protectionist policies, firms tend to make choices based on comparative advantages. This leads them to compete in areas where cheap raw materials, labor, or transportation costs appear to provide an advantage in competition. But to achieve sustainable competitive advantage—which can improve the wealth of the average citizen—firms must compete by constantly striving to innovate in terms of how they deliver value to customers. We can define value in several ways—delivering a low-cost product, a highly differentiated product, or a certain level of service—but for that value to be sustainable, the product must continually respond to customers' evolving needs.

Making choices about how and where to compete before entering the competitive battlefield may sound like simple advice. But our experience in the developing world has shown that people usually decide to compete before determining what customers they are competing for. A mindset of comparative advantage combined with protectionist policies has led business leaders to make assumptions about the marketplace that are not tested and are often untrue.

NOT TO CHOOSE IS TO CHOOSE: THE EXAMPLE OF COLOMBIAN LEATHER

On a sunny day in May 1993, 100 of the most important members of the Colombian leather industry gathered in a meeting room in Bogotá to plot their escape. There were no locks on the doors, no bars on the windows, and no guards in the halls outside, but these ranchers, tanners, manufacturers, distributors, exporters, and advertisers felt themselves to be caught in a very real trap with no clear way out. As one delegate after another outlined the dimensions of the dilemma, emotions rose and tempers flared. Occasional moans of desperation made the mood in the room almost unbearable.

Things had not always been so bad for the Colombian leather industry. From 1986 to 1991, exports of leather manufactured goods had grown by an average of almost 19 percent each year. Foreign sales of shoes, handbags, and other products had more than doubled the size of the industry in that time and had brought revenues of $140 million to the men and women in that Bogotá meeting room. Industry leaders were proud of their ability to compete in North America, Europe, and Asia; in 1991, Colombia was a "net exporter"—exporting more leather goods to the United States than it imported.

But in 1992, exports of leather products began to fall. When this happened again in 1993, fear of economic stagnation began to spread in the industry, and people wondered: Could the future of Colombian leather be in jeopardy?

The Colombians' strategy had been to offer what was until then an attractive combination of threshold-level quality and moderate price. The strategy was grounded in their basic advantages, such as inexpensive labor, low-cost, locally produced hides, and a favorable exchange rate. Relying on these basic factor advantages, manufacturers had compensated for the somewhat poorer quality of their products with lower prices. This strategy proved successful until other manufacturers, largely from China, taking advantage of labor rates far below those in Bogotá, offered similar quality along with much lower prices. The Colombians had advantages such as inexpensive wage rates, but they also had the disadvantages of expensive internal transportation and rising labor costs.

China and Korea pushed Colombian brands out of one retail and mass-market channel after another. At the same time, the higher-end markets dominated by Italian leather products were out of reach. The inconsistent quality and peculiar designs of Colombian leather bags represented little threat to the dominance of Gucci or Devecchi. Moreover, what the Colombians had heard about the Italian leather industry's strength in design, manufacturing, and interfirm cooperation led them to believe that their own industry was years away from presenting any kind of a challenge to the Italians. Squeezed out of the international markets above and below them, the Colombians seemed to have nowhere to go.

At the Bogotá meeting, one delegate expressed his pessimism regarding the Colombian industry: "It is clear that we must beat the Chinese or the Italians to stay in business. But my friends, I cannot use chopsticks and my tastes are not for pasta, so bankruptcy appears the only choice available to me." In his expression of ultimate frustration, this delegate had unwittingly introduced an idea that would ultimately show the Colombians the solution to their problem. This revolutionary idea? The notion of choice.

Let's revisit the strategies of the Colombians, the Italians, and the Chinese and ask two questions about *strategic choices*. First, what kind of competitive advantage did firms in each of the countries pursue? Second, what approach to technology and innovation did those firms take? The answers to these questions uncover the root of the Colombians' problem.

Consider first the Italians. Italian leather manufacturers benefit from two strengths in their local environment: very demanding consumers of fashion and very competent designers. Those strengths have enabled the manufacturers to develop sophisticated, high-end products that can satisfy the most demanding customers in the world. And it is these customers that they have chosen to serve.

Now consider the Chinese. With a wage rate of about one-sixth that of the Colombians (at the time of the Colombian leather sector's meeting), they hold a tremendous comparative advantage in the leather industry, and they have *chosen* to pursue a low-cost strategy while maintaining just enough design and manufacturing capability to remain at an average level of quality for the world industry. This enables them to compete very effectively for price-conscious consumers worldwide.

Now consider the Colombians again. They had made no clear choices regarding for whom they wished to compete or how best to compete.

Other than relying on a historically devalued currency and inexpensive labor, they had not pursued strategies to maintain a low-cost position nor had they invested enough in design, manufacturing, or marketing technology to achieve high-quality, differentiated products. What they had done, in fact, was to cede the strategic battlefield to others like the Chinese and Italians and had thus lost their ability to determine their own market position.

If we were to map the relationship among the leather industry competitors, we would end up with a picture like that shown in figure 2-1. In this figure, the most successful players are those whose strategies land them in corners. Put another way, those in the corners have made clear strategic choices. Both the Italians and the Chinese are located firmly in a corner, but the Colombians have allowed themselves to drift to the center.

When we showed this picture to Colombian leather industry leaders, they had one of two responses. The first was, "Why did you put us in the middle? We didn't choose to be there." The second was, "What's wrong with being in the middle? Obviously there are customers who would like a decent product at moderate price."

Figure 2-1   Strategic Positioning in the Leather Handbag Industry (U.S. Market)

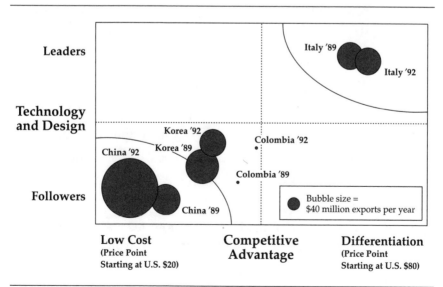

Source: Monitor Research, U.S. Department of Commerce.

Our response to the first question is that not making a choice is making a choice. In a dynamic, competitive battlefield, the players who do not make choices enable others to make choices for them. In response to the second objection to this chart, we can only reflect that there may in fact be customers who desire a combination of price and quality that the Colombians could serve. The problem is that the Colombians had not made any efforts to ensure that those were the customers they were serving. They did not know whether or not that was even an attractive market for them. Assumptions about who might be buying a product can be helpful, but they are not enough to identify the market segment in which to position a firm solidly against the competition. To reiterate, it is critical to make explicit choices about which segments to serve, and then to serve them. Otherwise, a firm inevitably is left in the middle—the least competitive place to be.

The Colombians clearly needed to begin making explicit strategic choices about what kinds of competitive advantages they wanted to develop. As we have seen, the two obvious choices—the low-cost position and the differentiated high-end position—were firmly in the grasp of the Chinese and the Italians. What's more, the Colombians were also becoming more and more burdened by an increasingly unfavorable exchange-rate environment, poor infrastructure, and an unreliable source of quality supply, owing to guerrilla activity around the country's cattle ranches. What *real* choices, then, were there for the Colombians to make?

SUMMARY

There are three fundamental reasons the Colombian leather industry leaders had worked themselves into such a difficult position:

1. They had not made *explicit choices* about customer segments.

2. They did not try to understand *customers' different needs.*

3. They did not seek the *most attractive customers* that they could serve.

In the days when the local markets were protected and export markets were easier to penetrate because of favorable exchange rates and government incentives, the issues listed above were not so critical. They are now.

Firms that fail to choose specific segments are essentially enabling the competition to choose for them. Whether we are discussing state-owned tourism in the Colca Valley of Peru, or the leather sector in Colombia, very predictable and consistent patterns will result. In failing to choose the most attractive segments that they can serve, firms will be forced into segments where average profit margins are lower, where competition on cost will be fierce, and where dependence on exogenous variables such as exchange rates will be high. These are the patterns associated with competing in basic factor-dependent industries, and they are inconsistent with creating a high and rising standard of living for the average citizen.

Moreover, there will continue to be little incentive for innovation or cooperation among industry participants because they will perceive that the number of customers is limited and that one firm can succeed only if another does not. The ability to create wealth, in other words, tends to be viewed as finite. Furthermore, firms will redouble their efforts to ensure that the government is providing them every source of advantage to continue competing in these unattractive segments. The eyes of the productive sector will be on the government—not on the market—and that will further reinforce the pattern of neglecting to make proactive choices about the best segments in which to compete.

CHAPTER THREE

Know Your Relative Competitive Position

Competition never occurs in a vacuum.
—*Colombian Petrochemical Plant Manager*

In Colombia, we conducted a three-month study on the relative competitiveness of the country's petrochemical industry, a project that had been financed jointly by the Petrochemical Industry Association and the Minister of Economic Development. The study took place as Colombia's Minister of Foreign Trade was beginning negotiations for the Group of Three trade accord between his country, Mexico, and Venezuela.

We presented the results of our work first to the industry association's board of directors. We had expected that presentation to be difficult; our analysis showed that Colombia's relative cost position was very poor compared with Venezuela and Mexico, and that polypropylene, the plastic we had studied, was not a very attractive industry at the time.[1] In fact, we concluded that the Colombians were at an 18 percent cost disadvantage, with few hopes of improving either their relative position or the attractiveness of the customer segments they were serving in the immediate future.

To our surprise, the board members received the presentation well, and they agreed with our analysis. They seemed to focus most, however, on one particular aspect of our message: that the government of Colombia was allowing one of its critical industries to lose competitiveness to its historic rivals. Of course, the government's part in the problem was not our entire message. But for the moment we had won the board members' confidence; they were certain we would be able to convince President Gaviria, with whom we would meet soon, to do his part to ensure the industry's survival.

We arrived at the President's Palace and took our seats at the Council of Ministers' table. The room filled with people, including our clients—the Minister of Development, and twenty of the board members from the Petrochemical Industry Association. We expected President Gaviria to be skeptical of us. He had received many foreign visitors, particularly from the World Bank and the IMF, to advise him on his *apertura*. Spanish for opening, *apertura* was the process of opening the Colombian economy initiated by President Barco in the late 1980s and largely accomplished by President Gaviria and his young and talented cabinet. We suspected that he anticipated from us a combination of lobbying on behalf of the petrochemical industry and some meddling in his management of the macroeconomics surrounding that industry. It was no surprise, then, that the President did not seem overly interested in what we had to say; still, it was clear he was listening carefully.

We focused on what we call relative cost analysis, an approach we use to determine the level of a firm's competitiveness in a cost-sensitive industry. Our analysis had enabled us to clarify what choices both the government and private sector had to make if the petrochemical industry was to survive, let alone prosper. And the choices were not easy.

Reflecting back on the situation, it is remarkable that the government and industry were able to engage in a productive dialogue. The industry association wanted the government to know how much its actions had hurt the relative position of Colombian petrochemicals. At the same time, the government had doubts about whether there would be any kind of future for certain parts of the petrochemical industry. Despite the different perspectives from which they viewed the problem, both parties were able to appreciate the importance of understanding the country's relative position in petrochemicals: their blindness to the competitive situation had hurt them long enough. If there were tough choices to make, at least, with the understanding of relative position, the choices would be fully informed, and together the government and the industry association would bite the bullet and make them.

This seems like an obvious point—that, before taking any strategic action, industry and government would want to know where they stood vis-à-vis the competition. But our experience in developing countries has proved otherwise; too often, critical decisions are made in a vacuum. These countries never had to become skilled in this type of knowledge capture and creation because in their protected, small economies, it was not important.

Companies that do not understand their position relative to the competition can fail in an industry. Alternatively, governments that understand relative position can help firms make better choices about where and how to compete. But if none of the key decision makers in an economy understands relative position, there is no one to set accurate priorities for improving the competitive environment and ensuring that firms have a platform from which they can compete globally.

Recall how this pattern of failing to appreciate relative position emerged in the story of the flower industry: the Colombians lost market share in the United States because they did not understand where they stood relative to other flower producers, particularly the Dutch. Similar examples abound throughout the developing world. In our experience, poor knowledge about relative position leads to three kinds of problems:

1. A habit of *ineffective communication* that inhibits productive dialogue within the private sector and between the private sector and the government: people spend more time lobbying and less time learning.

2. A tendency to make *uninformed choices* based on poor understanding (or inaccurate assumptions) about relative capabilities that lead to untenable positions in unattractive industries.

3. A high degree of *vulnerability to competition* that can easily erode advantages often thought to be sustainable.

INEFFECTIVE COMMUNICATION

When there is no clear understanding of an industry's relative position, unproductive dialogue between the government and private sector ensues. Ministers of government grow impatient with what they hear as the industry associations' droning cry: that they need government help to compete. If any data accompany those cries, a Minister will typically dismiss it as information selected simply to support the point of the lobbyist. And while the Minister gets frustrated at the private sector's inability to create compelling presentations of why, how, and for how long the government should act in an industry's behalf, the private sector develops the impression that the government simply does not give a damn.

As our story concerning President Gaviria's openness to learning about the Colombian petrochemicals industry illustrates, we have found that a rigorous analysis of relative position actually provides both sides of such a debate an opportunity to have a more constructive dialogue.

Uninformed Choices

Not knowing one's position relative to other competitors creates two types of uninformed and often detrimental choices. The first type is the choice *not* to act on certain opportunities that might present themselves to firms in a given country. The second type is choosing to make investments in areas where critical variables are unknown.

Let's begin with the first choice: not to enter the competitive battlefield. Remember what García Márquez said about knowing the great author by looking through his garbage can. So too with competitiveness; choosing not to compete in a certain arena can be good strategy. More often, however, rather than making a reasoned choice not to compete, firms in developing countries choose not to compete out of fear. That fear is often driven by inaccurate assumptions about how capable one firm is versus the other. Again, fear is not bad. But choosing not to compete because you are afraid of a competitor whose strengths or weaknesses you do not understand can hurt your business.

We observed that tendency to avoid competition during our work in Bolivia, and we decided to survey a group of influential Bolivian business leaders to uncover the underlying beliefs driving such behavior. The business leaders assessed their country relative to other Andean nations on a number of dimensions. One of the dimensions was national prestige. What we found in Bolivia was a nation whose leaders possessed very low self-esteem regarding export competitiveness. Those participating in the survey saw Bolivia as inferior to six out of the seven countries considered, and found themselves only equal to the seventh.[2]

In reviewing the data, one prominent Bolivian businessman re-marked: "Bolivia has a defeatist attitude. Losing is accepted here." Another leader said: "We have so few successes in business outside our own country that winning almost doesn't seem possible. Sometimes I think we don't try to export because we don't know if we even have a chance to become competitive. How others do it is a mystery to us, and we almost always start by thinking of ourselves as behind and not up to the challenge."

Indeed, many business leaders in the developing world often assume that their companies are incompetent relative to competition from com-panies in other countries. The attitude is: "If we are not winning we are losing, and if we are losing it must be because, in some way, we do not measure up." That seems like a reasonable hypothesis, but it is only a hypothesis. It implies the existence of a benchmark these leaders' com-panies are failing to meet or exceed, yet that benchmark cannot be explicitly stated or quantified. A business leader with that mind-set cannot say, "We are 20 percent less efficient than our primary competi-tor" or, "We need to cut our costs in this area by $4 per ton to have a cost advantage in this business." The only thing that leader knows is that his company does not measure up to a standard that is largely defined in his own mind.

When managers do not know where they stand relative to competi-tors, they lack information that could help them invest in new industry segments or seek new and innovative ways to compete that could actually break the patterns described here.

The second type of uninformed choice that companies and industries often make is actually easier to remedy than the first type. Firms that do choose to make investments are often unsure of the two critical variables we mentioned in the story of the Colombian leather industry: (1) the industry's structural attractiveness for the average player, and (2) the firm's competitive position relative to the other players in the industry. Those variables can be plotted on a chart, as shown in fig-ure 3-1.

Before any firm in any country invests in any opportunity, it should know the answers to the questions implied by these two variables. The legacy of heavy-handed government involvement in developing indus-tries throughout the Third World, however, has kept both government and business leaders from doing the work necessary to understand the

Figure 3-1 Industry Structure and Relative Cost Position

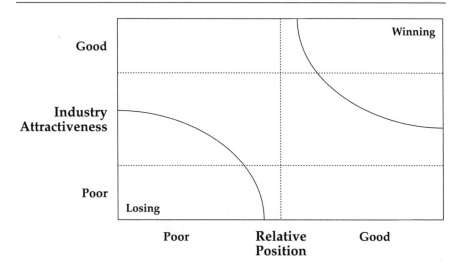

relative strengths and weaknesses of a particular industry. The incentives that governments and multilateral organizations have provided for firms to develop industries often make great *macro*economic sense but very little *micro*economic sense. A good example is the current environment in Venezuela, where leaders in the private and the public sector are preoccupied with inflation rates, balance of trade data, and the latest Brady bond[3] prices denominated in *bolivares* (the local currency), instead of building specialized infrastructure, developing firm-level strategies, and focusing on human capital improvements.

Another example is Colombian petrochemicals. Careful analysis of relative position would have been particularly useful *before* the industry invested millions of dollars. As we have said, our analysis showed that Colombian petrochemicals—specifically the manufacture of polypropylene, a product that serves as a good representative for the industry overall—were at a significant cost disadvantage compared with other countries. Figure 3-2 summarizes that position. Three main elements drove Colombia's cost disadvantage: (1) raw materials prices, (2) utility prices, and (3) transportation costs. In one sectoral analysis, we studied the cash cost position of one Colombian petrochemical company, relative to three of the firm's most important regional competitors—Vene-

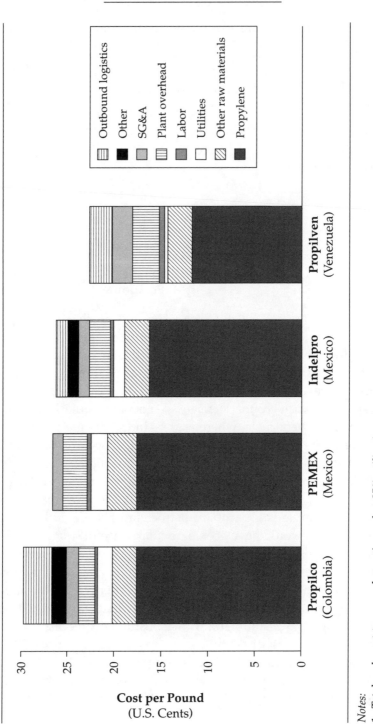

Figure 3-2 Polypropylene Industry Relative Cost Position: Colombia, Venezuela, and Mexico, 1992

Notes:

1. Total cash cost to serve domestic market 85% utilization rate.

2. Information concerning Propilco is made public with permission of client from previously published materials. The information used in this figure is over five years old and no longer reflects Propilco's current positioning.

zuela's Propilven and Mexico's PEMEX and Indelpro—and found that the Colombian firm could not be cost competitive with any of those firms in their domestic markets.

Some industry leaders believed that the problems Propilco faced in the marketplace were constraints that Colombian government policies imposed on the firm. Whether that was entirely true or not, we believed that without active government support and increased assistance, Propilco could never keep its doors open or continue to compete at all in the Latin American polypropylene industry. Propilco's power costs were high because the national power utility rates were high. Logistics costs were high because the nation's transport infrastructure was inadequate and getting worse. Insurance costs were high because there was little sense of security in Colombia, a country whose guerrillas and drug traffickers made it explosively and perpetually violent. Propylene was the raw material, or *feedstock*, and its costs were high because the state-owned petrochemical plant, Ecopetrol, did not produce polymer-grade propylene; consequently Propilco had to import its feedstock from the Texas-Louisiana coast in the United States.

By way of contrast, Venezuela's state-owned oil company, Pequiven, subsidized Propilven's already low power costs, sold it polymer-grade propylene feedstock at discounted transfer prices, and levied no royalty. Adding insult to injury, Propilven could then export polypropylene into the Colombian market and pay no compensating import tariff. Not surprisingly, at that time Propilven thought polypropylene was a good business and was seeking foreign partners to build another 100,000-plus metric tons of capacity.

While Propilco had a strong, dynamic position within a protected economy, its success ultimately depended on exogenous variables: the government's decisions about the petroleum industry, the nationally established utility rates, and a constant vulnerability to guerrillas who regularly captured oil trucks on the highways. At the same time, Propilco faced competitors in Mexico and Venezuela that had invested large sums of money and much national pride in creating strong petrochemical industries. Moreover, those competitors had proven they would do whatever was necessary (even to the point of pricing below costs) to keep employment strong and capacity utilization high.

Of course, having a good relative position is only part of what a firm needs to succeed, as we have indicated in chapters 1 and 2, where we warn against relying on factor advantages and stress the need for customer segmentation. In fact, recent research by Michael Porter (unpublished at the time of this book) shows that in the United States about 50 percent of a firm's success can be attributed to its choice of industry segment and about 50 percent to its relative position within an industry. We now understand why the petrochemical industry association members were pleased by our meeting with President Gaviria: they believed their success lay *100 percent* in improving their relative position. Even though it happened that the government was indeed largely responsible for their poor relative position, that was only half of the equation. The other half was about the original choice of industry segment in which to compete.

As is the case in many of the patterns we discuss in this book, it is increasingly important to see competitiveness as a system in which a thousand small things—not one or two big things—are done right. For example, petrochemicals might not be an attractive industry for most players because there are almost three dozen competitors in polypropylene in the Western hemisphere, many of which are state-owned and hence not forced to make all strategic decisions based on profit. Barriers to entry are small, as only 2 percent share of the world market is required to achieve economy of scale in production. Barriers to exit are high, however, because the physical plant must be large to even compete. In addition, the social issues surrounding employment are intractable in many of the producing nations.

Leaders who hope to make a lasting difference in their economies in the future need to begin thinking about microeconomic issues and business-level strategies in all of their complexity, especially relative positioning. They need to begin basing policy decisions on a sound understanding of what it takes to win, and they must develop their abilities to create productive, informed discussions between the public and the private sector.

VULNERABILITY TO THE COMPETITION

The final problem that emerges when relative position is unknown concerns competitor behavior. When economies move from being protected to being open to the forces of global competition, knowing what the competition is doing or planning to do is critical. And knowing how one stacks up against the competition is a key component of that analysis.

Kenichi Ohmae, author, former McKinsey consultant, and one-time political candidate in Japan, writes that in fact firms should *not* focus on analyzing the competition for its own sake; rather they should find ways to serve their customers to the customers' complete satisfaction and relative to the competition.[4] Competition, he writes, is the fundamental dynamic of customer satisfaction. We agree with Ohmae that it is easy to become distracted simply by what the competition is doing, or what the customer prefers and in the process lose track of the real dynamic of customer satisfaction relative to the competition.

Ohmae's advice applies to developing countries as well. As we saw in chapter 2, the last thing that most companies in the developing world think about is how best to serve customers (recall the Peruvian tourist hotel, for example). To understand how best to serve their customers, firms in these countries can begin by looking at the competition. They must keep in mind what other companies in the world are doing that might threaten their plans about where and how to compete. The following examples of two Mexican industries and the threat they pose to those same industries in Colombia illustrate this concept.

The Mexican Flower Industry

In the story about the flower industry, Colombia is competing not just against the Dutch but also against competitors closer to home—the Mexicans. Colombia has shown little concern about the threat that Mexican flower growers present, yet we estimate that Mexico can potentially—and soon—become competitive with other Latin American flower producers by strategically leveraging its transportation advantage to U.S. markets. Already Mexico flies a large portion of its flowers to Texas-based brokers who distribute them, much like the Miami brokers do for Colombia. A small number of Mexican flowers even travel on direct flights from Mexico City to major U.S. cities.

The Mexicans do not truck their flowers to the U.S. border because they do not yet have the volume to consistently supply full truckloads. (In the trucking business, full loads are necessary to justify in economic terms the establishment of a new route.) We estimate that in three to five years, however, Mexico will achieve the volume needed to begin shipping directly by truck. Moreover, with the passage of NAFTA, Mexican trucks may no longer be required to stop for inspection at the U.S.-Mexico border. This would mean that Mexico would be able to truck flowers nonstop to major U.S. cities, with the flowers arriving more quickly and in better condition than if they had been unpacked for inspection and then repacked.

Although countries like Colombia may still have a logistics cost advantage in serving East Coast markets, Mexico will have a logistics cost advantage in serving Midwest and West Coast markets. For example, our analysis shows that Mexico will have an advantage of 1.9 cents per stem in serving Chicago, which has 21 percent of U.S. demand for flowers within just a five-hour drive. In addition, Mexican growers are developing direct relationships with wholesalers and supermarkets, enabling them to further cut costs by eliminating or greatly reducing the broker function. Thus the cost advantage that Colombia now has over Mexico will become less relevant as the Mexicans directly target nearby U.S. markets and continue to lower costs in their flower production processes.

When representatives from the Colombian flower industry heard of these developments, they agreed that the relative position analysis we had done was important. But rather than use our results to develop a strategy, they hoped to use them to lobby the Colombian government for support. The Colombian growers suspected that the Mexican government was giving its flower producers certain benefits, and they wanted the same. Additionally, some of them wanted the information to invest in Mexican flower production themselves.

Time will tell what will happen between the Mexican and Colombian flower industries, but unless the Colombians take a proactive approach to deterring Mexico from penetrating their traditional markets, they may well lose the advantages they have worked so hard to build.

Printing and Publishing in Mexico

Colombia has traditionally boasted a thriving industry in printing and publishing that has seen particular success in producing children's pop-up books. In 1992, NAFTA loomed on the horizon, and North American printer R.R. Donnelley & Sons, which already owned Mexican *maquila* (light manufacturing with subsidies and incentives to export) plants, appeared to be positioning itself even more intensely in Mexico. The Colombian printing leaders, fearing that a Mexican-based operation of R.R. Donnelley would soon capture much of their market share in the United States, asked us to determine how much of a threat they actually faced.

We found that while Mexican printers had managed to recover from the economic upheavals their country experienced during the 1980s, most still used machinery that was nearly obsolete and faced serious problems finding the highly skilled labor needed to operate their presses. Mexico already exported more books to the United States than Colombia did, but 51 percent of those (in 1992) were children's picture books printed primarily by the R.R. Donnelley *maquila* plant. Moreover, export growth had been concentrated in the hands of only a few firms, while most Mexican printers, including R.R. Donnelley's plant, focused on the domestic market. That concentration at home was the result of an industry-wide belief that Mexico's internal growth under the influence of NAFTA and generally sound macroeconomic trends would spur increased domestic printing consumption, primarily of business forms and magazines.

Some Mexican printers were in fact trying to increase exports to the United States. Most of those firms had already created, or were actively seeking, partnerships with U.S. printers to help them obtain market knowledge and capital investment. Still, Mexican printers faced certain disadvantages compared with their Colombian competition. Our research indicated that Colombian printers maintained a lower overall cost position and enjoyed a better reputation for quality than Mexican printers did.

But in the process of discovering that bit of good news for Colombia, we learned that the real threat to the country's printing industry was actually coming from Asia. The Colombians, it seems, had been so concerned about Mexico that they had ignored the gradual but steady rise of the printing industry in the East.

SUMMARY

It is important for firms to analyze their position relative to competitors for three main reasons: (1) it can facilitate productive dialogue between the public sector and the private sector; (2) it can help firm managers make more informed choices; and (3) it can help firms anticipate areas in which they may be vulnerable to the competition.

There are two components to relative position analysis that we should make explicit. First, it is important to understand a given firm's basis of competition—that is, is it competing on the basis of costs, or competing as a differentiated player who can charge more for the product by adding unique value for the consumer? If the basis of the competition is cost, then *relative cost position* analysis is most critical. If the basis of the competition is differentiation, then analysis of *customer satisfaction* relative to the competition is most critical. Either way, the challenge is to know and understand one's own position so as to determine the likelihood of success in the competitive battlefield.

The second critical point regards competitors. "Competition never occurs in a vacuum." And a lack of knowledge about the competition's goals and capabilities in terms of serving customers may leave a firm very vulnerable.

When it comes to market demand, developing nations have to upgrade themselves from being *responders* to *seekers*, and ultimately, to *creators*. Instead of extracting and exporting the basic wealth of their countries—again, a strategy that leaves the countries vulnerable to imitation, price fluctuations, and exchange-rate management—firms need to learn how to understand demand and the dynamics of competition better so that they might find more attractive customer segments. That is what we mean by *seeking*.

Furthermore, if firms in developing countries understood customer preferences so intimately that they could anticipate them, and perhaps even help shape them, they would be on their way to becoming *creators*. Italy's high-end fashion designers and manufacturers are creators in the sense that what they make tends to shape the tastes and preferences of consumers—and to influence competitors—in a portion of their market. Very often, they make excellent profit margins doing just that.

The essence of this upgrading process involves becoming competent at ascertaining *relative position*. As we have said, the lack of this knowledge is one of the reasons firms in developing countries find themselves competing in unattractive industry segments. It also makes impossible the kind of high-quality discussion that must take place between senior public and private sector decision makers as they make increasingly complex decisions about opportunities that will come and go with increasing rapidity. With a clear understanding of relative position, these decision makers will be able to begin creating their own opportunities that promise even greater rewards.

CHAPTER FOUR

Know When and When Not to Forward Integrate

When we sell our goods, we never know what happens after they leave our farm. It's like they go into a big black box.

—Peruvian agriculture producer

In 1992, the fruit juice processors of Colombia faced a predicament. The price of their primary export product, passion fruit concentrate, had fluctuated wildly during the preceding five years. The price per pound of passion fruit pulp they could earn from U.S. buyers, for example, had gone from $2.90 in 1988 down to $0.98 in 1991 and back up to $1.55 in 1993.

These large fluctuations were due to Colombia's status as a relatively small supplier of commodity juice concentrate. Brazil, on the other hand, a world leader in juice production, could make international demand soar just by selling to its home market rather than the world market. When Brazil did sell on the world market, however, demand and price for the Colombian product plummeted. In addition to the power Brazil exerted over the commodity market, those closest to the consumer, including Miami brokers, bottlers, and distributors, seemed to be in a better position to earn stable, long-term profits than the Colombians were. As one Miami broker put it, "We can get passion fruit from wherever we want." The Colombian processors felt like they were on a tiny vessel, tossed and turned in a tumultuous commodity sea.

Recall how the Colombian flower industry faced a similar problem, with U.S. brokers, wholesalers, and retailers earning surplus profits that the growers could never hope to see. The juice processors debated whether investing in a production and possible distribution facility in the United States would help them gain power in the long chain to the consumer. If the Colombians could brand, bottle, and distribute their own product, they felt they might have a chance of capturing the profits that had eluded them for so long.

Where to Compete? The Challenge of Vertical Positioning

In the developing world, producers have consistently been unable to gain leverage in the distribution of their products and are often taken advantage of by big multinational corporations. How can one explain the dominance of the United Fruit Company in the history of Central America or the huge trading companies in sub-Saharan Africa? Why do the powerful consistently exploit those who, at least by measures of comparative advantage, should be considered the wealthy?

Part of the answer is that the developing world's business leaders have profited handsomely by taking advantage of their countries' factor endowments, a situation that creates little incentive for change. As a result, the captains of industry have almost without exception failed to develop the *strategic positioning* necessary to change the balance of power. It is this poor positioning, especially with respect to vertical scope, that has made this fourth pattern of business behavior—failing to forward integrate—one of the most pervasive, unjust, and difficult to change.

Vertical scope, which later in the book we will identify as one of eight generic areas in which firms must make explicit choices, relates to how a firm chooses to position itself among its suppliers and buyers. The decision to be made in most developing countries, although not all of the time, concerns how to move closer to the end-user, or how to *forward integrate* to improve the firm's competitive position. Increasingly, vertical—or specifically, forward—integration has come to include not just ownership but also partnership, cooperation, electronic knowledge-based linkages, and other forms of "virtual integration." For example, Benetton, the Italian clothing group, has epitomized the concept of "virtual" forward integration. Having placed its retail shops throughout the world, the company uses informational linkages that instantly convey customer information to the Benetton factories; customer segmentation and strategic planning occur at a rate faster than most retailers can manage. Benetton has achieved this level of vertical integration without having to actually own the production chain: they are vertically integrated through information, not ownership.

The Colombian flower industry is an archetypal Third World story in its lack of forward integration. For the most part, the flower sector is restricted to the "upstream" part of the value system, that is, the part having to do with converting inputs into products. Moving "downstream," or forward, would give the growers more control over actually selling their products to end-consumers and manipulating market information (as the U.S. wholesalers and retailers do now). We don't intend to discuss here theories of vertical positioning but rather want to address the issue of why so much of the learning that exists on the subject has failed to create fundamentally different patterns of competition in the developing world. One reason, perhaps, is that strategy practitioners in the developed world have adroitly managed their suppliers and kept control of industries for themselves. This has had dire consequences for firms in the developing world, and it is a situation that must be addressed explicitly. There are several micropatterns of vertical integration that consistently reveal themselves in developing countries and that represent critical challenges for Latin American business owners and managers. Those micropatterns are:

- Failure to understand or inability to meet distribution channel needs.

- Failure to see distribution channels as a tool for leveraging unique sources of competitive advantage.

- Failure to use distribution channels to get consistent and accurate market feedback about trends and industry dynamics.

In this chapter we will illustrate these micropatterns by drawing from case studies in Colombia and Peru and suggest that there are better ways for producers in the developing world to think about choices of vertical scope. Many of these producers have not chosen the best distribution system for their products, as illustrated by their tendency to rely mainly on brokers for the sale and distribution of goods. In the case of the Colombian flower industry, this was appropriate during the 1970s and 1980s. At that time, the brokers in Miami added tremendous value: they opened up markets, they provided tax shelters for the producers, and they created successful strategies to fight the dominant U.S. and Dutch producers. But the same strategy has proved remarkably inefficient for the Colombian flower industry in the 1990s. It is unclear what real value the brokers currently add to the Colombian flower industry that the producers, given the advances in technology and communications, could not take care of themselves from Colombia. Instead, the Miami brokers have developed an increasingly bureaucratic, often hostile, and unresponsive system that has tremendous incentives for self-preservation and very little incentive to help the Colombian flower producers develop more sustainable sources of advantage.

Sellers must learn two critical skills with regard to channels of distribution: what to provide them with and what to get from them. As computing power has given more leverage to consumers and more information to producers, and as distribution systems have become more efficient, the distance between the producer and the consumer is rapidly shrinking. We believe the days of allowing middlemen to control the wealth of exports is fast coming to an end, and there is no better time than now for firms in the developing world to seize control of their industries. This is part of the key to moving away from basic factor dependency: learning how to compete not only close to where the value is created but also close to where it is captured—oftener than not, closer to the end-user.

Giving Distribution Channels What They Need: A Lesson from the Fruit Juice Industry

In the early 1990s, the fruit juice producers in Colombia, though small in number, were committed to moving themselves away from being occasional exporters to global fruit juice companies, and toward becoming providers of unique and exotic fruit juices to end-consumers. The desire to move away from the problems inherent in the first pattern of business behavior we discussed a few chapters ago—competing on the basis of comparative advantage in commodity-like industries—to competing in more complex industries is admirable and correct. It is also very difficult to achieve.

The Colombians have many fruits that no other country grows, and they produce many products for the export market, including guanabana, guayaba, lulo, mango, maracuyá, mora, and papaya. But the processed fruit product with the highest external sales is passion fruit concentrate. The export market for Colombian passion fruit in processed form is relatively new, although a domestic juice market has existed for hundreds of years. The domestic market, however, does not consume much processed or concentrated juice since most Colombian households buy fresh fruit and squeeze it themselves.

Growers are generally small, autonomous enterprises that provide fruit to the local market or to fruit juice processors, depending on the prices in each market. Growers therefore behave much like speculators, which leads to two results that hurt Colombian processors. The first is that the growers tend to plant a lot of passion fruit when it appears that world demand (and prices) are going to be favorable, and they pull out their crops as prices decline. Because a mature passion fruit plant takes significant time to grow, it is hard to coordinate Colombian supply with world demand precisely. Second, if the local price for passion fruit rises above the international price, growers tend to sell to the local market instead of the export market. Both of these behaviors lead to an unstable Colombian supply that hurts the image of processors in the eyes of foreign buyers.

Growers are geographically dispersed, with seven different types of fruit grown in seventeen regions. Often the same fruit is grown in three or more parts of the country. For example, passion fruit production is spread among the regions of Risaralda (5 percent), Cauca (5.9 percent), Valle de Cauca (22.2 percent), Huila (25.2 percent), and other regions (26.2 percent). Many of these regions are separated by rugged, mountainous terrain, and the roads connecting them are often unpaved and primitive. Fruit deliveries are therefore costly and full of delays, and the result is often damaged fruit.

The scenario we have just presented can be summed up in a few words indicative of many other industries in the region: rudimentary, unplanned, and uncoordinated. It is important to acknowledge the chaotic nature of the Colombian competitive environment. As we see later, it both influences the strategic choices now being made by the industry and holds the key to the execution of a strategy that will extract more value from the production chain in the future.

Weighing the Opportunity to Forward Integrate

Because of the poor transportation conditions, unpredictable supply, and the broad dispersion of growers across the country, Colombian juice processors have a hard time guaranteeing the price, quality, and supply of their product. That is why brokers in Miami play such a vital role for U.S. fruit juice producers: brokers can consolidate supply from a number of sources and absorb all of the quality risks from suppliers. A full 90 percent of concentrate supply, therefore, goes to those brokers.

In 1992, Corporación Colombia Internacional (CCI) was formed to promote the export of Colombian agricultural products. CCI, which had several fruit juice processors on its board, worked with us to examine the processors' problem. The challenge was to find a way to move the processors away from exporting commodity juice concentrate, a product at the mercy of all sorts of external price variables, as we have described. But did the answer lie in branding their own product and establishing factories and distribution networks in the United States? Or was an alliance with an established U.S. fruit juice producer a more intelligent option? Both options fall under the rubric of viability of forward integration into the U.S. market, and that is what we set out to analyze for the Colombian producers.

We began by looking at the channels through which the Colombians might sell their product, starting with supermarkets, which represented 85 percent of total sales in the U.S. juice market. The top five supermarkets had considerable buying power, averaging 1,000 outlets and $15.9 billion in total annual sales. Not surprisingly, we found that when it came to gaining shelf space in most of these supermarket chains, large U.S. fruit juice producers had the scale and bargaining power to edge out smaller competitors easily.

In addition, those large branded fruit juice companies spent a huge amount of money on advertising. For example, in 1991, the annual advertising expenditures for the top U.S. fruit juice companies ranged between $3 million and $21 million each.

Concluding that large supermarket channels were not very attractive, we turned to smaller, niche distribution channels. The most attractive seemed to be the *bodega* channel, which served ethnically diverse consumers (including many Hispanics) in small U.S. neighborhood supermarkets. Our initial analysis showed that *bodegas* did offer a broader and more extensive assortment of tropical flavors and that Hispanics tended to consume more juice than the average population sample. Closer analysis, however, revealed a number of unattractive elements lurking within that channel. First, even though the *bodega* was a niche channel, it was locked up by one relatively giant competitor: Goya. With $453 million in sales in 1992 and an advertising budget of $1.2 million, it also boasted a large, extensive sales and distribution network.

Moreover, our research showed that of the Latin American *bodega* patrons, the majority were Mexican, which was unfortunate since Mexicans were not highly familiar with passion fruit (fewer than 10 hectares of the fruit is grown in Mexico). Suddenly the *bodega* channel wasn't looking as good as it had. In fact, the idea of the Colombians bottling their own product and then battling entrenched U.S. competitors did not seem to make strategic sense at all.

Understanding How Channels Add Value

We began looking at other options with the processors. Could the growers and processors establish such an outstanding reputation of quality and stable supply that they could sell directly to the large branded juice producers in the United States? We interviewed a number of U.S. fruit juice purchasing heads to find out.

The purchasing representative for Very Fine was intent on continuing to buy from his brokers and did not seem interested in dealing directly with the Colombians. Ocean Spray, which manufactures a number of fruit drinks using passion fruit, was more receptive to the idea of creating a direct relationship. The company's requirements in establishing such a relationship were "price, quality, and stable supply," according to one purchasing manager.

For the Colombians, this was not good news. As they thought more about the concerns of companies like Ocean Spray, they concluded that they were not yet in a position to meet those requirements. In other words, the brokers in this system did add real value in a situation where the producers were unable to do so. The distribution channels, therefore, were actually beneficial to both fruit juice producers and end-customers. It made no strategic sense to try to restructure this industry—yet. As long as the current system of distribution added value to all parties involved, we concluded, it should be kept and leveraged.

The experience reinforced some valuable lessons. First, it is critical to *test the value that is being added* by the current distribution system. If the distributors/brokers are adding value that the buyers of the product want, they should be considered an ally that can be leveraged. In many cases, the distributors are extracting profits without adding value. The second lesson is similar to that taught by analysis of the second pattern of business behavior we discussed: the importance of choosing segments in which to compete and developing an understanding of the needs of that segment. The Colombian producers were unable to meet the needs of Ocean Spray, which wanted reliability and low financial risk. But this knowledge does present the Colombians with the opportunity to configure themselves in a way that might position them to compete farther downstream.

Forward integration requires firms to move into a different competitive arena. It is not easy, and it is not always the right way to go. In general, however, it is true that the closer one is to the customer, the easier it is to understand the customers' purchasing criteria. This knowledge then presents the opportunity to develop products and services for which customers may be willing to pay more.

Leveraging Distribution Channels: More Reflections from the Flower Industry

The distribution strategy the Colombian flower industry pioneered in the United States was a remarkable success in that it dethroned the United States from its position of market dominance. But as we have shown, what began as a good strategy and a tremendous source of learning for the large, forward-integrated growers, selling flowers in the United States became over time an unresponsive, overly structured system that destroyed value for the producers.

For example, more than 21 percent of U.S. flower consumption was concentrated in and around Chicago in 1992. To better serve that area and the surrounding midwestern market, why shouldn't the Colombians export directly to Chicago and then truck flowers to nearby customers instead of exporting to Miami and then transporting flowers by truck cross-country?

Direct shipments to Chicago would enable the flower growers to be more responsive, to provide a fresher flower, and to better learn the vagaries of the midwestern market. But that change could take place only if Colombia established direct flights to Chicago, and that decision fell under the purview of the government, since it involved trading airline landing rights. In addition, the huge private sector investment required to make Chicago a viable hub represented a significant risk. Unfortunately, this was not a risk the private sector was willing to take, given many years of comfortable and successful operation in Miami. The Colombians had developed a strategy that worked, and they could see no clear reason why they should risk a system they knew for one that might jeopardize their current success.

But the industry faced at least two looming challenges. The first was the increased threat posed by new competitors entering the market. For example, as we mentioned in chapter 3, on relative position, the Colombian flower industry faced a possible threat from the Mexican industry, particularly with regard to the then imminent passage of NAFTA. Mexicans might well be able to ship flowers directly to the western United States much more cost-effectively and rapidly than the Colombians could.

A more urgent short-term concern was the Colombian macroeconomic environment. With an effective real revaluation of the peso, it was becoming harder for the growers to make any money exporting flowers. There was an economic imperative to find ways to capture more of the wealth in the cut flower distribution chain. Figure 4-1 illustrates how revenues are distributed for one cut rose. Though the growers made almost 15 cents per rose stem, their costs were almost 13 cents per stem. In this industry, the closer one is to the end-consumer, the more wealth can be captured: the wholesalers and retailers are the ones making the real profits.

Some Colombian flower pioneers had reached that conclusion early and ventured into broker operations and later to direct sales with several large supermarket chains, with varying degrees of success. The majority of Colombia's producers, however, were intent on making the current strategy of Miami brokers succeed and were unwilling to invest in learning how to fundamentally rethink their vertical positioning. Whereas the fruit juice producers found that the broker system was in fact adding value, our analysis of the flower brokerage system showed that it had ceased being a major source of advantage for the Colombian flower industry.

All of this points to a disequilibrium between the value created throughout the flower distribution channel system and the rewards

Figure 4-1 Colombian Cut Flower Value System, 1993

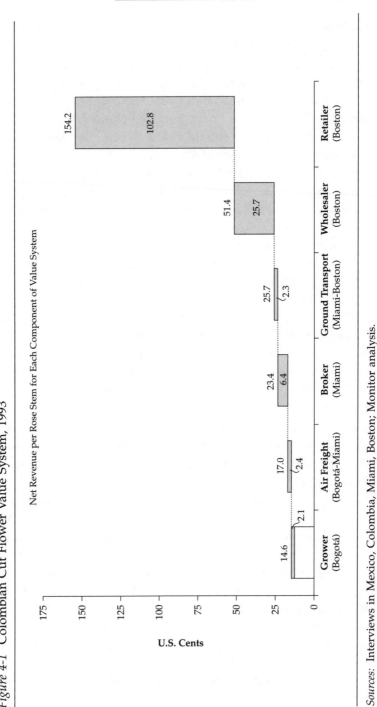

Net Revenue per Rose Stem for Each Component of Value System

Sources: Interviews in Mexico, Colombia, Miami, Boston; Monitor analysis.

received. But where there is disequilibrium, there is also opportunity. The challenge is for the exporter to realize that a particular part of the distribution channel no longer provides unique advantage. Using a particular channel is worthwhile only if it gives something back—advantages that help a firm position itself better vis-à-vis the competition or that provide valuable information about end-consumers. This second point is that channels should help firms understand the needs of their final consumers by providing market feedback.

GETTING MARKET FEEDBACK: WHAT PERUVIAN ASPARAGUS GROWERS DIDN'T KNOW

Michael Porter refers to market feedback as *economies of information:* a seller can respond to customer needs only if positioned to know the constantly changing nature of end-consumers. Indeed, many exporters describe the brokerage system as a "black box"—once their product leaves the factory, they have no idea what happens to it. The broker charges them a fee and sells the product, but they do not know if the work is being done well or poorly. Part of the reason these exporters see the system as a black box is because they have developed a channel strategy that does not provide them with any market feedback.

Most of the exporters we have come to know are not competing close enough to the end-consumer to be able to influence demand. They *respond* to demand. They are accustomed to waiting for others to tell them what demand will be. As we have indicated, instead of simply responding to demand, exporters should seek it out or actually create it. Forward positioning is a critical component in both seeking and creating demand. A firm has to design a vertical or forward integration strategy that enables it to capture critical market information that will ultimately improve its ability to compete effectively.

The Peruvian agricultural industry, for example, has experienced a boom in recent years, especially in its exports of asparagus. Our research reveals, however, that 95 percent of Peru's agro-industry exports are sold through brokers. Traditionally, this approach has made the most sense. But Peru is changing, and Peruvian capabilities are changing. We believe that the broker system is no longer the best route for Peruvians to get their agricultural product to market. The diagram in figure 4-2 represents other options producers in Peru have for selling their product. These are now untapped markets that offer the exporters

Figure 4-2 Distribution Possibilities for Peruvian Asparagus

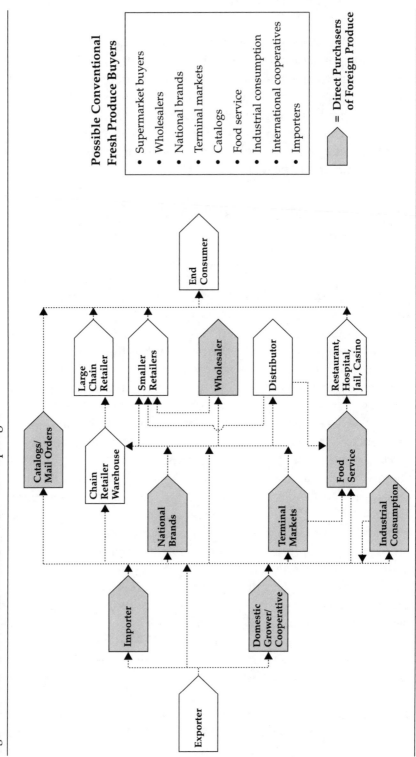

**Possible Conventional
Fresh Produce Buyers**

- Supermarket buyers
- Wholesalers
- National brands
- Terminal markets
- Catalogs
- Food service
- Industrial consumption
- International cooperatives
- Importers

= Direct Purchasers
of Foreign Produce

potentially many more benefits—in terms of both competitive advantage and market knowledge—than the current system.

The Peruvian asparagus industry, the third largest supplier of the vegetable to the United States, offers a good example of how important it is for firms to reconsider their thinking about vertical scope. Asparagus consumption in the United States is highly cyclical, yet we found that the Peruvian producers knew little about the underlying patterns of U.S. demand, not to mention the possibility of actually increasing demand. Figure 4-3 demonstrates where opportunities for the Peruvian growers lie.

Asparagus consumption is cyclical for the simple reason that U.S. producers can grow the vegetable only during certain months of the year, so that is when asparagus is most plentiful in supermarkets. It is a matter of what consumers are accustomed to. But consumers can be educated to buy asparagus year-round. By launching an aggressive marketing and distribution strategy, Peru could sell a great deal more

Figure 4-3 1993 U.S. Market Asparagus Consumption

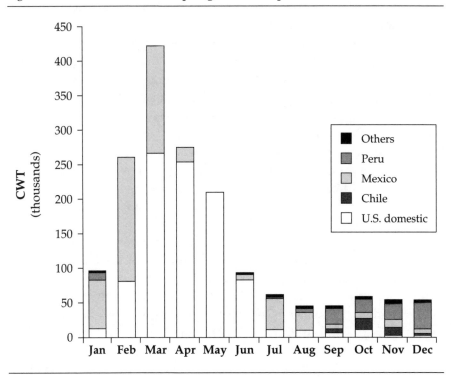

Note: 1 CWT = 100 lbs.

asparagus during the traditional low-consumption season in the United States.

Why is the Peruvian pattern relevant in a discussion about forward integration? Primarily because it reveals that the Peruvian producers had little understanding of the dynamics and sheer size of their principal export market. This raises the possibility that their current distribution system is failing to add value in one critical dimension—that of bringing Peruvian firms closer to where demand can be developed and shaped. Chile experienced a similar dynamic with its exports of grapes in the 1980s. Through a combination of marketing and partnering with distribution channels, however, Chile was able to increase year-round consumption of grapes in the U.S. market.

SUMMARY

Exporters from the developing world face a wide variety of challenges not only in the production of their goods but also in the distribution and sales of the goods. Wide variations in the macroeconomic environment, political and social instability, inconsistent government policies, and poor infrastructure are the problems most often associated with poor export performance. Correcting these problems is a prerequisite to creating sustainable and profitable growth in many exporting industries, but it is not enough. The many strategic challenges firms face cannot be postponed any longer; as companies wait to make decisions about critical strategic issues, they actually cede control of their future to more nimble competitors and to buyers.

If exporting firms in the developing world are to have any hope of capturing more of the economic rewards they now create for others, they must address the three problems we have just discussed: poor knowledge of channel needs, a failure to leverage channels, and a failure to capture market feedback.

Because exporters rely on brokers and distributors that typically do not pass along valuable information about market trends and dynamics, they are inherently less able to understand customers' needs than either the brokers or the competition. This reduces both their ability to differentiate themselves in the marketplace through service and better understanding and fulfillment of customers' needs, and their ability to anticipate market trends. In light of changing market dynamics, this lack of information also poses a problem because exporting firms tend to be unaware of the relative performance of their competition in key market areas, which could mean they will face some unexpected and painful realizations about their industry's development down the road.

Lack of forward positioning contributes to yet another problem we have observed: groups of companies in the same industry are unable to cooperate with each other to improve the consistency of supply, the quality of products, and the scale needed to export efficiently. That fact has hampered the growth of dynamic groups of industries that could help upgrade the broader competitive environment. We call these kinds of dynamic industry groups *clusters,* and we will examine their value in more detail in the next chapter when we discuss the specific problem of interfirm cooperation.

Poor thinking about forward integration is part of a system engendered by other patterns we discuss in this book. For example, a tradition of depending on natural-resource-based products—what we have called factor or comparative advantages—forces competition to be based simply on price and scale. That, combined with a historical dependency on government policies to facilitate exports, has inhibited firms' ability to think "outside of the box" about how to distribute their products. Forward integration would go a long way toward mitigating some of the challenges facing firms and industries in developing nations, and for this reason we consider it an underutilized strategy, another hidden source of growth.

CHAPTER FIVE

Improve Interfirm Cooperation

Competitive advantage emerges from close working relationships between
world-class suppliers and the industry.
—*Michael E. Porter*

The Colombian leather industry, which we introduced in our discussion
of customer segmentation in chapter 2, illustrates how poor cooperation
between firms in the same industry can contribute to lackluster market
performance. The following story recounts our efforts to ascertain why
Colombian handbags were not doing better in the U.S. market.

"No Es Nuestra Culpa"

We began by surveying New York City purchasing managers to find
out what they thought about handbags from Colombia. They told us
that a critical purchasing criterion was leather quality and that the
leather of the Colombian bags was generally poor. If quality could be
improved, the buyers suggested, the Colombian leather industry would
fare much better in the U.S. market.

We returned to Colombia to inform the leather manufacturers that
their principal problem was one of quality. They agreed, but suggested
that there was little they could do about it. "*No es nuestra culpa*—it's not
our fault," they said, "*es la culpa de los curtiembres*—it's the tanneries'
fault." They consistently supply the industry with substandard hides.
Moreover, the manufacturers could not import quality hides from
places like Argentina, which produced the best hides in South America,

because of prohibitively high tariffs. The Colombian manufacturers encouraged us to take up the matter with the tanneries.

Armed with our market research from New York and the information we had previously learned first-hand from the leather manufacturers, we arranged for a series of interviews with people in the Colombian tanning industry. When we told them about the problem of quality in hides leaving their tanneries, they readily agreed with us, and added: "But you must understand, *no es nuestra culpa.*" They elaborated: "We do a remarkably good job of curing and tanning the hides—but you should see the state of the hides when they come to us. *Es la culpa de los mataderos*—it's the slaughterhouses' fault. Those people do not know how to kill a cow in order to preserve the hide; they are interested only in the meat."

So the problem, we learned, was actually farther upstream than we had imagined. The quality problem experienced in New York began with the slaughterhouses in Colombia, not with the manufacturers. With this insight, we went to meet with the slaughterhouses to see if we might be able find a solution.

The slaughterhouse managers gave us a warm reception and listened closely as we explained the complexity of the problem facing the Colombian leather industry. We told them about the critical role they could play to help turn things around. This was their response: "We can understand why the tanneries would think we were to blame. But the problem is quite simple, actually: *No es nuestra culpa, es la culpa de los rancheros*—it's the ranchers' fault. The countryside is so full of thieves, the ranchers have to brand the cow a hundred times before they are content it will not be stolen. Imagine what all of that branding does to the hide of a cow!"

Increasingly perplexed by the seemingly intractable nature of the problem, we packed our briefcases and went to the *campo* to talk with some ranchers. After a long ride and many discussions, we discovered a pattern of responses that can be summed up in the words of one ranch owner. He claimed that ranchers were not to blame for the problem: "*No es nuestra culpa,*" he said. "*Es la culpa de la vaca*—it's the cow's fault." The cows constantly rubbed themselves against the barbed-wire, damaging their hides and making it difficult to create a quality leather product.

So we had come full-circle. The problem with Colombian leather bags was that Colombian cows are stupid. What we found in the Colombian leather industry was a dynamic of *blame*. Indeed, in the short run, it can seem easier to "blame the cow" than to accept responsibility for improving the performance of the entire industry. The culture of blaming the cow is especially pervasive in small protected countries that have lacked an outward orientation, where companies have learned to compete on the basis of the low prices made possible by cheap raw materials and cheap human resources. Sometimes the cow is the supplier, sometimes it is the government, and sometimes it is a foreign government; but there is always a cow to blame.

If industries in developing countries can ever hope to become globally competitive, they must create a new kind of environment. Instead of assigning blame, participants in an industry must accept the responsibility to learn and to cooperate to improve the overall performance of their sector.

"THE CLUSTER"

Michael Porter expresses the concept of industry cooperation in what he calls "the cluster." Porter describes it this way:

> The presence of internationally competitive supplier industries in a nation creates advantages in downstream industries in several ways. The first is via efficient, early, rapid and sometimes preferential access to the most cost-effective inputs. . . . Mere access or availability of machinery inputs, however, is not the most significant benefit. . . . Perhaps the most important benefit of home-based suppliers . . . is in the process of innovation and upgrading. Competitive advantage emerges from close working relationships between world-class suppliers and the industry. Firms gain quick access to information, to new ideas and insights, and to supplier innovations . . . the exchange of R&D and joint problem solving lead to faster and more efficient solutions.[1]

In the Latin American industries we have observed, we noticed a profound absence of clusters of related and supporting industries and a corresponding lack of innovation: firms that do not cooperate with each other cannot learn from each other.

Economies that have long been protected by the government from competition tend to "trust no one" and to perform most activities in-house. Lack of trust and cooperation limits supplier and purchaser firms' ability to specialize in the development of specific critical industry inputs, and, ultimately, this impedes the ability of the industry to innovate and upgrade. In a protected environment, firms are not forced to make choices—that is, they do not have to focus. They can try to be both low cost and differentiated, and if that does not work, they can pass the burden on to consumers. (Recall that in chapter 2 we discussed how a company must usually decide whether to offer low-cost products *or* differentiated products that add unique value for which customers will pay more; companies do not often offer both successfully.) In an environment where explicit choices have not had to be made, firms often do not see how working closely with others can be a source of competitive advantage. As a result, no cluster develops around them.

For example, the plastics sector in Colombia could benefit greatly from specialty mold shops that could design, manufacture, and repair plastic molds. Plastics manufacturers, however, do not trust anyone outside the firm with responsibility for such a critical activity. Consequently, every major manufacturer has established a mold-making and repair facility. This is not bad in itself, but it represents a missed opportunity to create a dynamic industry that could support the plastics manufacturers in such a way that each could better focus on its core activities, such as product design, or manufacturing and distribution.

We have observed three opportunities to resolve the problems that stem from the absence of a cooperating cluster of firms:

1. Create explicit strategies for competing; that is, related and supporting industries should make decisions that are aligned and complementary with other firms in a cluster.

2. View related and supporting industries as both a unit of analysis and as a mechanism for upgrading the industry and improving the development of a nation.

3. Treat cooperation, coordination, and/or transfer of advantages between related and supporting industries as a source of competitive advantage.

In all three cases, our experience has been that the Latin American culture of *autosuficiencia* (self-sufficiency) inhibits the growth of interdependent relationships and limits firms' ability to make innovative responses to strategic and competitive challenges. The story is not unique to Latin America. We have observed similar dynamics in industries as far afield as the Kenyan flower industry and the Irish tourism industry. Moreover, poor cluster development means that business owners in the region are missing many of the associated benefits of clusters, including lower input costs, better qualified and educated workers, and improved logistical efficiency. Table 5-1 lists potential sources of advantage for firms competing within robust clusters. We will devote the rest of this chapter to examining these advantages of cluster development, using examples from the Bolivian soy, Colombian fruit juice, and Peruvian alpaca industries.

MAKING STRATEGY EXPLICIT: THE BOLIVIAN SOY CLUSTER

The Bolivian soy industry, introduced in chapter 1, offers insight into how a healthy cluster could help create an explicit strategy to improve

Table 5-1 Representative Cluster Linkages and Their Potential Benefits

Cluster Linkage	Description
Product Design	Involves sharing ideas—specifically, technological know-how in the development or fabrication of products
Reputation	Affords enhanced reputation of cluster participants through association with other participants or via certification, accreditation
Process Technology	Involves sharing ideas—specifically, technological know-how in the development of process technology
Access	Depends on cooperation that results in obtaining early, secure, and/or preferential access to, or distribution of, products or services
Market Information	Involves sharing information about buyer demographics, buyer needs, market trends
Logistics	Involves cooperation in the movement of goods or information among cluster participants
Education and Training	Involves upgrading human resources with skills and knowledge to meet the needs of the cluster: for example, market knowledge, specialized technical training

competitive position. As we have seen, soy is a commodity, which means the industry has no choice but to compete in a cost game rather than trying to differentiate itself in any way. The cost position of any agricultural commodity product depends on farm and labor costs as well as transportation costs. The transportation infrastructure in Bolivia is a disaster, for a simple reason: the government, the private sector, and the multilateral organizations whose decisions affect the soy industry do not share a vision of the railroad system and soy farms as a cluster. It is only in working within such a cluster that soy producers can hope to remain price competitive.

ENFE, the formerly state-run Bolivian railroad, is inefficient, corrupt, and expensive. In discussions with Santa Cruz businesspeople who dominate the soy cluster, we heard the same tales over and over again: "The route that should take two days to complete takes two weeks, if they are lucky." "The boxcars are often held at the border to load contraband goods from Brazil." "We must pay ENFE officials $200 to $400 per car just to 'reserve' them for soy." The list of stories goes on, but perhaps the situation was summed up best by the businessman who said: "We don't have a railroad here, we have a little toy train."

Highway construction and road maintenance are no better. There is still no paved road connecting Santa Cruz with Puerto Suarez on the Eastern border, and no paved connection with Brazil or Paraguay. Though everyone—the government, the private sector, and the multilaterals—agrees that the roads are a critical priority for the region, nothing changes. Thus ENFE keeps its stranglehold on the region, and the private sector's lobbying efforts to dismantle ENFE continue.

The condition of local roads in the Santa Cruz region also directly and severely affects the cost position of Santa Cruz businesses. Even in the heart of the city, the roads are erratically paved and after a storm intersections typically remain under three or more feet of water. Outside of the city, especially during the rainy season, the local roads are one giant mud slide; not one is paved.

The message here is simple: the broader cluster in this case—the government, the private sector, and the multilateral funding agencies—must agree on three things if the Bolivian soy industry is to become truly competitive. First, what is the core strategy? Is it to begin to compete on the basis of low cost, or is it to compete on some differentiated dimension of customer preferences? As already mentioned, in the case of soy, the strategy can be based on only a low-cost structure.

Second, what is the source of competitive advantage? In soy it comes not from transportation but from low farm costs and government-provided advantages in the form of protection, which will not be sustainable. And third, how can the broader cluster of these three groups work together to upgrade the weak link, in this case, transportation? For example, the railroad was recently privatized, but track access to a new Pacific port needs to be built.

In the long run, however, as competitive forces from other countries grow, competing on costs might not be a feasible strategy for Bolivian soy producers hampered by such grave transportation problems. The cluster will have to agree on what is necessary to build advantages in more productive, "downstream" segments such as soy-based cosmetics or mayonnaise, for example. This means the cluster will have to learn more about strategy, engage in more productive dialogues, and learn to make more complicated choices. But primarily the cluster will need to understand that competitive advantage starts with an explicit strategy shared within the cluster itself.

THE "MOTHER FIRM" AS A MECHANISM FOR UPGRADING

Colombian fruit juice producers, you will recall, suffered from significant quality and reliability problems. Before we return to that industry, it will be useful to look at the Italian textile industry to illustrate how the Colombian fruit juice producers could use the cluster to continually upgrade their product.

In the 1970s, the Italians faced strong competition with China, which was shifting the terms of the competition in the low-cost segments of long-run textiles and mass-produced garments. The Italians foresaw no sustainable competitive advantage for themselves. Instead of exiting, however, the large, core textile firms redefined strategies around three elements: fashion, high quality, and flexibility. Their customers, which included the fashion houses of Milan, were some of the most sophisticated consumers of textiles in the world. The large, core manufacturers decided to make it a priority to understand those customers' needs and serve them with innovative designs, quality, consistency, and rapid delivery to market. To do that, the firms increasingly began to outsource discrete activities to smaller suppliers while maintaining coordinating functions for themselves. As a result, the small firms profited, the large firms resolved their problem, and the entire set-up worked to build needed flexibility into the industry. Moreover, the suppliers began learning about such issues as quality from the large firms. Soon those large "mother firms" became focused solely on coordinating and outsourcing the production of garments, advertising, monitoring quality, and transferring learning. Eventually, the manufacturers' use of clusters led the Italian fashion industry to reinvent itself from being a "seeker" of demand segments to a "creator" of demand.

Traditionally, industries in the developing world have worked with suppliers only as a last resort; the fear has been that outsourcing opens a firm to risks of uncertain quality and unreliability. A typical response to this threat has been to remove the uncertainty by integrating backward; that is, attempting to control if not outright own the suppliers. But that kind of heavy vertical integration may run counter to what the most competitive firms and clusters do, especially when the industry needs to offer the end-user flexibility and therefore must learn from him continually. Indeed, heavy backward integration may keep industry clusters from emerging or growing, and consequently, impede competitiveness instead of reinforcing it.

So what is a firm to do? Manage uncertainty by improving the quality and reliability of the independent suppliers. Pursuing this kind of mother-firm philosophy is time-consuming, but it is often necessary to achieving the quality, reliability, and flexibility sustainable competitiveness requires, especially in uncertain economies.

The Italian textile industry model of upgrading clusters implies that a small group of firms will help structure and align many layers of suppliers and other related industries around one strategy. While that is an effective approach, it is not the only one. Another alternative, for example, is for relatively equal *competitors* to band together—not to restrict competition but to jointly improve quality and collectively upgrade the competitiveness of the entire industry, even remaining competitive.

That is where the Colombian fruit juice producers come in. Recall how the major U.S. fruit juice companies doubted the Colombians' ability to deliver quality fruit and fruit juice concentrate consistently. The cutthroat competition the Colombians faced from other countries like Brazil did not help to improve quality or the reliability of suppliers;

instead it created incentives to push prices as low as possible to compensate for generally poor quality.

Our analysis of the distribution system showed that the U.S. fruit juice companies viewed Colombian suppliers as a group; it appeared unlikely that any one or two Colombian companies would be able to establish significant independent brands or market positions with supermarkets or Hispanic neighborhood stores (the two target markets for the Colombian producers, as discussed in chapter 4). The challenge facing the Colombian suppliers therefore became a challenge to *jointly* improve their reputation—as a cluster. No one firm could accomplish the task alone.

The consortium the suppliers formed in 1992, Corporación Colombia Internacional, was designed to meet the two key needs of the U.S. purchasers—quality and consistency—without sacrificing competition between Colombians or applying downward pressure on the profit margins. By pooling supply, the producers hoped to deliver quality juice consistently and to eventually rehabilitate the reputation of their industry.

The consortium might serve the Colombian fruit juice producers in the same way that the mother-firm concept helped Italian textile manufacturers upgrade and innovate their way to becoming the world's leading producer of high-end garments. If the Colombians can use the consortium as a mechanism for upgrading quality and consistency, it could help the cluster begin to build even more sophisticated advantages, such as certified quality and improved transportation logistics, on top of its already considerable natural advantages.

COOPERATING AND COORDINATING: THE PERUVIAN ALPACA CLUSTER

Robust clusters can also be a means for sharing the advantages enjoyed by individual firms, which can enhance the overall competitive advantage of an industry and a nation. The alpaca industry of Peru, for example, could greatly benefit from such cluster cooperation.

The alpaca, whose wool is among the softest in the world, is an Andean cousin to the camel. It is a partially domesticated South American hoofed mammal bred by the highland ethnic groups of Bolivia, Chile, and Peru. Some people may be familiar with alpaca from the Peruvian fur tapestries that were popular internationally in the 1970s.

Using white- and black-colored pieces of baby alpaca fur sewn together, Peruvian artisans created rural scenes with peasants and alpacas bordered by abstract geometric shapes. Such fur pieces are prized, though; Peruvians make them from only the hides of baby alpacas that have died of natural causes. Since the fur of baby alpacas is even softer than the adults', they are far more valuable alive, so they can be sheared annually and their wool sold.

After copper, alpaca has been southern Peru's dominant export since the nineteenth century, when British trading houses exported wool from the region to feed the textile mills in the United Kingdom. The city of Arequipa, the commercial center of southern Peru and northern Bolivia[2] has long been the alpaca industry's major market and transport hub as well as the center for processing and value-added activities. The Arequipa region itself, however, produces few of the raw materials associated with either the alpaca or mining industries. It sits low in a desert valley, while the alpacas thrive in the Andean highlands that are more inland, near Cuzco and Lake Titicaca, as well as in Bolivia, where highland peasant communities tend their flocks. Yet Arequipa has played this role for more than a century because it is the nexus where the railroads and roads from all corners of southern Peru converge; producers have traditionally traded goods there before loading them onto trains headed for the nearby port of Mollendo.

In recent years, alpaca has provided Arequipa's best export results, not only in terms of sales but also sophistication. The industry is an example of the maxim that "local rivalry breeds sharper competitors." Unlike the monopolistic structures in Peruvian beer and dairy industries, local alpaca firms have been competing for more than a century. The two dominant alpaca houses, IncaTops and Michell & Co., both weave top-quality fabrics with dyed yarns and sew finished clothing. Their client lists include top designers in Europe, Japan, and the United States. Their factories use the latest computerized machines from Italy, and their sales representatives speak excellent Japanese, English, and French. Baby alpaca sweaters that the houses produce for U.S. department stores and catalogue distributors routinely sell for $300 each to the end-user.

Overall, the vision of the business has been relatively sophisticated. They recognized that alpaca could be marketed to the world's most sophisticated customers in the high-end fashion market. They see their product as not only the physical good but also a package that includes quality services. "I do not just sell alpaca tops [the pre-yarn stage] or fabrics. I sell on-time delivery. I sell customer-responsiveness. I sell quality control and the capacity to reproduce even the most complex fabric designs," says Derek Michell, grandson of the founder of Michell & Co., who now manages the sales department and will eventually head the company. "My customers tell me, 'We could order from one of the smaller alpaca companies for less, but it is worth paying a little extra for the reassurance of dealing with a professional company.' "

Despite that positive picture, the houses face tough markets. They constantly feel squeezed by the price demands of their customers, the large overseas clothing makers and retailers. They eventually may be able to reduce this pressure by overcoming the gap between final consumers and alpaca breeders that gives the clothing design houses so much market leverage. In other words, down the road the firms might be able to improve their marketing and distribution strategies, particularly by forward-integrating, to begin to capture retail margins and establish their own brands. For example, they should probably consider a joint venture with a U.S. retailing firm to do catalogue sales in the United States under their own brand name.

Distribution and marketing strategy, however, are the least of the barriers to increasing alpaca exports. Alpaca's growth is reaching limits, according to all the firms, because of difficulties with expanding production and improving cost position. Despite their premium product, the alpaca firms face substantial pressure to grow supply while staying price competitive, for two reasons:

- *Competition with cashmere from China and other Asian countries.* Cashmere is a better-known, higher-end wool that is a direct substitute for alpaca. Cashmere supply capacity by nimble Asian firms has expanded, forcing Peru to try to increase output and lower costs to hold world market share and build consumer recognition and momentum. (The situation is similar to that in the Peruvian textile industry, in which firms extol the unique virtues of pima cotton—their native species—while ignoring the fact that Egyptian species of extra-long staple cotton have similar characteristics at a competitive price.)

- *The need to cope with a high currency.* Substantial currency appreciation is almost inevitable during a successful stabilization program,[3] and various economists have estimated that the Peruvian *sol* has become overvalued by as much as 25 percent,[4] forcing the alpaca firms to change prices or maintain prices by squeezing profit margins.

Why is coordinating alpaca supply to meet new market pressures so difficult? As we've said, the alpaca industry has not suffered from too little rivalry, as many industries do. In fact, a root problem for alpaca has actually been too much rivalry. As a result, firms have been unable to distinguish areas suitable for fierce competition from areas suitable for cooperation.

In the alpaca industry, cooperation among key players, including manufacturing firms, public sector leaders, and worker associations, is absolutely vital. Three interlocking weaknesses, however, kept the Peruvians from developing a strong cluster:

- The inadequacy of the infrastructure in rural areas.

- The limited resources available to develop and teach the use of new technologies to increase the efficiency of highland producers.

- Poor cooperation and efficiency within the cluster of alpaca suppliers.

"Would You Want to Go up There and Live with the Campesinos*?"*

The first problem, basic infrastructure, is that inadequate roads make quick transport and communication between rural suppliers and urban-based purchasers difficult. It takes days to reach villages where alpacas are bred, around Juliaca or the other highland regions by Lake Titicaca and the dirt roads are strewn with rocks *como cancha*—like popcorn, as they say in Peru—making the journey hard on trucks as well as bodies. It is commonplace to lament the neglect of back-country areas, the suffering of the rural poor in twentieth-century Peru, and the long history of broken promises to improve the situation. But few people realize how much that neglect has cost the country in terms of export expansion and business upgrading. The isolation has made it difficult to oversee quality in rural areas and offer technical support from urban universities and company offices. It has contributed to the cultural divide between urban entrepreneurs and rural farmers; in the case of alpaca, the inconvenience of travel to farms discourages alpaca firm managers from trying to reach out to rural suppliers.

The alpaca houses therefore rely on independent roving brokers to purchase wool from the farmers and deliver it to the factories. The brokers speak Quechua and Aymara, the predominant indigenous languages, and know the villagers personally, but they are not acting as a source of communication that would help to upgrade the industry.

One alpaca executive we spoke with complained about the alpaca breeders' lack of sophistication. They made no attempt to improve stock through methods like artificial insemination. "And rather than improving the quality of the wool," he added, "they prefer tricks, like stuffing the wool with dirt to make the bags heavier, since they are paid by the kilo."

We asked him why he did not change his approach to purchasing to emphasize mutual benefit and better prices for wool that meet quality standards. And why not send his own people, or hire experts, to help the rural breeders learn about new methods of breeding?

"Would you want to go up there and live with the *campesinos*?" the executive replied, incredulous at the question. "It's in the middle of nowhere."

The Need for Technical Expertise

The seeming inaccessibility of the alpaca farmers is the source of another factor that impedes cluster development: the need for specialized human resources—technical experts—to help upgrade the industry. The alpaca executive couldn't believe that the kinds of experts we were talking about already existed—that there were people who would *want* to devote their lives to improving farm productivity. In fact, we had met many organizers from nongovernment organizations, Peruvians and foreigners alike, working in rural areas on just those kinds of issues and without many resources. If the alpaca firms could make the pay rewarding, they would have an even greater chance of finding and training those kinds of experts.

Caught in cycles of limited thinking, mistrust, and a tradition of deceitful game playing, the industry is ill-prepared to expand capacity and lower its raw materials costs. For example, the supply of alpaca wool available at any given time is never enough for the firms' needs. The brokers know that, and they know that Michell and IncaTops are always eager to buy more in an effort to deprive the other of supply. Whereas the two firms should join each other in insisting that brokers and suppliers adhere to certain standards or cooperate with technical experts, they have chosen to join each other in cutthroat competition. There is a healthy role for competition, but also a healthy limit.

The appearance of new outside competitors is making the need for specialized, sophisticated human resources to drive innovation and progress in Arequipa even more critical. A few years ago, the only country outside Peru to raise alpacas in significant numbers was Bolivia, and its alpaca population was a fraction of Peru's. Now, however, Australians are beginning to raise alpaca. In 1994, an Australian buyer paid $100,000 for a top-notch male alpaca for breeding.

The Australian was not purchasing a pet; this was a stud animal. And the Australians will apply modern technology to their ranching businesses. In particular, they are investing in genetic engineering to improve the quality of the wool and to breed an alpaca strain more adaptable to low elevations. But Arequipans dismiss this Australian development as a challenge. They believe it is positive, saying it will benefit alpaca to have wealthier First World companies promoting alpaca and raising customer awareness.

That will be true if the Peruvians can match Australian costs and quality, but not if they fall behind. The issue of genetic engineering, for instance, ties directly to costs. A single Peruvian alpaca has widely different patches of hair in terms of thickness and color. The smaller the hair measured in microns, the softer the resulting fabric woven from it. The process of sorting wool patches by grade and color is done by hundreds of peasant women sitting in the factories in Arequipa. Genetic engineering could lower processing costs and increase the proportion of the softest fibers, thereby better positioning the industry to compete with cashmere and to expand alpaca sales.

The alpaca houses have only in the past year begun to recognize the importance of such engineering. One of them is involved in a British-government-funded program that has brought a genetic scientist to Arequipa to work on alpaca. But that is not enough. A substantial effort is needed to tie universities to the effort and train the corps of local researchers and technicians to continually learn and to disseminate the learning. The campaign might include a variety of tools:

- Scholarships to send promising agronomists to study overseas in labs, contingent on their return to work in the region.

- Endowed "chairs" at universities that include explicit clauses requiring that graduate students work both in companies and on the academic campus.

- Visiting fellowships of international experts who would train local students and researchers as well as learn from the best of Andean peasant herding knowledge, which is extensive.

- Efforts to enhance the prestige of technical agricultural degrees at local universities and to tie agricultural expertise into the industry by offering seed money for cooperative field research and for the establishment of technical consulting firms.

- Partnerships between academic institutions, private firms, and government, funded by a mix of firms and industry associations, central government grants and loans, and local government discretionary budgets. We are talking about the kind of private-public-academic partnerships that have made Silicon Valley in California and the Research Triangle Park in North Carolina into high-tech industrial dynamos.

Specialized human resources are essential, and their development is distinct from the need to pursue basic education and investment in human capital in rural areas. Clearly, general education must be a priority. Literacy, numeracy, and the communication skills that schooling brings would be helpful in preparing the rural work force to work with technicians and apply, evaluate, and modify technologies for raising rural productivity. But to fund such social welfare programs, a nation must begin with an adequate revenue base. We believe the money could come from specialized human resource investments, such as advanced university-level research and work programs, which would pay off rapidly.

Many of the above suggestions fit under the heading of "the cluster" and the need to construct a productive dialogue at all levels of the supply chain. Both *campesino* producers and textile houses must show willingness to be partners. That means no more "dirt in the bags" thinking from the highlands, and in return the alpaca firms must lend support in upgrading productivity and incomes. The alpaca houses can learn from the example of Chile's half-dozen large agricultural export houses, which support their independent producers with loans and technical help in return for the right to inspect crops in progress. Likewise, as production expands in alpaca, for example, producers that do not meet quality standards would lose business, while those that comply would receive more. Technicians could augment villagers' traditional skills in growing flock size faster with diet supplements, vaccination, scientific breeding, genetic engineering, and artificial insemination.

The Need for Cooperation

None of the ideas we have just named is possible without a minimal degree of cooperation between the two alpaca houses, which is the third problem that the Peruvian industry faces. If one house continues to pressure brokers and producers to raise standards while the other house uses the opportunity to "steal" a larger share of suppliers, the industry will likely never upgrade at the rate at which it is capable.

Why does change fail to occur, or to come about only slowly and half-heartedly? One reason is that industry executives are perpetually trying to make ends meet and so naturally focus on the immediate problems at hand, like today's purchase order and tomorrow's shipment. Yet a lot has to do with individual perspectives or frames of reference—the easy stereotypes that people bring to their work each day: "the rival company" as the enemy, determined to back-stab even when it is in its interest to cooperate; the white-skinned *empresarios* as capitalist exploiters; the *campesino* peasants as lazy, disorganized, and incapable of learning. The most important barrier, we think, however, is a lack of awareness about the value created by cooperation.

SUMMARY

The three stories recounted in this chapter—soy, fruit juice, and alpaca—are actually the same story in one sense: they demonstrate that a company's competitiveness often depends heavily on the competitiveness of other firms and institutions in the same industry. That interdependence can be a source of weakness or strength, depending on the collective competitiveness of the industry. When thinking about implementing a sound strategy, companies must explicitly understand where their strategies are vulnerable to the actions of suppliers and buyers, and ensure that the chains of companies behind a product are all working together. Without strong related and supporting industries, achieving sustainable competitive advantage in the developing world will be much more difficult than it need be. In the past, it may have made sense not to cooperate, but in the increasingly competitive global economy, firms must seize the opportunity to create the conditions where buyers and suppliers no longer insist *"Es la culpa de la vaca."*

CHAPTER SIX

Overcome Defensiveness

My only hope for action from the government is through criticizing and fighting it.
—*Bolivian export manager*

Chris Argyris, Harvard Business School professor and specialist in organizational learning, defines defensive reasoning as follows: "[It is] when individuals hold *premises*, the validity of which is questionable yet they think it is not, make *inferences* that do not necessarily follow from the premises yet they think they do, and reach *conclusions* that they believe they have tested carefully yet they have not because the way they have been framed makes them untestable."[1] This definition of defensive reasoning works like a syllogism, and the purpose of this chapter is to explore this syllogism in greater detail both to understand how defensiveness occurs, and to introduce several tools that are critical in the effort to begin nurturing the hidden, intangible sources of growth. We begin with the phrase "premises, the validity of which is questionable."

THE VALIDITY OF PREMISES

In our studies of Latin American nations, Ireland, the nations in the Russian Federation, and African nations we have found there is an overwhelming propensity for the leaders, when confronted by poor results, to do the same things again, *only harder*—that is, with redoubled effort. For example, Bolivia's government leaders insist that they want to be less dependent on basic minerals, cheap labor, and commodity agricultural products—yet they are more dependent on a greater concentration of commodities than ever before. Colombia's leaders in the petrochemical sector opine that they must innovate, but they have spent as much time attempting to influence President Samper's government as with previous governments, and they have invested record-low amounts of money in research and development.

Irish leaders have said for decades that to expand the economy they must increase the rate of innovation of their underdeveloped indigenous entrepreneurs (versus the many foreign entrepreneurs who seem to have a grip on Irish-based exports). And yet they continue to overrely on the finite resources of European Union funds as the main engine of growth.

Russian Federation leaders say that if they could just get production up to the levels recorded in the 1950s and 1960s, they could take advantage of cheap labor and scale to send their manufactured products to less developed countries. That did not work before, when many of those countries were politically tied to the Soviets; why would it work now? In South Africa, government leaders have claimed, since a year before Nelson Mandela's election, that foreign investment was ready to flow in at any time. It never happened.

The truth is, each of these countries has had bad results: none has been able to create wealth for its average citizen by exporting sophisticated products and services to sophisticated countries. These bad results, while recognized, have not created the changes in behavior necessary to ameliorate the situation. The leaders work under certain premises about how things will happen, but these premises are questionable. This dynamic can be called *single-loop learning* and is depicted in figure 6-1.

An example of this dynamic can be found in many of the cases already presented. For instance, the response of leaders of the Bolivian soy industry to competitive pressures takes place in a single loop. Even though it is clear that their tariff protection is highly vulnerable, that their specific industry segments are not structurally attractive, and that their product prices have been declining steadily, they continue to believe that they would be competitive if only the government would fix the roads. If only transportation were more efficient, they could be very successful in this industry. This is a strategy of trying the same thing, only harder. It is single-loop learning; it is a failure to question the fundamental premises.

Recall from chapter 1 that Bolivia's share of the world market in

Figure 6-1 Single-Loop Learning

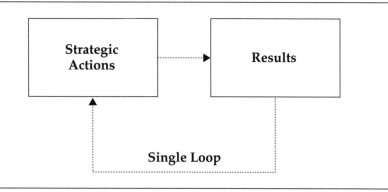

soybeans is only 0.26 percent. It is a very small player in a very big market. On average, world prices for soy have declined each year since 1973 by 5.8 percent—a true commodity business. And the Bolivians' key source of advantage is an artificial tariff barrier that keeps the Brazilians' product out of Colombia. Why would the land-locked Bolivians want to continue competing in such an unattractive environment? Because, in spite of the external constraints they face, they have developed an export industry worth $60 million per year. And the government has played a critical role—through trade policy and tax policy—in encouraging that success. And, because the industry is profitable, the government has not had to develop good infrastructure in the region.

But times are changing, and the government is no longer able to provide these kinds of supports—still the good infrastructure does not exist. The soy producers argue, quite convincingly, that they will be unable to compete without decent infrastructure. The government argues, equally convincingly, that it is doing all it can to help. And there is a great deal of animosity between them. There is a great deal of defensiveness, and it is inhibiting their ability to work productively together to resolve their problems. What could be interpreted as an historic opportunity for the government and industry to further diversify the economy—to build clusters of companies working closely together, to develop better knowledge bases about how to compete in this industry—instead is being played out as a bitter fight between industry and government, each fighting to blame the other for the current difficulties.

What choices do the leaders of government and industry have, then? They can continue to fight to succeed on the basis of premises that no longer apply, or they can reexamine their premises, their frames of reference, and develop new and innovative solutions to their problems. Such an approach would look something like double-loop learning depicted in figure 6-2.

In the terms of figure 6-2, double-loop learning is the capacity to "move farther left," to examine the *frames of reference* used to inform the actions and achieve results. The farther to the left in the process that a change is made, the more sustainable the results. In other words, change that is brought about by altering or informing the frames of reference is a more sustainable and more desirable form of change than that brought about by an uninformed shift in actions. Altering one's frame of reference—testing one's premises about how the world works—is an activity that taps into hidden sources of success. The answer is not necessarily to *do* things differently; it is to *think* differently about the things that need to be done.

Our criticism of defensiveness is not directed at the soy industry or the flower industry or even the natural tendency of any industry to try to protect its interests. Our point is that until leaders are able to *re*frame their problems, to look at them differently, to think about them differ-

Figure 6-2 Double-Loop Learning

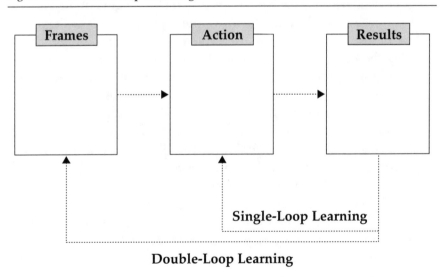

ently, they will be limited to reacting to crises and trying harder and harder at solutions that no longer will work.

THE LOGIC OF INFERENCES

The second part of Argyris's definition of defensive reasoning concerns the tendency to "make inferences that do not necessarily follow from the premises." Part of the problem with frames of reference lies in the way that the human mind works: based on partial information, people make inferences just to get through the day. Often, the inferences we make are correct enough to keep us on a course that is true. Yet when we stop to think about the evaluations and judgments we make so automatically, we realize that we are behaving as if they are more concrete, specific, and informed than they actually may be.

Chris Argyris suggests there is a "ladder of inference," on which there are four rungs to climb to any belief or assumption. The first rung holds the directly observable data in a given situation, such as actual conversations and observable nonverbal communication. An example is the generic complaint of the industry leader trying to succeed in an uncertain economy: "My appeals to the government for help have yielded no benefits."

The second rung, Argyris says, "represents culturally understood meanings that individuals with different views or axes to grind would agree were communicated during the conversation."[2] This is the paraphrase or the interpretation of the directly observable data. So the industry leader's statement in the above example might actually mean: "My industry is losing competitive advantage, and the government refuses to help us improve our competitiveness."

The third rung on the ladder represents the meanings that individuals impose on the second rung. It would be concluded by that industry leader, therefore: "The government does not have my best interests in mind."

The fourth rung represents "the theories of action individuals use to craft their conversations and understand the actions of other people."[3] So, as the quote with which we open this chapter states: "My only hope for action from the government is through criticizing and fighting it." Essentially, a misguided belief or assumption is what would inform this person's behavior.

As the above example shows, the evaluations and judgments that inform action are automatic, highly abstract, and inferential. What is frightening is how quickly individuals will jump to such judgments as if they were concrete and obvious conclusions, and how completely their behavior is guided by those conclusions.

The important point is that *inference making* is a "human program," as Argyris says; that we—government leaders, business leaders, husbands, wives, children—are inference-making machines. The implication of this finding for the uncertain economy is that if the world is more complex and the decisions to be made more crucial, then should not leaders be more aware of the high inferences they make so frequently—especially about one another?

Recall from the introductory chapter on the Colombian flower industry the miscommunications between the Cabinet Minister of Foreign Trade, and the president of the country's flower association, Asocolflores. The letters they exchanged are filled with negative attributions and an aspect of mutual aggression that shut down any real hope for learning.

What we did not explain in that chapter was how we contributed to that dysfunction—a story that we think illustrates well the concept of cycles of inference. Late one night in the airport in Caracas, Venezuela, we happened upon the Minister of Trade for Colombia, who was preparing a speech for a conference the next night in Bogotá. The Minister asked us how the study was going and we, only too happy to discuss the results, took the opportunity to try to shape the Minister's thinking concerning the competitiveness of the flower sector. We spent the next three hours in the executive lounge and on the airplane elaborating a plan for how the government and the private sector could work together to upgrade the sector's competitiveness, which until then had been based simply on basic advantages.

By the time the plane landed we felt that we had been able to construct a different, more productive new role for the government in the sector's future. Our temporary sense of accomplishment was shattered the following evening when on national television the Minister attacked the flower sector for its laziness and selectively quoted from the work our team had done. Soon after the Minister's speech, the flower association struck back in the press, ironically, also quoting our work—but only the parts that supported its attack against the government.

We tried to call the Minister to stop the letters running daily in the press from both sides, but the Minister stopped taking our calls, relaying instead elliptical messages to us such as: "Don't worry, everything is all right" and "The plan is working perfectly; we have created a debate." We were quite disturbed by two things: How can a public slugfest be "framed" as a productive debate? And why did his "plan" require elevating defensiveness instead of creating an environment where more learning could take place?

Figure 6-3 takes direct quotations from the public debate and reconstructs them as rungs on the ladder of inference. But there is an added complexity. In this case these are two separate ladders of inference, which become self-fulfilling cycles of inference. Thus the picture we show demonstrates how two highly competent, committed, and respected people made inferences about each other that while somewhat grounded in the facts were framed in such a way as to be very unproductive—to shut down learning and dialogue.

We believe that the cultural roles assigned to the sectors when Colombia was a closed economy—the government leader responsible for allocating benefits, the dynamic lobbyist for marshalling his or her influence—created a filtering mechanism, or a set of frames, by which they each selected and interpreted the data, drew conclusions, and created beliefs that informed their actions in ways that might now be considered fallacious, even invalid. Because the world and the basis of competitiveness has changed, those leaders' respective roles, and their interactions, have to change.

Both the Minister of Trade and the president of Asocolflores begin with what we call "selected data." In this case, the selected data comes directly from our report. Both then move up the ladder of inference—or forward in the cycle—to interpret these data: the Minister lauding the industry for exploiting its natural advantages to reach second place in the world; the industry official expressing surprise that it has succeeded despite the obstacles in place. From this interpretation, they both reach conclusions. The Minister concludes that the flower growers are lazy—that they are resting on their laurels. The industry leader concludes, on the other hand, that the country is failing as a platform for success in this industry. The final step up the ladder—or forward in the cycle—is to the arena of belief. The Minister now believes that if the flower growers do not innovate, they will disappear in five years. The industry leader believes that if the government doesn't help, they will lose their North American market. Ironically, the two sides agree on one point—

Figure 6-3 The Roots of Defensive Reasoning: Inference Cycle in the Colombian Flower Industry

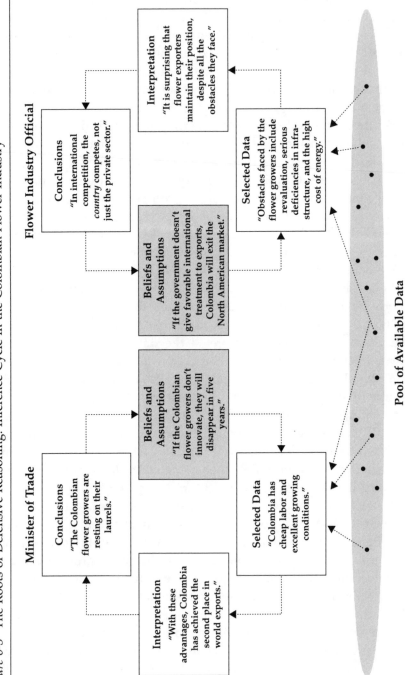

that the industry is in danger. But there is no agreement on what needs to be done.

That is unfortunate—and unnecessary. As long as two individuals carry on an argument at the level of belief, there is no hope for reconciliation, let alone cooperation. To develop productive interactions, it is critical for individuals to descend the ladder of inference and look anew at the pool of available data. That is to say, to reframe the problem and to be open to new data and new interpretations of old data. Insofar as the debate occurs at the top of the ladder of inference, the only thing that can be guaranteed is that people will behave defensively. Learning will stop. Problems will go unsolved. People will become frustrated. The situation will remain the same. But the competitive pressures will not let up; rather, they will continue to increase for as long as decisive action is not taken.

THE QUALITY OF CONCLUSIONS

Argyris completes his definition of defensive reasoning with the statement that the parties involved "reach conclusions that they believe they have tested carefully, yet they have not because the way they have been framed makes them untestable." The quality of conclusions reached by an individual in a given interaction is, to a large degree, limited by the quality of the frames of reference applied to that interaction. These frames will filter data in specific ways and create opportunities to pursue false conclusions. The quality of the conclusions each side reaches is limited by the quality of the inference making that led to those conclusions, as well as by the degree to which people are open to rethinking or reframing their original premises. Or, to use Argyris's language, to engage in "double-loop learning." When both frames of reference and inference making are distorted, there is no hope for the attainment of sound and relevant conclusions or for informed choice or timely action resulting from complex decisions.

The histories of developing countries are replete with chaotic swings in government behavior: between a focus on economic growth and a focus on social equity, between private sector leadership and a state capitalist model, between engagement with the world and almost complete isolationism. Some of these swings have occurred in just a single administration; for example, that of Alan García's in Peru in the late 1980s.

One way to explain this chaotic behavior is to examine the country's core frames of reference at the time and its ability to learn and make complex choices. García's time can be regarded as a masterpiece of highly reactive single-loop learning, culminating in policies that essentially closed Peru's doors to the rest of the world: outlawing foreign currency deposits, nationalizing many institutions, placing import restrictions on 539 items, creating 56 tariff rates and 14 different exchange rates, restricting repatriation, limiting debt service, and allowing 226 government-owned enterprises to dominate the economy. We can only wonder at the answers to the following questions:

- What kinds of inferences was the administration making to come to the belief that these policies, and the constant swings in policies were correct?

- How could García possibly have avoided the defensiveness that arose between Peru and the international financial community, and between his government and the private sector?

- And finally, could anyone have anticipated those results had they the tools to study the frames of reference, to judge the quality of inferences that were being made, and to understand the level of defensiveness that was about to occur?

SUMMARY

Overcoming defensive behavior is critical to the success of all enterprises, not just those in the developing world. To seize the opportunities identified in previous chapters, business and government leaders will need to develop more sophisticated sources of advantage. Gone are the days when cheap labor and access to raw materials—very visible and accessible advantages—will allow sustained success. Gone are the days when it is worthwhile to argue publicly about how to allocate finite resources. The challenge in the twenty-first century will be to work together to create sustainable sources of growth in a way that neither degrades the environment nor exploits human beings. This cannot be done in highly defensive environments. Today's sources of competitive advantage are more subtle than yesterday's. They are based on human relations, on productive reasoning, on knowledge and creation, on trust, on cooperation. They are some of the hidden sources of advantage that nations must learn to develop.

CHAPTER SEVEN

Avoid Paternalism

In the past, the government was there to protect us from the rest of the world.
It gave us employment; it cared for us. The question that we have to ask ourselves
now is: Why do they have to change that?

—*Bolivian soy bean producer*

As neither psychologists nor anthropologists, we find ourselves stretched to write about paternalism, with all its nuance, its interconnectedness with the other themes explored in this book, not to mention its historically deep roots in the cultures of many developing nations. And yet paternalism is a fundamental pattern that must be addressed; it is the 10,000 pound elephant standing in the room that no one wants to talk about. Our experience has led us to define paternalism *as a system that results when one group defers responsibility for its own welfare, indeed its future, to another group, in effect assigning to that other group the power to make complex decisions that it should be making for itself.*[1]

There are several kinds of paternalism we could examine. Government-to-government paternalism would start with a look at colonialism and communism's analog, the recently defunct Comecom trading group of Eastern European nations. Business-to-business paternalism would examine the case of corporate relationships to subsidiaries, especially cross-border subsidiaries and especially those in developing countries. We have chosen to focus on government–private sector paternalism, since that is what we have observed and experienced the most, and it is the area where the greatest tension is being felt as government leaders begin to embrace open economies and competition rather than shield their industries from them.

GOVERNMENT AND THE PRIVATE SECTOR

In developing countries, we have encountered three micropatterns of paternalistic behavior:

1. Devaluation of a currency perceived to be a source of competitive advantage
2. Government as "master economic strategist"
3. Protectionism

These micropatterns of behavior have resulted in a false sense of competitiveness through exchange rate policy; a crowding out of the private sector in key areas of the economy, both financially and intellectually, owing to state intervention in companies and industries; and finally, little innovation on the part of the private sector owing to the lack of competitive pressure. The opportunities for the private sector to break from these patterns and develop the skills necessary to compete without the heavy hand of the state are great, but understanding the effects of paternalism is a necessary first step.

Devaluation in the Colombian Flower Sector

Devaluing the currency is like smoking dope.

Throughout this book, the Colombian flower sector has been held up as a morality tale of competitiveness. Everything in a sector that could go right and wrong has. Its biggest risk is classic in competitiveness: it is not in danger, necessarily, of doing the wrong thing; it is in danger of doing the right thing for too long. The reason is precisely that the sector has been so successful: export penetration, market share, and increases in employment, not to mention the 40 percent margins on simple cut roses many of the big exporters were making in the mid-1980s.

From the beginning, the flower growers' basic sources of advantage were its natural resources: sunshine, cheap labor, and proximity to the world's biggest flower market, the United States. They had other advantages as well, one of which was their position as first movers among developing nations to compete for the lucrative U.S. market.

Another "advantage" that the flower growers had was an extremely undervalued currency. Cheap currency is something that any government can give its exporters, and there are two things wrong with it. First, since any government can provide it, it is an extremely imitable advantage that is really neither strategic nor sustainable. For example, figure 7-1 shows that the appreciation of the guilder destroyed the advantage of the Dutch in the U.S. chrysanthemum market, clearing the way for the Colombians to take control. But how attractive was that market segment and how sustainable that advantage if the exchange rate could determine the winners and losers so abruptly?

If the Ecuadorians, blessed with the same natural advantages and even cheaper labor, decide to undervalue their currency to compete with the Colombians, they could do so by government fiat overnight. Thus would begin a vicious cycle of price competition, with horrible consequences: both Ecuador and Colombia would be exporting the wealth of their countries to richer countries. That is, purchasers in the United States, for example, would get to buy Andean flowers at very low prices, thus capturing the wealth of those countries extremely

Figure 7-1 Real Dutch Guilder Exchange Rates (versus U.S. Dollar) and Dutch Chrysanthemum Exports to the United States, 1980–1992

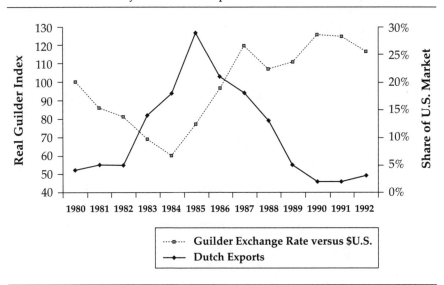

Sources: U.S. Department of Commerce, U.S. Department of Agriculture.

cheaply. The vicious cycle would continue because the price of admission to that game is so low: yet a third government of a developing country wishing to promote its industry could also devalue its currency. The result? The new entrant to the market would place still more downward pressure on the prices—in the long run, a losing proposition.

The second thing wrong with competing on the basis of cheapened currency is that it reduces the initiative to innovate—both the incentive and, indeed, the resources with which to invest in innovation. To state the point as clearly as possible; we offer the following syllogism.[2]

1. Competition spurs innovation

2. Undervalued currencies reduce pressure from competition for export industries

3. Therefore, undervalued currencies reduce innovation

We have observed that firms, sectors, and nations that compete on the basis of an undervalued currency have a tendency to underinvest in developing their human resources. Unfortunately, investment in human resources is the one investment that actually has the potential to provide infinite returns as witnessed by increased productivity. Failing to invest in a nation's human resources is part of the first pattern of uncompetitive behavior discussed in chapter 1—overreliance on basic factor advantages.

Perhaps the problem was stated best by one Colombian senior government official, the owner of a successful conglomerate and a man wizened by many political fights. "Devaluing the currency is like smoking dope," he said. "You don't have to do anything, and you're happy."

A Story of State Ownership in Peru

Government as "master economic strategist."

Between 1968 and 1990, three common themes defined the national objectives of Peru, all of them destructive for the economy. The first was *stimulating domestic production* to achieve economic growth through both import substitution and picking winners and losers, that is, having the government choose sectors to support with subsidies.

The second theme was *isolating the domestic economy* as thoroughly as possible from foreign pressure, including protecting Peru from import pressure, foreign investment and control, and worldwide price fluctuations of the commodities Peru produced.

The third theme was *managing economic activity* to achieve very specific outcomes in the market. In less palatable words: the government acted as the "master economic strategist." That meant the government increased regulation, became the main allocator of economic resources, and became an owner of the means of production.

We will focus here on the third theme of substituting government economic management for market dynamics, a type of paternalism whose recent history is dramatic.

In 1968, President Velasco observed a predominance of non-Peruvian firms in Peru's economy: more than 300 firms were owned by U.S. stockholders, direct foreign investment comprised more than $1.2 billion, and much of the most modern infrastructure, such as roads and bridges, had been created and controlled by either U.S. corporate interests or the Peruvian elite. Since Velasco's military stewardship was designed to redistribute the country's wealth, he began by ending the historic foreign control of the economy and initiating what would be a long history of protecting the domestic economy from foreign interests. The objective articulated at the time was to replace the economic system with a "new mix" of a socially responsible private sector and an "expanded" public sector.

Between 1975 and 1983, a period of vacillation ensued as the leadership took the country back to a more growth-oriented strategy. But then in 1985, President Alan García noticed a 13 percent drop in wealth for the average citizen over the previous two years, a low industry capacity utilization of 55 percent, inflation accelerating to 200 percent (in early 1985), unemployment rising to more than 50 percent, and huge government debt-servicing pressures to the tune of more than $2 billion. García attempted to reactivate the economy by promoting domestic production and import substitution policies, winning repayment concessions from international lenders, and positioning the state as an owner of the means of economic production. Fundamentally, García had moved to thoroughly assert the government's control as the master strategist for the economy.

As can be seen from table 7-1, the entire portfolio of government tools was designed to disengage the country from the rest of the world, in

Table 7-1 Competitiveness Legacy of Peruvian Government Policy (García Administration), 1985–1990

Policy Instruments \ Policy Areas	Monetary	Fiscal	Trade	Foreign Direct Investment	Incomes	Sectoral
Legal	• Foreign currency savings deposits outlawed • Capital allocated through network of development banks	• 170 different federal and local taxes	• 539 items subject to import restrictions • Many trade certifications, authorizations, other controls	• Foreign-owned assests nationalized • Discrimination against foreign investments part of code of law	• Employment guaranteed with restrictive hiring policies • Regulated labor participation in firm profits, management	• Concentrated industry structures legally bestowed • Government monopolies legislated
Administrative	• Low interest rates to stimulate investment • Money printing to fund deficit, not manage growth	• Complex tax structure, poor enforcement yield revenue of 4.5% of GDP in 1990	• 14 general, hundreds of specific exchange rates • 56 tariff rates between 15% and 108%	• Repatriation of profits restricted	• Direct price controls • Wage indexing • Consumption subsidies for basic goods • Labor firing restrictions	• Commercial regulations to micromanage industry competition and evolution
Direct Market	• Attempted nationalization of banking system • Central Bank used as source for industrial loans	• Underfunding of health care, education, infrastructure	• CERTEX subsidies directly supported selected exports • Freight reserve requirement	• Partnerships with foreign firms discouraged • Foreign debt repayment formally limited to 10% of exports	• Government assumed role of employer of last resort	• 226 SOEs* generating 20% of GDP by 1990 in oil, transportation, minerals, telecom, other industries

Sources: Template from James Austin, *Managing in Developing Countries* (New York: Free Press, 1990); World Bank, *Peru at the Crossroads* (Report no. 11943-PE, 1994); World Bank, *Peru Establishing a Competitive Market Environment* (Report no. 11446-PE, 1993); Monitor analysis.

*State-owned enterprises.

three basic ways: (1) discriminating against foreign investment; (2) encumbering trade through import restrictions, specific exchange rates, and subsidies; and (3) enacting legislation to establish monopolies and to create more than 200 state-owned enterprises that generated one-fifth of the wealth of the nation.

In 1990, President Fujimori came to power in an electoral upset: as a nonpolitician, an academic, and an ethnic Japanese, he had the moral authority of an outsider. He took on the leadership of a Peru that had been economically disengaged from the world for some time and was undergoing an internal assault by the *Sendero Luminoso* guerrilla movement. By international standards, the nation was virtually an economic and political basket case. President Fujimori took decisive, often controversial, steps to restore political and social order by systematically capturing the leadership and supporters of the *Sendero Luminoso* and suspending congress and the judiciary to rid them of what he has called "corrupt and incompetent" leaders. Economically, President Fujimori opened the economy and began to dismantle a large, inefficient state accustomed to corruption and paternalism, to develop a more transparent and efficient government, and to remove what he felt was one of the greatest obstacles to economic growth—Peru's long history of paternalism.[3]

Protectionism in the Bolivian Soy Sector

> Only 100 sons-of-bitches run this country. I should know—
> they're all my best friends.

We return now to the story of the Bolivian soy industry related in previous chapters. To recap: Bolivian soybean production has taken off during the last two decades; with a compounded annual growth rate of 27 percent since 1973, it should be by all rights one of the country's great success stories. In the 1970s, President Banzer's statist policies initiated soy production, and in 1986 it received financial support for agricultural development from the World Bank. Soy is thoroughly protected by the Andean Trade Pact agreement, which provides Bolivia with a $37 per metric ton advantage over Brazil in the lucrative Colombian market, amounting to a $6 overall cost advantage.

The story here is simple: the competitive environment for soybean production in Bolivia never upgraded, specifically because of the trade protection it received from Bolivia and other Andean governments.

Moreover, the multilateral institutions' policies enabled that stagnation by supporting the focus on soy as a short-term substitute for tin production, whose exports had been waning.[4]

In 1974, the Bolivian soy environment was characterized by Banzer's unqualified support, excellent growing conditions, low wage rates, an adequate supply of cheap labor, and high transport costs owing to the lack of roads, nonexistent port infrastructure, and poor rail transportation (including the fact that all of the train cars were designed for mineral transport only). There was virtually no investment in agricultural research, capital for small farmers was limited, agrochemical inputs were scarce and prohibitively expensive, and domestic demand for soy was zero.

By 1995, nothing had changed. One Brazilian investor commented that the number one reason to invest in soy in Bolivia was still because "the land is so cheap," rather than because of more sustainable advantages. Small farmers still could not use their land for collateral; all the other countries in the region spent from two to eight times as much as Bolivia in research and development as a percentage of GDP. Local demand has never improved, and the soy industry's strategies were simply to remain the low-cost producer in only four out of the hundreds of possible soy products they could potentially produce.

Furthermore, the Bolivians relied on an artificial price umbrella, making it possible for them to sell in the Andean market any amount of soy they produced. Therefore, *quantity* became the soy producers' metric of success. Together, the producers and the government created an implicit system of thinking, organizing, and choice making that achieved perfectly what they had designed the system to do. The resulting false sense of security, however, has kept the industry from investing in the kinds of continuous improvements it must make to survive in a competitive environment.

The Bolivian soy industry illustrates important facts about paternalism. First, government protection is not a sustainable advantage because it can be threatened by new government administrations with different ideas, it can be made obsolete by bilateral agreements, or, as in the case of soy, it can be threatened by multilateral agreements like the Mercosur trade and investment agreement among the southern cone countries of South America (Mercosur would override the benefits Bolivia now receives as part of the Andean Trade Pact). Second, focusing on strategies that are a function of protection distracts management attention away from the subtle business of creating and accumulating true sustainable advantages.

PATERNALISM: TWO LEVELS OF IMPACT

In all three of the countries just examined—Colombia, Peru, and Bolivia—paternalistic environments had two distinct levels of impact. The first was on the ways firms chose to compete; paternalism effectively inhibited firms from taking advantage of the opportunities described in the preceding chapters. The second level of impact was on the overall structure of the economies; many unintended consequences of government policies arose, including slowing economic growth and increasing concentration of wealth among people with access to government leaders.

Impact on Competitiveness and Strategy

Because paternalism limits competitive pressures, neither the government nor firms have much incentive to invest heavily in improving their competitive environment (infrastructure, human resources, interfirm cooperation, and so forth). This environment also constrains the strategy choices available for firms. Companies in this type of environment have practically no chance for sustained growth. Paternalism, as practiced through government-imposed market distortions, can limit firms' ability to take advantage of opportunities such as moving beyond reliance on basic factor advantages; choosing better customer segments in which to compete; gaining a new understanding of relative positioning; building better interfirm cooperation; and overcoming defensiveness.

Moving Beyond Reliance on Factor Advantages

In developing countries, which are often shielded from competitive pressure by cheapened currencies or tariff protection, factor conditions do not tend to become specialized and upgraded. For example, during the 1980s wages in Peru fell 65 percent in real terms. This made labor a very attractive substitute for machinery investments, since no premium was placed on productivity. That resulted in a 43 percent decline in machinery investments over the same period of time. And as shown in the case of Bolivian soy, the basic advantages of fertile soil and cheap labor were never upgraded, and advanced or specific advantages in transportation or in training people never became objectives.

Removing the constraints of paternalism does not mean removing the influence of government from the economic domain—the government will have a critical role to play in helping to create an environment where it is easier to compete in more complex industries. This will require investment in basic infrastructure, education and training, and close collaboration with industry enabling firms to build unique, sustainable competitive advantages in addition to the comparative advantages they possess in abundance.

Choosing Better Segments in Which to Compete

In environments where the government makes most economic decisions, market learning is virtually nonexistent. When the basis of competitiveness is factor conditions and exchange rate management, why spend time figuring out market segments? As one flower exporter in Colombia said, "There's one segment that we serve, and that is the price-sensitive segment." And again, in Bolivian soy, market learning could help producers compete in dozens of segments more attractive segments than the four basic ones on which they now focus.

As paternalism recedes, firms will need to invest heavily in determining where they are best able to compete without government help—and the speed of the changes in many countries has necessitated that they already have. This is a fantastic opportunity for firms to reinvent the way business is done in their countries and to fundamentally reshape their strategies in light of the rapid changes occurring in the structure of the global economy.

Gaining a New Understanding of Relative Positioning

Bolivian soy industry leaders face a classic relative position issue: the source of their competitive advantage is the protection they get from the Andean Trade Pact, which allows them to compete in the large Colombian market against the Brazilians. When that protection ends, Bolivia's relative position will decline inside of a deteriorating industry structure. Another way to express it is that the trade pact among the five Andean governments is artificially shaping and protecting the industry structure in which the Bolivians export; it suppresses rivalry, keeping out the threat of new entrants and, to a lesser extent, the threat of substitutes.

In the Colombian flower industry, revenues continued to grow even as profit margins shrank because the undervalued currency was changed almost overnight by the administration of President Gaviria. Other reasons profit margins in the Colombian industry continue to shrink are because, as we have already examined, its failure to undertake the necessary quality and logistic upgrading to compete with the Dutch and the price pressures stemming from other countries' low cost advantages in transportation (such as Mexico) and labor (such as Ecuador).

By developing a better understanding of relative position, firms will have two distinct opportunities: they will have accurate, reliable data to better inform the government–private sector debate about important policy decisions facing industry, and they will have a better understanding of where it makes sense to invest or to grow their companies.

Building Interfirm Cooperation

The following is a common example of how paternalism stifles the kind of interfirm cooperation needed to create a competitive export. In both Bolivia and Peru, government-owned raw materials and metals exporters took over critical suppliers to mitigate supply disruptions. That type of strategy often distracts management attention from higher-ordered strategic thinking. Also, that kind of government-driven concentration of wealth in a few exporting segments limits the wealth diffusion needed to develop related and supporting industries. For example, in Bolivian soy, producers had no extra capital to invest in learning about packaging and marketing—or to invest in suppliers who could do that learning for them. That might be what has prevented Bolivia from moving into more attractive segments of soy production. We have discovered at least 110 products that are based on soy; paying more attention to developing related industries could allow Bolivia to refocus downstream on more diverse and structurally attractive industries.

Overcoming Defensiveness

In the Bolivian soy industry, it is ironic that the soy producers are very antagonistic toward the government, which provides the tariff protection that sustains them. As figure 7-2 illustrates, both the soy industry and the government are caught in battling cycles of inference—each selectively interpreting the available data to support its view. This has the result of escalating tension and decreasing the possibility that a mutually beneficial solution to the sector's strategic challenges will be found.

Figure 7-2 The Roots of Defensive Reasoning: The Inference Cycle for the Bolivian Soy Industry

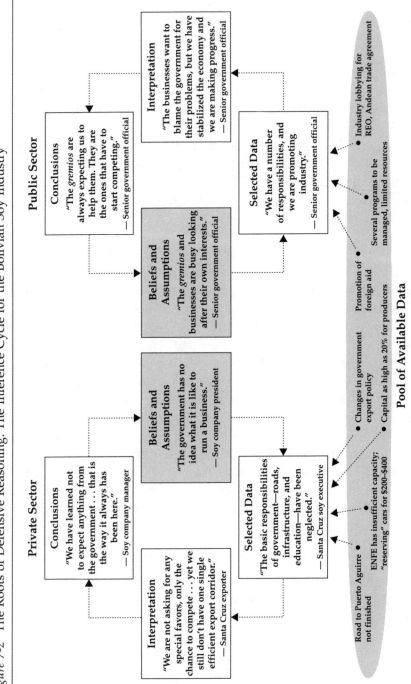

The figure suggests that paternalism and defensiveness can be considered the opposite sides of the same coin; where there is one, there is the other. Going forward, government and business leaders must hold each other accountable for establishing more productive discussions of critical strategic issues. This will be particularly important if the historic patterns of paternalism are to be left behind.

Impact on Wealth Creation and Competitiveness

Paternalism, especially the forms discussed in this chapter—devaluation of currency, government behaving as master economic strategist, and protectionism—squashes competition. Firms that have fewer strategic choices available to them will often compete by exporting very simple things that other nations can easily imitate. Thus prices are driven down, only limited wealth gets created, and the opportunity to reinvest in more complex exports and to redistribute wealth to the average citizen is lost.

In the case of Colombia, Peru, and Bolivia their capacities to export complex products are around 5 percent, 2 percent, and 2 percent, respectively, of total exports.[5] As already established in earlier chapters, low amounts of complex manufactured exports correlate with low standards of living. For example, in Bolivia between 1982 and 1993, and across three presidential administrations, the compounded annual growth rate for per capita income was negative.

The world has changed: computing power and communications are becoming cheap, and learning, as Microsoft's Bill Gates says, has become "frictionless."[6] The rules of the game are indeed changing. But the way that decision makers in small countries are playing the game is not changing fast enough. When nations and industries find a formula for success, they cannot presume that formula will remain appropriate. And when the terms of competition shift and success is jeopardized, industry leaders often assume it must be someone else's fault—and someone else's responsibility to fix.

As figure 7-3 indicates, factor-driven and paternalistic policies create some initial success, and because human nature is the way it is, everyone presumes that these policies will continue to create success. Therefore, leaders of governments and the private sectors institutionalize these formulas for success and prepare to fight for them. If the industries make any profit at all, this profit is noticed, and competitors

Figure 7-3 Preserving the Status Quo and the Loss of Competitiveness

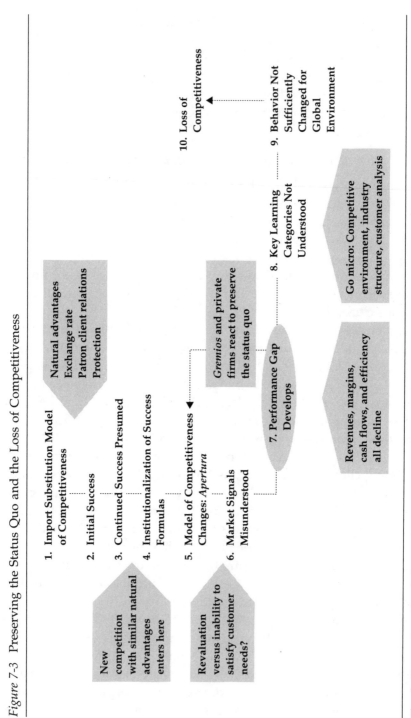

The choices are investing in innovation or attempting to return to the status quo.

prepare to enter the industry. Those competitors will enter the field with less experience, perhaps, but also with a less rigid sense of what it takes to win. If they look at the market with a fresh eye and position themselves accordingly, both they and the industry, ultimately, will benefit. But this is not the usual development. More often these entrants frame their data selection in the same way as their predecessors, and they will blame the government, or the World Bank, or the international economic order for the nontrivial effects paternalism has on their companies. They will end up lobbying the government to do what it always has done or to just help create "a level playing field" for them.

And so the vicious cycle continues. The government fights back because it feels considerable pressure from the international multilateral funding agencies. Or it fights because the winds of neoliberal thinking that have swept the multilateral institutions, focusing people on limited government and unfettered business sectors, have really convinced it that the rules of the game have changed.

SUMMARY

Two choices: Take the Minister to breakfast or reshape the industry.

In Peru, we once gave a presentation to several hundred business and government leaders in a grand hall, darkened except for the raised stage on which we were speaking. After relating some preliminary analysis about the country's export performance, some survey results about patterns of decision making, and some hypotheses concerning the future of the country, we stated that the businesspeople in the audience had two choices as they went forward. The first choice was that they could simply wake up tomorrow and take to breakfast whichever minister in the government showed an interest in their particular industry.

"You know the Minister," we said. "On weekends you give a friendly nod to the Minister from across the tennis court at the club or on the golf course. You can take the Minister to breakfast and ask him for a favor. *That's one choice.*"

"But there's another choice," we continued. And we asked if someone in the audience could articulate it. From the back of the room, a man raised his hand timidly and addressed us from deep within the anonymity of the darkened hall.

"We can take the Minister to *lunch.*" And the audience laughed in a sublime moment of self-recognition.

The second choice open to businesspeople, of course, is that they can try to reframe their perspective so they do not interpret events from a paternalistic frame. Specifically, they can learn how to judge the attractiveness of industry structures, they can work on developing their competitive environment to improve their relative position inside those industry structures, and they can focus on learning about competitor behavior and customer preferences. In a phrase, they can learn to reshape the industry structure in which they compete.

PART TWO

UNDERSTANDING THE ROOT
CAUSES OF THE SEVEN
PATTERNS

The seven deadly patterns discussed in part 1 arose from the interaction of thousands of variables that make up business life in developing nations—economic, political, cultural, demographic.[1] Much time and energy have been spent and thousands of approaches tried in the effort to improve the conditions in the developing world. Each approach—from heavy-handed government policies that tie humanitarian aid to politics to the grassroots efforts of the early 1990s to focus on "Trade, not Aid"—has its own merits and underlying logic. In fact, there have been hundreds of economic models created over the years that attempt to explain the challenges of development. Our learning has convinced us that among all of the efforts to alter the economic structures in the developing world, the microeconomic message has not gotten through. The fundamental dynamic of what it takes to create and sustain wealth—the message of firm-level economics—does not appear to have stuck with the leaders of the developing world.

A few questions arise from this observation: What are the firm-level lessons that should be foremost in the minds of these leaders? Why is it that this message, if and when delivered, seems to disappear so quickly from the collective imagination of that leadership? We have several hypotheses. First, that perhaps the message itself has been neither well delivered nor well understood. Second, that the very nature of the political process may create a degree of institutional and structural instability that makes it difficult for people, no matter how they think they *should* behave, to opt for anything but short-term thinking and profit maximization. Finally, it may be that the microeconomic message has gotten through but has not been internalized, owing to the leaders' deeply held mental models about how wealth is created and distributed.

The second part of the book addresses these hypotheses in detail. Chapter 8 focuses on one component of the microeconomic message: business strategy. This is a fundamental starting point; if businesses are to succeed in an era of total competition, they will need to have good strategies. This is followed by a chapter on firm-level learning. In addition to choosing their strategy, firms need to get better at investing in learning in several critical areas: customers, costs, and competitors. This is the essence of firm-level competition: what strategic choices are made and how well a firm is able to act on those choices in light of both customer needs and competitor behavior.

Chapter 10 takes a step back to examine the context within which firms are playing out their strategies. As we have sought to understand why firms have not taken advantage of the opportunities described in part 1 of this book, we have realized that the institutional heritage in many developing countries inhibits long-term thinking. Government policies and institutional mechanisms have impeded the ability of firms to develop more sophisticated and sustainable strategies. We examine these themes in a detailed look at Bolivia from 1952 to the present.

Chapter 11 goes a step further to examine the implications of the strategies and structures in place on the way business, government, academic, and union leaders think about innovation, productivity, wealth creation, and distribution. We argued in chapter 6 that defensiveness limits the ability of a nation to upgrade its sources of advantage. Chapter 11 analyzes the theme of defensiveness and divisiveness in much more detail, drawing on extensive research conducted with almost 500 government, business, academic, and union leaders in Venezuela.

Chapter 12 examines what we refer to as "The Old Way of Thinking" and makes recommendations on how things will need to change if the hidden sources of growth so abundant in the developing world are to be upgraded.

CHAPTER EIGHT

Strategic Actions—Not Making Choices Is Making Choices

Strategy is informed choice and timely action.
—*Mark Fuller, chairman and CEO of Monitor Company*

Where does one begin the task of changing the seven patterns of uncompetitive behavior into opportunities for sustained growth? By waiting for the context to improve so that one can make better choices? Or by making better choices that will help improve the context? That is a classic chicken or egg dilemma that has paralyzed many leaders. What must be done, we believe, is for both the government and private sector leadership to assume responsibility for making changes to improve the economic and social results achieved throughout the nation. That partnership must be based on explicit choices, on strategy.

STRATEGIC ACTION DEFINED

Every organization makes choices and takes action. The type of action taken is often in response to pressures created from the results of previous actions. Effective action is the result of good choices: good strategy. *Good strategy is converting informed choice into timely action.* Given the very real constraints that senior decision makers face in government and business, making good strategic choices is not easy.

The failure to take advantage of the seven opportunities for positive economic change is not simply the result of a productivity problem; firms that have fallen into the patterns of uncompetitive behavior described in part 1 must do more than simply do what they are doing more effectively. What is needed is a fundamentally new approach to doing business that is not overly conditioned by strategies that were successful in the past. Part of that new approach should involve a fundamental assessment of the strategic positioning of the firm along three broad dimensions:

1. Choice of advantage
2. Choice of scope
3. Choice of technology

Management of human resources, operations, finance, and sourcing can be critical to improving operational productivity. But it will be effective only inasmuch as it is aligned with the choices of advantage, scope, and technology.

For both the private sector and the public sector, it is important to understand that *not* making choices *is* making choices. If leaders do not make clear, explicit choices, they risk letting the competition decide for them.

The choices made by firms and industry leaders in preceding decades were choices that made perfect sense in the old context, the old way of doing business. But they often make little sense today and need to be revisited. What do we mean by choices? Broad, strategic choices, such as which industries to compete in, which products to produce, how to distribute the products, what human resource strategies to pursue. The choices made in these areas are fundamental to the success of any business enterprise and must be understood as building blocks for creating and sustaining wealth. We will now revisit some of these choices in light of the patterns just described in part 1 and suggest that there are viable solutions to the strategic problems we presented. There is a solution that falls somewhere between government paternalism and bankruptcy.

Strategic action is the combination of the strategy choices that organizations make regarding how they will position themselves and the actions they will take to convert those choices into results. Why the distinction between strategy choices and actions? Ideally, strategy and action would be the same thing. But it is easy to confuse progress with motion, and in the world of global competition, it is easy to confuse good strategy with operational effectiveness. When the competitive pressures mount, it is far easier to keep busy working harder or trying to become more efficient than to step back and think about the choices that are being made. For this reason, it is valuable to talk about both choice and action.

The terms *strategy, operational productivity,* and *competitiveness* are three concepts which are often used loosely, creating more confusion than clarity. *Strategy* is about turning informed choices into timely action. *Operational productivity* is about utilizing all of the inputs of an operation—labor, capital, raw materials, energy, and knowledge—to generate output more efficiently.[1] As figure 8-1 illustrates, *competitiveness* results where good strategy and high operational productivity intersect.

Sustainability is also relevant. It is possible for a firm to be highly productive by depleting natural resources and degrading human resources, and it is possible for this firm to make millions of dollars. But these strategies are not sustainable, nor in our opinion, desirable. Exploiting the visible sources of growth in the developing world is easy and has been done very effectively, but the net result is that countries

Figure 8-1 Strategy, Operational Productivity, and Competitiveness

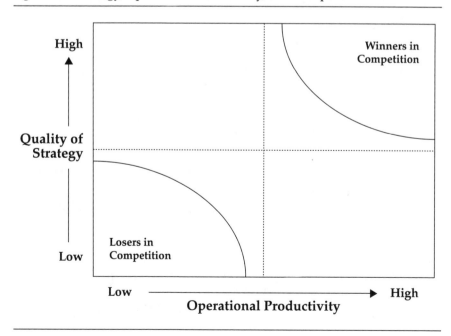

in Africa and most of Latin America are poorer today than they were twenty years ago. And in the midst of that poverty, there are pockets of tremendous wealth.

The environmental degradation and social tension that result from exploitative strategies have created two rather predictable outcomes in the Andes: social chaos (ranging from strikes to guerrilla terrorism) and political chaos (resulting from government attempts to correct the vast inequities in the distribution of wealth). Peru experienced both during the presidency of Alan García, and his reactions sparked the banking crisis of the 1980s.

Good strategy is sustainable and very difficult to imitate. And the challenge to be competitive is not simply the challenge to exploit laborers or the environment. The challenge is to make better decisions about how to alter the mix of inputs in order to achieve better strategic results.

As will become increasingly clear, we believe that good strategy forces firms and nations to upgrade their pool of available resources, primarily their knowledge resources, which will have tremendous spillover effects on the way other resources are allocated to economic activity. Given the constraints of a capitalist system, the trend toward increasingly open economies, and the lack of a viable alternative, we advise those interested in economic development to think about the following syllogism:

1. Good strategy is critical to successful businesses;

2. Successful businesses create wealth and employment;

3. Therefore, good strategy is critical to wealth and employment.

Types of Strategic Choices

What follows is a review of the elements of basic strategy. Though we have mentioned them in part 1, they need to be made explicit. As already said, firms must make choices in three primary areas to develop clear strategies. Those areas are advantage, scope, and technology.

Choice of Advantage: Strategy 101

Conventional strategy theory has it that there are really only two clear options when it comes to choice of advantage: to be low cost or to be differentiated. *Low cost* can be defined as a strategy that minimizes costs to offer low prices, while addressing as well as possible the buyer's other needs. *Differentiation*, on the other hand, can be defined as adding unique value for which the customer is willing to pay.[2]

There is no right choice of competitive advantage. Each company in each industry must make a careful assessment of its competitive environment and industry structure to determine which strategic approach is most viable and sustainable. In that sense, it is possible to speak of strategic choices that are better aligned than others, or more appropriate given the unique circumstances an industry faces.

Low Cost

Low-cost strategies, for example, are sustainable only if based on innovation. Low-cost strategies that are based on passively inherited factors of production, such as labor rates or access to inexpensive raw materials, are effective in the short term but are not sustainable. And a low-cost strategy based on a favorable exchange rate is a potential disaster because, as we argued earlier, it is the single most easily imitated advantage firms can have from a national platform and is therefore the most easily defeated.

Among exporters, a common complaint is that their government has hurt them by revaluing the currency. But why would one want to compete based on advantages that the government, which is revaluing, or another government, which is devaluing, can take away in a single day, by fiat? Firms in any national platform need to do a better job of picking their segments and bases of competitiveness. That is the lesson drawn from the first and second chapters of the book, which discuss the problems inherent to competing solely on the basis of basic factor advantages and the corresponding failure to focus on specific customer segments within chosen industries.

Competitive environments are going to change, wage rates are going to rise, raw material sources will dry up. By creating low-cost strategies based on higher-order advantages, such as distribution efficiency, sourcing strategy, manufacturing processes, or focused customer strategies, firms would be able to build lasting sources of advantage. For example, the flower growers have been some of the most innovative and successful exporters in Colombia over the past two decades. As stated earlier, they based their advantages on sunshine, cheap labor, location, and good soil. They also created a distribution system that competed very successfully on the eastern seaboard of the United States against the Dutch. That innovation was perhaps partially due to a transfer-pricing scheme to avoid Colombian taxes, but it also served to get the Colombians closer to their U.S.-based customers, and that provided market driven, strategic advantages. Now, with Ecuadorian and Mexican growers gaining strength and doing some innovating of their own, the distribution logistics system is under pressure to improve. The Colombian flower industry is at a cross-roads; it has the chance to invest in upgrading its distribution and to learn about sophisticated customer needs, but it may also spend its energy complaining to the government about the Colombian context—things like exchange rates or labor laws.

Developing countries tend to rely on competitive strategies based on inherited factor conditions. In other words, most "Third World" strategies are low-cost strategies because that is where their *comparative* advantages lie. The Peruvian fishmeal industry, discussed in chapter 1, continues to dominate that segment, but we would maintain they are winning the battle and losing the war. The long-term, wealth-generating potential is not in the fishmeal industry; it is in developing the capacity to compete in increasingly sophisticated markets.

As leaders think about developing more sustainable sources of advantage, they will have to think about developing more sophisticated knowledge assets; they will need to nurture the development of competitive advantages based on human capital and innovation, which take full advantage of the tremendous comparative advantages they possess. The *mix* of inputs used throughout the economy—raw materials, capital, human resources, institutional support, even culture—will need to reflect a deeper understanding of how wealth is created and *sustained*.

Differentiation

"A firm differentiates itself from its competitors," writes Michael Porter in *Competitive Advantage*, "when it provides something unique that is valuable to buyers beyond simply offering a low price. Differentiation allows the firm to command a premium price, to sell more of its product at a given price, or to gain equivalent benefits such as greater buyer loyalty during cyclical or seasonal downturns.[3] Perhaps the most common refrain repeated by leaders in the developing world is that firms cannot compete on any basis other than low cost. There is no question that achieving differentiation is difficult, but that is precisely why differentiated strategies tend to be more sustainable.

Differentiated strategies can be based on brand name, design, technology, service, features, or other dimensions required by the customer. The key to building a differentiation strategy is to invest heavily in understanding what product attributes a customer will value. Differentiation is in the eye of the purchaser, not the manufacturer. When the Colombian flower industry leaders heard this, they responded that Colombian flowers were actually both low cost and differentiated. The growers' belief that their product was differentiated, however, came from their assumptions about customer desires rather than from research. For example, on Valentine's Day in Boston, a dozen roses from the Netherlands sold for $60, while a dozen roses from Colombia sold for only $24. Clearly, in the eye of the consumer, there was a difference between the Dutch and the Colombian rose—a richer color, a nicer scent, a stronger stem—and that was a difference the customer was willing to pay for. This is the test of differentiation: *when customers are willing to pay more for a value they perceive.* A product is not differentiated simply because the producer thinks it is.

Choice of Scope

Generally speaking, questions of strategic scope fall into one of four broad categories of choice: vertical scope, segment or product scope, geographic scope, or business scope. Again, fundamental to a firm's success is its ability to make clear choices along those four basic dimensions.

As should be clear by now, factor-driven economies that have been protected for a long time reveal certain familiar patterns. In general, the decisions made in factor-driven environments are toward broad product scope, narrow geographic scope, wide vertical scope, and unsophisticated segments of the market. Why is that so?

These choices are explained in part by the economic legacy of the import substitution approach to economic development found in many developing countries. In an environment where producers are not constrained by competition, they have freedom to produce their goods and then to think about what to charge and to whom to sell. There are no real trade-offs to be made in a protected environment.

Vertical Scope

The choice of vertical scope is of such fundamental importance to managers in the developing world that we devoted an entire chapter to it in part 1. In our discussion of forward integration, we discussed vertical scope in terms of distribution systems and determining how much value distribution systems were actually creating for the producer, both in terms of market knowledge and real sources of advantage. We also argued that many firms suffer because they do not know the needs of the distribution channels they serve.

There is another dimension to vertical scope that merits further discussion at this point. Vertical scope usually focuses on where in the value system a company wants to compete. This includes not only choices about how to distribute a product but about how integrated a company wants to be in the production of downstream products. There are more than 110 different potential products farther downstream where the Bolivian soybean industry could be competing (see figure 8-2), yet it now produces products in just four categories: soybean oil products, refined soy oil, whole soybeans, and soybean meal. Given their rich and fertile soil, the Bolivian producers have a unique opportunity to develop processed soy goods such as oils, inks, pharmaceuticals, or food products that might be much more attractive industries for them—and industries in which their source of advantage would not be government policies but their own rates of innovation.

Investing energy in determining what strategic choices should be made regarding positioning in the value system has the potential to yield far greater returns than spending time, energy, and money lobbying the government to try to sustain a position that, in the long run, is neither desirable nor competitive.

Segment Scope

To choose one of those 110 products in which to compete, a soy producer would need to assess the attractiveness of each product group and to determine what segments in each group are the most attractive. For example, there might be a way to develop a mayonnaise spread that combines the unique spice combinations highly valued by local consumers throughout a given region. Or it might be wise to think of a joint-venture manufacturing scheme with a company such as CPC International (the maker of Hellmann's mayonnaise) that could provide

Figure 8-2 Potential Product Choices for the Soy Industry

Soybeans

Soybean Oil Products

Refined Soy Oil

Glycerol
Fatty acids
Steroids

EDIBLE USES
Coffee creamers
Cooking oils
Filled milks
Margarine
Mayonnaise
Medicinals
Pharmaceuticals
Salad dressings
Salad oils
Sandwich spreads
Shortenings

TECHNICAL USES
Core oils
Diesel fuel
Disinfectants
Epoxies
Fungicides
Inks
Oiled fabrics
Paints
Pesticides
Plasticizers
Soap

Whole Soybean Products

Soybean Lecithin

EDIBLE USES
Emulsifying agents
Bakery products
Candy
Pharmaceuticals
Nutritional uses
Dietary
Medical

TECHNICAL USES
Anti-foam agents
Alcohol
Yeast
Dispersing agents
Paint
Inks
Insecticides
Rubber
Stabilizing agents
Shortening
Wetting agents
Calf milk replacers
Cosmetics
Paint pigments

EDIBLE USES
Seed
Stock feeds
Soy sprouts
Baked soybeans
Full fat soy flour
Bread
Candy
Doughnut mix
Frozen desserts
Instant milk drinks
Low-cost gruels
Pancake flour
Pie crust
Sweet goods
Roasted soybeans
Cookie ingredients
Crackers
Dietary items
Soynut butter
Soy coffee
Traditional foods
Miso
Soymilk
Soy sauce
Tofu

Soybean Protein Products

Soy Flour Concentrates and Isolates

TECHNICAL USES
Adhesives
Analytic reagents
Antibiotics
Asphalt emulsions
Cleansing materials
Cosmetics
Inks
Leather substitutes
Paints
Plastics
Polyesters
Pharmaceuticals
Textiles

EDIBLE USES
Alimentary pastes
Baby food
Bakery ingredients
Beer and ale
Candy products
Cereals
Diet food products
Food drinks
Grits
Meat products
Noodles
Prepared mixes
Sausage castings
Yeast

Soybean Meal

FEED USES
Aquaculture
Bee foods
Cattle feeds
Dairy feeds
Fish food
Pet foods
Poultry feeds
Protein concentrate
Swine feeds

HULLS
Dairy feed
Filter material
High-fiber breads

Source: Monitor Research, U.S. Department of Commerce, *1996 Soya Blue Book* (Michigan: American Soybean Association, 1996).

entry into surrounding markets. There are thousands of ways to compete, but for each possibility, it is critical that producers research the particular segment's structural attractiveness and how well they can serve it. Chapter 2, which emphasized the opportunities available to firms that invest in customer learning, argued that managers must actively choose to compete for those parts of the market most attractive to their firm.

Another dimension of segment scope includes deciding on specific products. That is another choice made difficult by past government policies; in a protected environment, it was not uncommon for a firm to widen, or proliferate, its product scope rapidly as it sought either to leverage its production technology or to reach a wider and wider group of customers. In the era when producers could sell their products for their cost plus some predetermined margin, this was not an unreasonable strategy. Today, however, it is not possible to serve all customers at all times with all products. Again, the discipline of focus is critical. One textile company we know in Medellín produced 2,000 products and managed to make a profit. They were probably making a profit on about 10 percent of their product line, but they were not sure which 10 percent of the products. In the future, it will be much more difficult, if not impossible, to compete effectively in such a wide variety of products.

Several problems stem from proliferating product lines. There is an obvious increase in shop-floor complexity that reduces efficiency and throughput. Also due to product proliferation and inadequate accounting systems, companies are no longer able to track just how much profit an individual product will provide. In fact, in large manufacturing companies in the United States, where product scope has proliferated, the companies have created incentives to sell the highest-priced products—products that actually lost them money.[4]

In the future, firms in the developing world will need to choose carefully which customers they want to serve and which products they will sell. Understanding what customers really value makes it easier to decide on product scope.

Geographic Scope

Where, geographically, should firms compete? Although this is generally a question whose answer is critical to the life of a business, the issue of geographic scope has not been among the main challenges facing firms in the Andean region. As long as firms had the benefit of protected environments, they did not need to think hard about geographic scope; they were effectively ensured the ability to compete at home and were often offered such incentives to export that it didn't really matter where they competed abroad, either. As those advantages have disappeared, however, firms are actively having to consider where they will look for growth—and this has meant thinking about expanding into new markets.

A characteristic of those countries known as the Asian tigers—Hong Kong, Korea, Singapore, and Taiwan—is worth pointing out: because their national strategies were focused on economic growth through exporting manufactured goods, their firms have had to develop broad geographic scope to compete with much larger rivals in many countries simultaneously.[5] To effectively develop, produce, and market a manufactured product globally requires tremendous managerial dexterity and commitment. These are skills that may not come quickly to firms in Latin America, which have on the whole been successful primarily in exporting natural-resource-based products, which require few of the human resource skills necessary to compete in many locations around the world.

Business Scope

The final choice with regard to scope that firms must make concerns the type of business in which to compete. Again, history has played a role in shaping this choice. The protected environments in which Latin American firms have operated have enabled firms to enter many unrelated businesses and compete in them effectively. Many firms, largely owned by family groups or associations of friends, are now in a position of being unable to make money in all of their businesses, and they must make fundamental choices about which arenas they want to compete in and how.

Choice of Technology

Technology is a principal driver of change. As such, firm leaders need to think about it carefully and manage it properly. Many companies in the developing world appear smitten by the desire to acquire technology to become more competitive. While it is true that technology can be a great equalizer, it can also cause tremendous strain on limited resources. Leaders often misunderstand the relationship between technology and competitiveness.[6] Technology tends to be viewed as valuable for its own sake, when in fact it is valuable only insofar as it enables a firm to more effectively pursue its strategy.

There are two broad categories of technology strategy a firm might adopt: to be a technology leader or to be a technology follower. Neither choice is better than the other. As we will see, what is important is that a firm be explicit about making that choice and resolved to stick with it.

Technology is desirable for a firm only insofar as it:

1. Creates a sustainable competitive advantage.

2. Shifts cost or uniqueness drivers in favor of the firm.

3. Provides first-mover advantages to the firm.

4. Improves overall industry structure.[7]

The story of Colombian textile leaders, who spent millions of dollars on equipment in the 1980s to upgrade factories, provides an interesting example of technology strategy. They had a very clear strategy in mind: buy the best used equipment available on the market and use it to improve operational productivity and to enhance product-line quality. Coincidentally, Colombian firms went on this purchasing spree at the same time that U.S. firms were in the middle of a huge downsizing effort, and the U.S. firms were happy to find eager buyers in Colombia for their equipment. The problem was that U.S. firms were selling that equipment for a reason: it was no longer able to help them compete globally. It was good for competing in segments of the market that required long runs of single products, and, typically, of cotton products; it was perfect for segments such as T-shirts, underwear, and other simple, commodity-type products. The U.S. firms had realized the hard way, however, that strategies based on long-run, low-end products were not sustainable; Asian competitors beat them on price every time—in spite of the distance their product had to travel and a complex international system of trade agreements and quotas. And price was the only basis of competition in those segments.

So the U.S. firms sold their machinery and invested in highly flexible machines that could run both cotton and synthetics, machines that were very good at manufacturing items like linens and bedding. Because consumers valued fashion and design in those particular segments (an edge that U.S. firms had over Asian firms), and because the end product was actually physically very heavy, the Asians were unable to get their product to the United States and remain price competitive. By switching segments, the U.S. firms were able to improve the structural attractiveness of the industries they served. Meanwhile, by buying the U.S. machinery, the South American firms placed themselves in the same position in which the U.S. firms had been, except that, at the time, South America's local markets were protected from Asian competitors. It was only after the economy opened in the 1990s that the Colombians realized the grave mistake they had made; they had not understood how their enormous investments in technology would measure up to the tests of desirability.

SUMMARY

Strategy is making discrete choices along clear dimensions, a critical first step toward nurturing hidden sources of growth. Not making choices is, indeed, allowing others to make choices for you. More than once we have shown a client his firm's competitive position on a map relative to all of the firm's competitors only to hear, "We didn't decide to be there." Our response is always the same: "No you didn't, but your competitor decided for you."

Competing by making better choices about *where* to compete, *how* to compete, *what* products to produce—this is the way to build sustainable sources of advantage. The next chapter looks more deeply into the type of learning firms must engage in if they are to make informed choices and take timely action.

CHAPTER NINE

Firm-Level Learning

For a man to attain to an eminent degree in learning costs him time,
watching, hunger, nakedness, dizziness in the head, weakness in the stomach,
and other inconveniences.

—*Miguel de Cervantes (1547–1616)*

The inability of leaders in the developing world to take advantage of the opportunities highlighted throughout this book is both understandable and unfortunate. It is understandable given the political and social tensions, which have created unstable environments that do not support investment in knowledge assets. And that is unfortunate, because the failure to invest in more sophisticated ways of competing has contributed to declining standards of living in developing countries. Developing these opportunities requires a combination of better strategic positioning, firm-level learning, and fundamental improvement in the quality of the dialogue within leadership circles. We have discussed strategic positioning and would now like to focus on firm-level learning; the task of improving the quality of the dialogue will be addressed later in the book. What follows is a look at what could be called the three C's of firm-level learning vital to sustained growth: customers, costs, and competitors. It is difficult to know where to position oneself on the strategic battlefield without high-quality information about customer needs, relative cost structure, and competitor positioning. Firms knowledgeable in these areas will likely make good choices.

CUSTOMERS

As argued in chapter 2, the choice of segment focus is a critical starting point for creating a company's competitive advantage, but it is often misunderstood and rarely executed. This section of the chapter will show the underlying principles of customer segmentation. More important, perhaps, we will assert that only by identifying and serving the most sophisticated customers in the most sophisticated markets will developing countries create a growing export base that is less susceptible to political and macroeconomic trends that can produce a higher per capita income.

In serving any given industry segment, a company must identify customer requirements in the segment and develop a plan to meet them. Regardless of geography, demographics, or products, a company's ultimate success is only as strong as its understanding of what drives the behavior and economics of the market segments in which it competes and its ability to act on those requirements. That means understanding customer needs in the given industry segment. Developing strategy from that perspective enables companies to derive competitive advantage by competing in those segments where they are uniquely capable of meeting customer needs.

How can a segment of customers be defined? There are many variables on which a market can be segmented: by geography, by demographics, by product, or by consumer needs. This discussion will focus on "needs-based segmentation" because success will likely come to firms that not only identify who their customers are, where they live, and how much they earn but that also learn *why* they purchase the particular product.

A segment is an identifiable group of customers with shared requirements that are significant to achieving competitive advantage. Needs-based segmentation has three basic principles:

1. Customer needs and purchasing criteria drive segment identification.

2. Each segment has a different set of buying requirements.

3. Within each distinct segment, customers have similar buying requirements.

Why is needs-based segmentation important? Because understanding the needs of specific customer groups is the first step in creating competitive advantage. There are several ways to look at any industry. In one view, an industry consists of hundreds of individual customers with different sets of needs. In another, it is understood as homogenous and easily classifiable. In a third view—the one we consider the most accurate and useful—an industry is thought to be made up of many segments of individuals that share common characteristics or needs. Customers with similar criteria form distinct segments. Determining what those groups of individuals value in terms of things like product, pricing, and service enables a firm to effectively target its resources to compete where it knows it can win.

Getting Unstuck from the Middle

A return to the example of the Colombian leather industry will illustrate how different types of segmentation can work to enhance competitiveness. As discussed in chapter 2, Colombian leather manufacturers believe themselves to be competing as low-cost producers in the U.S. market. But as the dominance of Asian imports in the U.S. market implies, the Asians are much lower-cost producers of leather handbags than the Colombians are. As long as labor remains a significant component of total production costs, that trend will continue. What is critical for the Colombian leather manufacturers, however, is to identify *why* U.S. purchasers are buying 46 percent of their product from Asia and only 17 percent from South America. The answer has little or nothing to do with geography but rather with how well certain producers from certain areas deliver on key elements of success.

In the chapter about interfirm cooperation, we show that Colombian leather goods producers are constrained by a number of factors beyond their control, and most consider themselves to be competing in the low-cost market, with some spillover in the more differentiated market segments. Let us revisit the chart presented in chapter 2 (shown here as figure 9-1) that compares the leather industries of Colombia, Italy, China, and Korea. Colombia is clearly not cost-competitive with China or Korea in leather handbags, and because labor rates drive much of the cost structure in leather goods, Colombia will likely never be able to compete with China on a cost basis. Korea, meanwhile, is losing market share to China as its wage rates are becoming less competitive.

Figure 9-1 Strategic Choices in the Leather Goods Industry: Handbag
Exports to the United States

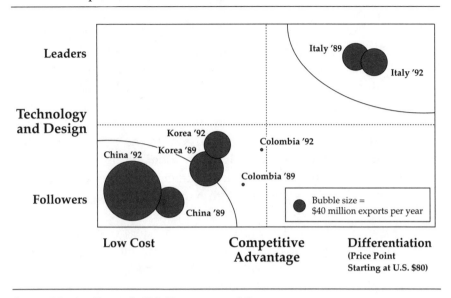

Source: Monitor Research, U.S. Department of Commerce.

Korea is positioned near the middle of this map—the worst place to be.
A firm whose technology or design strategy is that of neither leader nor
follower risks positioning itself uniquely to serve the needs of no one.

Italy, you will recall, maintains market share because it consistently
produces sophisticated products that appeal to customers who are
willing to pay premium prices for cutting-edge fashion and design.
That makes the Italian leather producers somewhat "macroeconomic
proof." Exchange rates, inflation, and wage rates affect the cost structures of Italian producers less than they do other nations, because the
Italians can preserve their margins by charging higher prices.

Colombia is clearly stuck in the middle of the chart. This is a perfect
example of industry-level strategy not being aligned with a competitive
environment. There are natural constraints on Colombia's ability to
produce high-end leather products; specifically, they lack a fashion and
design culture as well as high-quality domestic leather. Given these
constraints, Colombian producers have tended to produce what they
can and then look for markets for those goods. What they should be
doing is to consider first what the market is looking for—its needs—and

then configure their strategies to meet those existing needs. In the leather industry, being neither low cost nor differentiated makes it very difficult to win.

The challenge for Colombia is to get "unstuck" from its position in the middle through strategic positioning and choice of segment. In chapter 5, on interfirm cooperation, we stated that the Colombian leather industry appeared to be stuck in the middle because customers were not satisfied with the quality of its product. While that is true, in and of itself it is not a helpful, actionable answer. Quality is subjective and difficult to measure. To be more useful to the Colombian leather manufacturers, we needed to help them identify the ways in which customers were unsatisfied with the product they were trying to sell.

To put the industry's dilemma into more context, keep in mind that there was an import duty of 15 percent on leather hides; many leather manufacturers therefore felt captive to their domestic suppliers, whom they believed were not providing high-quality hides at competitive prices. The leather industry had responded to that raw material disadvantage either by paying a tax (that forced up their prices) on imported hides from Argentina and elsewhere or by developing product lines from the lower-quality Colombian leather and pricing themselves out of certain markets. In that way, the Colombians essentially allowed external forces to dictate competitive strategies that, as has been said, place firms at risk to become "stuck in the middle."

Strategically speaking, firms must identify what strategies will best enable them to serve the segments they desire. If external variables (import duties on raw materials, prohibitive transportation costs) make it difficult to serve a given segment, the firm must do one of two things: (1) innovate to compensate for the disadvantages, or (2) abandon the segment as currently defined. The Colombian leather manufacturers needed to identify which segments of the U.S. leather market they would best be able to serve to improve their performance. What they were focused on, however, was not the challenge of learning more about customers but the uphill fight to get the government to improve their competitiveness by changing the exchange rate and lowering import tariffs for raw materials.

To help Colombian leather industry leaders, we designed a survey instrument to test our various hypotheses about the leather market and to get views from buyers representing 2,000 U.S. retail outlets. With that survey we hoped to help the industry ascertain its most attractive segments; more important, however, we wanted to demonstrate to the leather industry the importance of performing segmentation analysis to identify market opportunities.

What do the results of a customer segmentation analysis looks like? Before examining a chart that summarizes our findings about leather handbags, we will revisit two questions raised in earlier chapters that we also asked individual leather producers:

- How structurally attractive is a particular segment?
- What is my relative capability to serve that segment?

These two questions should serve as the basis for making decisions about product, design, distribution, and levels of service.

Identifying Attractive Segments

The "five forces" model is most useful when thinking about segment and industry attractiveness. It suggests that at any given time, there are five constituencies that determine the attractiveness of an industry. They are:

1. Buyer power.
2. Rivalry among competitors.
3. Threat of new entrants.
4. Threat of product or service substitution.
5. Supplier power.[1]

Figure 9-2 summarizes the factors that determine the power of each force.

Conceived in 1980 this model has received criticism over the years for being too basic or simple or for enduring beyond its useful life, yet it remains one of the most helpful conceptual tools in the strategist's toolbox and is a constant source of commentary. Astonishingly, it also remains one of the least-used tools by government and multilateral officials who oversee the investment of billions of dollars in industries throughout the developing world.

The five forces can be used as a simple ten-minute diagnostic exercise or as a quantitatively intense six- or nine-month study. Essentially, it

Figure 9-2 Industry Structure: Summary of Key Drivers

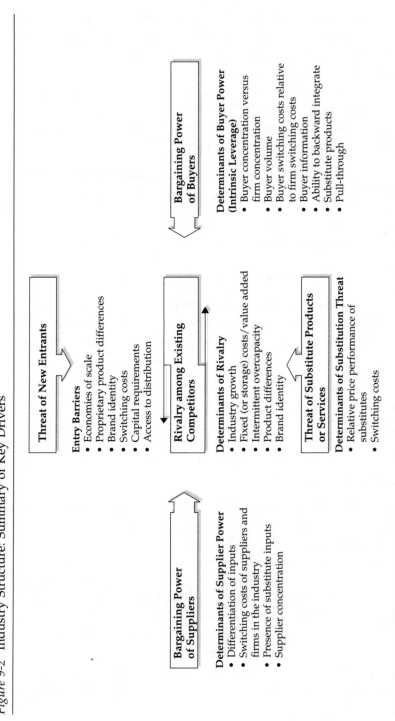

Source: Michael E. Porter, *Competitive Strategy* (New York: Free Press, 1980).

provides insight into what an industry's competitive dynamics are and, ultimately, how much wealth-creating potential an industry has. We are not suggesting that governments use it to pick winners and losers for their government investment dollars or to provide specific export credits. But it would be useful in giving governments and the private sector a shared vision of what is competitive and not competitive; that way they would at least be speaking the same language, thus improving learning and inhibiting the defensiveness that impedes complex decision making.

To explain how the five forces work, we will briefly discuss relevant examples from previous chapters relating to each force. When *buyer power* is low or fragmented, industries are more attractive to producers. During the days of import substitution, buyers had very little power because they had few choices in the protected markets. When an economy opens up, consumers are able to exercise their choices and demand more from producers. In the case of leather, the people who buy Italian leather bags tend to be very discriminating on quality, name brand, and service. They are demanding purchasers who, because of their relative price insensitivity, tend to define the segment they are in. They become one of the dominant forces determining industry attractiveness (defined as a specific segment of this industry).

An industry with intense *rivalry* tends to be a difficult industry in which to compete. Again, during the years of protected environments, competition was limited and polite. In these days of global competition, that has changed. For example, in scale-intensive and capital-intensive industries such as petrochemicals, producers are willing to sell their product at marginal cost just to keep their equipment running or, at times, to sell at a loss to boost market share. Such intense rivalry often signals an unattractive industry.

The *threat of new entrants* is very real for industries such as tourism or flowers, where the markets are large and customers demonstrate little loyalty to the source of production. While Machu Picchu might be a leading destination for tourists this year, other destinations can easily enter the competition—the Mayan ruins or the Egyptian pyramids, for example. Closely related to the threat of new entrants is the *threat of substitute products*. This is a threat facing the Peruvian cotton industry, which has a unique product in Pima cotton. Although Pima is a high-quality cotton, other producers of extra-long staple-length cotton, such as Egypt, can easily substitute for it. When buyers can easily substitute one product for another, the structural attractiveness of the industry is diminished.

It is interesting that in the Andean region there are not many examples of industries with high *supplier* power. Perhaps the Colombian tanneries, mentioned earlier in the book, could qualify, because the leather manufacturers have no real alternative to the Colombian product unless they are willing to pay high tariffs for Argentine goods. But this is an artificial advantage given to the suppliers.

A strategic problem that goes hand in hand with competing in natural resource-based industries is that one is usually a supplier of commodity goods, and there are rarely strategic advantages in that position. We also spoke earlier of the opportunity to become more forward integrated; the strategic rationale for this is to begin competing in industry segments where firms have more power and to shed the shackles of subservience to the overwhelming power of buyers in commodity industries.

In general, then, producers in developing countries find themselves in relatively unattractive segments, owing to a high level of rivalry, high threat of new entrants and substitutes, and enormous buyer power—the unattractive "five forces." A sociologist or "dependency" theorist might see this dynamic as an example of rich countries having power over poor countries. A business strategist, however, sees it as a poor choice of segment—or five forces—and the inability of a country's firms to learn their way out of their dilemma by coming to understand customer preferences.

Choosing Where to Compete

Returning to the Colombian leather example, table 9-1 is a summary of the customer segments we identified in the U.S. market broadly classified into five main groupings based on similar characteristics and identifiable traits. Each of the five segments is discussed below.

Segment 1: Price

Because the Colombian leather producers had no real sustainable basis for competing on price, it was clear that it would be difficult for them to serve segment 1. Their cost of labor was high relative to that of the cheaper Asian producers, and the Colombians accrued no cost advantages in any other part of their production and distribution system that could offset that labor disadvantage.

Table 9-1 Summary of a Needs-Based Segmentation of the U.S. Market for Leather Handbags

	Segment 1	Segment 2	Segment 3	Segment 4	Segment 5
Dominant Criteria	Price	Design and Quality	Design, Brand, and Service	Price and Brand	Quality
Description	The low-cost segment, looking for a product with a low unit price and volume discounts	The primarily fashion-focused segment, looking for good product styling with product functionality and high-quality leather	The "I want it all" segment, looking for an established brand name, timely delivery, consistent lot quality, and a willingness to adjust designs	The segment looking for low unit prices and established brand names	The practical, functional segment looking primarily for high-quality workmanship

Segment 2: Design and Quality

The customers in segment 2, on the other hand, were principally concerned with leather design, secondarily with leather quality, and not at all with price. The competitive environment for Colombian leather was not conducive to producing design-oriented products, largely because it lacked key elements such as specialized human resources in design, institutional mechanisms like universities or institutes to support a fledgling design institute, and an overall "culture" of design leadership. Because segment 2 was the least price sensitive of all the segments identified, it seemed an attractive segment in which to try to compete; however, competition in that high end of the market was fierce, and Colombia brought no relative strengths to the field. Moreover, that segment also valued leather quality, something Colombian producers were hard pressed to provide.

Segment 3: Service, Brand, and Design ("I Want It All")

Segment 3 valued service, brand, and design and was not price sensitive. Servicing this segment of customers meant providing timely delivery, consistent quality of lots, a willingness to adjust designs, and an easy return policy. In most of these areas, Colombian firms were at a competitive disadvantage. Timely delivery from Colombia was difficult to ensure because of security and port problems. Consistency in hide quality was also difficult to ensure because the numerous smaller tanneries in Colombia were relatively unsophisticated. The Colombian producers told us they had an easy return policy, but the consumers in the United States did not know that. In general, then, it would have been very difficult for the Colombian leather industry to effectively serve this segment.

Segment 4: Price and Brand

Segment 4 was price sensitive and was looking for branded products and high levels of service. Again, as the industry was configured, most Colombian companies were unable to compete for U.S. business on a price basis with the Asians, and developing well-known brands had been difficult for the leather producers.

Segment 5: Quality

Finally, this segment valued quality above all else and was only moderately price sensitive. More than the quality of the leather itself, however, the segment valued the quality of the workmanship. That was good news for Colombian leather handbag producers, because Colombia had an abundance of artisanship, and the country was generally well regarded for its workmanship in many industries (for example, construction). Furthermore, this segment was not overly concerned about price, so the Colombian producers' price disadvantages were not as relevant. Segment 5, then would be an excellent place for the leather handbag producers to start investing their profits in developing the capabilities to serve more sophisticated consumers who were willing to pay an even higher price premium for the value Colombians could add to their handbags (customers represented in segments 2 or 3, for example).

In conversations with Colombian leather manufacturers about the process of segmenting buyers on the basis of needs, most said they believed they had an intuitive sense for how a market would break out. Thus they made implicit assumptions about which segments they would serve and what the key drivers of success for that particular segment would be.

Explicit and well-articulated choices can actually help shape the nature of public policy decisions political leaders are considering to improve a country's infrastructure. It is possible to make informed, strategic investments that will provide the kind of assistance industry needs to effectively compete in sophisticated markets. In the Colombian leather sector, there are many policy decisions that could be made to provide incentives, for example, for Italian designers to help establish a Colombian design institute or that could help create scholarships for aspiring designers to study abroad.

Such exercises in obtaining customer knowledge, then, are helpful not only for firms but also for regions, nations, and multilateral organizations. Customer knowledge is a powerful tool that can be used to ensure that resources are used efficiently and effectively.

In the era of protected markets, customer needs were not a high priority for most companies. As the protective barriers drop, and as the competition enters, consumers have an increasing variety of choices to make about what they will buy. It is critical for firms today to realize that they cannot serve everyone. They must choose which customer segments to serve, and realize that not making those choices is allowing the competition to choose for them.

This means that customer learning must be considered one of the critical disciplines in the organization. When most economic activity is based on commodities, it is easy to satisfy customer needs; when competing in protected environments, it is unnecessary to satisfy customer needs; but when competing in the era of total competition, only those who truly understand their customers and serve them will survive. If firms don't begin to get that lesson right, there is little hope they will be able to move out of their dependence on natural resources.

The *solution* for the Colombian leather goods industry as a whole is very complex. The work we did focused on one portion of the market and was limited in nature. What is critical to understand is that as simple as that analysis can be to perform, it is rarely done. By clearly identifying market segments to serve, firms force themselves to make explicit choices about their use of resources and the future direction their firms should take. Failure to do this type of work results in something akin to throwing darts at a dart board while blindfolded. When detailed analysis of customers does not take place, no one wins: not the customer, whose needs are still unmet, not the firm, whose returns are not optimized, not the creditors, whose money is backing the firms, and not the government, which would like to see the commensurate benefits of employment, training, and added income accrue to the general population. Customer segmentation, then, is a critical step toward fully developing the competitive strengths of a nation's industry and commerce.

Summing Up: Customer Knowledge Learning Points

The list that follows sums up the major points that readers should take away from the discussion of customer knowledge and segmentation.

1. As pointed out in the discussion of customers in part 1 of this book, the true road to development may very well be not in teaching others how to fish but in teaching them how to manufacture high-quality fishing rods to export to the most sophisticated fishermen in the world.

2. Development efforts should focus on understanding what a country needs to compete globally—on how competitive environments should be upgraded to help firms serve attractive customer segments.

3. Value can be defined as a low-cost strategy, a differentiated strategy, or a service-oriented strategy, or some combination of

the three. But to be sustainable, its definition must constantly adapt to the evolving nature of customer needs.

4. There are many ways to segment buyers. Segmentation can, for example, be based on geographic location, demographic trends, product or technology characteristics, or customer behavior. The most meaningful segmentation is that which creates a clearer understanding of who the customers are and why they behave the way they do.

5. Regardless of geography, demographics, or products, a company's ultimate success in an industry depends on its understanding of what drives the market segments in which it competes and how it meets those requirements.

6. Customer knowledge exercises are helpful not only for the firms but also for regions, nations, and multilateral organizations. It is a powerful tool in helping to ensure that firms use resources efficiently and effectively.

COSTS

Cost management is strategically important for private firms and interested government entities. The interest for private firms should be clear. If a firm has chosen a low-cost strategy, delivering products in a low-cost fashion is critical to success. By the same token, if firms have chosen to produce differentiated products, good cost management will increase their margins.

The government, too, has a vested interest in understanding how costs fit into the overarching strategy of a firm. Governments play indirect roles in determining how capable a particular region is in supporting firms that compete on costs. While public policy decision makers do not need to be intimately familiar with costing methodologies, they should be familiar with cost analysis outputs, and they should be prepared to force industry representatives to provide adequate information about the industry's evolving cost structures.

What follows are some principles of cost learning and a discussion of how developing those capabilities will help firms.

Cost Management Should Be Strategic

The entrance of foreign competition in developing markets usually triggers two predictable responses from domestic firms already in those markets. The first is to ask for government assistance to deal with the changing nature of competition; for example, quotas, price floors, or other protectionist policies. In addition to political efforts, most firms acknowledge that they must simultaneously undertake significant efforts at cost reduction themselves. Unfortunately, the first approaches to cost reduction are usually the wrong ones. They occur across the board, they eliminate the wrong people, or they fail to restructure the fundamental approach to doing business. Cost management should be strategic in nature. There is a saying that "if you don't measure it, you probably aren't managing it." And that "if you are managing it without measurement, you may be lucky, but you are probably wrong."

The Use and Misuse of Cost Data

As discussed in the chapter about relative position, industry associations often try to provide their government with data about their cost positions relative to competitor countries and/or other industries. Nevertheless, governments remain skeptical of those cost data, which they see as being used to make a particular point. And the government is usually not wrong to be skeptical; it is easy to manipulate data, and industry associations are particularly adept at making data appear to support their position. What is needed is a consensus about why cost information is important, about what types of cost information are useful for the public decision maker, and about how to perform the analysis and to package the results in a way that is credible to all interested parties.

Cost in a Broader Sense

Managers recognize the importance of cost, and many strategic plans establish cost leadership or cost reduction as goals. The behavior of costs, however, is rarely understood. There tends to be wide disagreement among managers over what is a firm's cost position relative to the competition and what are the reasons for it. This disagreement results partly from the fact that cost studies tend to look at manufacturing costs and to overlook the impact that other factors, such as marketing, services, and infrastructure, have on relative cost position. Moreover, the cost of individual activities is often analyzed sequentially, without recognizing the linkages between activities that can affect cost.

In most firms, the absence of a systematic framework for analyzing costs underlies these problems. There are many analytical frameworks for analyzing costs, and it is not our intent here to lay forth a specific approach to understanding costs. Understanding and managing costs, however, is a core discipline that will become increasingly critical in the developing world in the era of total competition. In particular, relative cost position analysis will help business and government leaders understand how to make better-informed choices about how to compete in the future.

The Benefits of Relative Cost Position Analysis

Understanding firm-level costs is critical for reasons already explained. When cost analysis becomes interesting at the industry/regional/national level is when it is put in relative perspective. The relative cost position of a firm reveals the amount of erosion that has occurred in an industry's or firm's *comparative advantage*. As such, relative cost position analysis can provide valuable insights for the private and public sectors along the following dimensions:

At the firm level:

- The strengths and weaknesses of a firm versus its competitors (across all functional areas).
- Potential areas for cost reduction.
- Strategic opportunities to exploit new segments or defend areas most vulnerable to attack by competitors.
- Costs and benefits of strategic choices.

At the industry level:

- Knowledge of shifting patterns of competitiveness.
- Competitor information to stay informed about industry evolution.
- A clear sense of direction for industry-wide competitiveness programs.
- Opportunities for foreign alliances.
- Knowledge of opportunities for promoting competitive exports.

At the government level:

- Public policy priorities such as infrastructure and education (a function of transportation and human resources costs).

- Trade negotiation opportunities and pitfalls vis-à-vis competitor countries.

- Foreign direct investment campaigns targeted at industries that would benefit from a competitive home-base platform.

- Industrial policies linked toward providing incentives to bring cost parity to industry dynamics.

As the points above illustrate, relative cost analysis is critical to strategy formulation for firms, industry associations, and nations. That should come as no surprise, but the work in this area is nevertheless often inadequate or inaccurate or both. Relative cost analysis is difficult to perform, and it is meaningful only if it identifies an industry's fundamental drivers of success and if the data are grounded in rigorous research. Ultimately, one of the great services that industry associations will offer their constituents is high-quality analysis about relative position, which they can use to better prepare themselves for more firm-specific efforts to improve their cost structures.

The Example of the Colombian Petrochemical Cluster

In the story of the Colombian petrochemical industry begun in chapter 3, we chose Mexico and Venezuela as the competitors for Colombia because of their strong hydrocarbon base, major petrochemical potential, and their degree of vertical integration. At the time, the Colombian Ministry of Foreign Trade was also in the process of negotiating the Group of Three (G3) negotiations between the governments of Colombia, Venezuela, and Mexico, and petrochemicals was one of the items on its agenda. We focused on the chemical polypropylene because plants in all three countries were relatively new, the export potential from each country was high, each country used different technologies, and they all used similar raw materials. The lessons learned from studying polypropylene, therefore, could be applied to other product lines in the sector, such as polyvinyl chloride.

Performing a relative cost position (RCP) analysis requires learning about the entire competitive environment (including things like government policy, investment plans, and quality of factor conditions). We spent a lot of time in Venezuela and Mexico visiting petrochemical plants, talking to industry executives, and gathering data from industry associations, petrochemical firms, industry experts, newspapers, libraries, and the like. That research helped us identify and measure Colombia's current state of competitiveness vis-à-vis its principal competitors in that business arena. In the process, we also gained information that would help the Colombian firms focus their efforts on key areas of needed internal improvement.

Table 9-2 summarizes the cost drivers in petrochemicals identified *before* we performed the competitor field investigation. While traditional cost accounting can often take into consideration the right cost categories, it does not provide the level of detail seen with the cost drivers. The cost drivers listed in the table help a firm identify the implications of its managerial decisions. For example, electricity costs are largely a function of the unit price of electricity in a given area. A specific firm's consumption of electricity, however, is also a function of its efficiency in converting raw materials, which is driven largely by the type of technology used.

The graph in figure 9-3 was first shown in chapter 3 in a discussion about the importance of relative position. The bars depict three principal drivers of cost: raw materials, transportation, and utilities. In each of these cases, the Colombian firm is constrained by the competitive environment in which it operates. For example, utility rates in Colombia were between 7 and 9 cents per kilowatt hour, compared with 4.5 in Mexico and between 1.5 and 2 in Venezuela. While Venezuela clearly benefits from its abundance of natural gas, there is some evidence that the Venezuelan government is subsidizing its electricity costs.

As illustrated in figure 9-4, the electricity rates of the Colombian producer Propilco are higher than those of all of its competitors in Mexico (PEMEX and Indelpro) and Venezuela (Propliven). Despite the fact that the company employs competitive technology to manage its rate of consumption, the national platform did not provide competitive rates at the time this analysis was done in 1992.

In fact, when we looked at the impact of the electricity rates on outputs of the individual companies, PEMEX's cost structure was most hampered by its older technology, whereas Propilco was hurt most by actual electricity cost. It has been said that the Venezuelan government is subsidizing polypropylene production. Propilven had the lowest

Table 9-2 Representative Polypropylene Cost Drivers

Cost Categories	Drivers
Propylene	• Procurement cost per unit • Inbound logistics • Yield of propylene
Other raw materials	• Procurement cost per unit • Polypropylene manufacturing technology
Electricity	• Price per kilowatt • Polypropylene manufacturing technology
Outbound logistics/freight	• Cost per truck per mile • Truck utilization
Maintenance	• Polypropylene manufacturing technology • Plant scale
Plant labor	• Number of employees • Cost per employee
Royalties	• Polypropylene manufacturing technology • Production volume
Insurance	• Country risk
Sales, general and administrative	• Number of employees • Cost per employee
Inventory carrying costs	• Average inventory value • Cost of capital
Depreciation	• Fixed investment • Production volume

cost, owing to natural advantages. The Venezuelan platform was more supportive of Propilven regarding electricity costs than the Colombian platform was of Propilco. (See figure 9-5.)

Another way to look at a national platform is to focus on the cost of logistics. For example, the transportation costs per mile for the average company are lower in Venezuela than in Colombia because of Colombia's poor roads. What's more, because of Colombia's guerrilla violence, trucking companies are few and far between and insurance rates have been known to increase more than 200 percent in a single year. (See figure 9-6.)

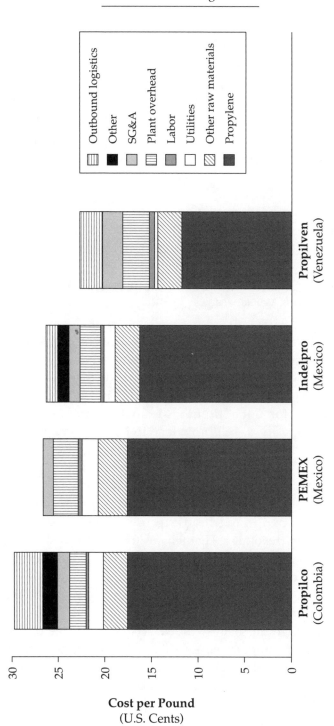

Figure 9-3 Total Cash Cost to Serve Domestic Market (85% Utilization Rate)

Figure 9-4 Electricity Cost

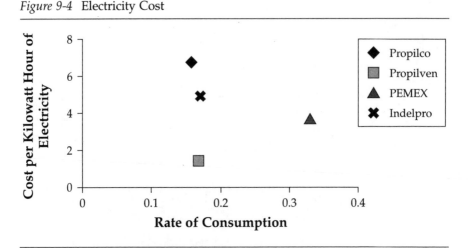

Sources: Propilco, Chemical Systems, Dow Chemicals, Pequiven, Mexican Federal Energy Commission, Monitor analysis.

Colombia also has disadvantages in its cost of raw materials. At the time of our research, both Mexico and Colombia had to import propylene, while the Colombian government had made the clear commitment not to produce propylene for industry so that it could produce greater amounts of gas for domestic use. Meanwhile, Mexico was actively pursuing the capacity to sell propylene to its two polypropylene producers. In this instance, Colombia's overriding national objective of bringing gas to residential areas was given a greater priority than bringing raw materials to the petrochemical industry.

It must be noted that in two other key areas, general and administrative expenses, and in overhead expenses, the Colombian firm was doing better than the others. That tells us that the Colombian firm may be the best managed of all the firms on an operating basis, even though it was the least cost-competitive.

Cost analysis, then, makes it possible to measure relative competitive position over time, which makes it very obvious when sources of comparative advantage are being eroded. The significance of this point should be clear: if comparative advantage is eroding, then a firm needs to develop a more sustainable source of competitive advantage. There are many steps involved in doing that, but one clear place to start is with a complete understanding of cost positions. The Colombian firm is at a comparative disadvantage because the national platform (elec-

Figure 9-5 Total Utilities Cost per Pound of Polypropylene

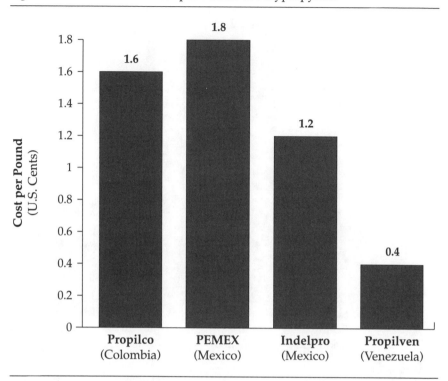

Sources: Propilco, Chemical Systems, Dow Chemicals, Pequiven, Mexican Federal Energy Commission, Monitor analysis.

tricity, raw materials, and transportation) does not provide the reasonably managed firm with the advantages it needs to compete in such a competitive industry segment. Analysis such as this both lowers the defensiveness between government and industry and enables industry to think more clearly about what types of investments it should make to compete effectively.

Summing Up: Cost Knowledge Learning Points

The following list summarizes the key points made in this section on costs.

1. Cost management should be strategic in nature. In other words, "if you don't measure it, you probably aren't managing it." And

Figure 9-6 Outbound Logistics (Domestic Transport)

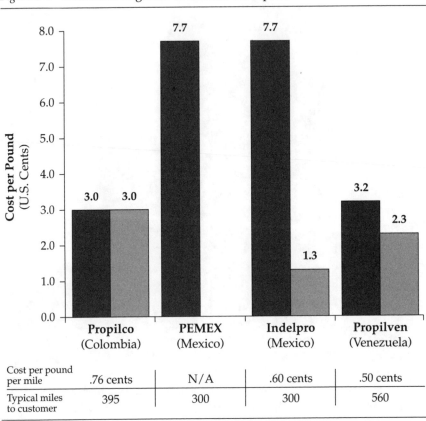

	Propilco (Colombia)	PEMEX (Mexico)	Indelpro (Mexico)	Propilven (Venezuela)
Cost per pound per mile	.76 cents	N/A	.60 cents	.50 cents
Typical miles to customer	395	300	300	560

Sources: Propilco, PEMEX, Indelpro, Propilven, various trucking companies, Monitor analysis.

Note: The left bar is all-in costs delivering to home country; the right bar is delivering to Colombia.

"if you are managing it without measurement, you may be lucky, but you are probably wrong."

2. Cost data are often incorrect and misused. There needs to be a consensus about why cost information is important, what types of cost information are useful for the public policy decision maker, and how to perform the analysis and to package the results in a way that is credible for all interested parties.

3. The behavior of costs, however, is rarely understood. There tends to be wide disagreement with managers over a firm's relative cost position and the reasons underlying it. One reason

is that cost studies tend to look at manufacturing costs and to overlook the impact that other factors have on relative cost position.

4. Relative cost analysis is critical to strategy formulation for firms, industry associations, and nations. The work we have seen in this area is often inadequate or inaccurate or both. Relative cost analysis is difficult to perform, and it is meaningful only if it identifies an industry's fundamental drivers of success.

COMPETITORS

Competitor analysis completes the three C's of firm-level learning vital to sustained growth. It is useful both for improving current firm practices in the developing world and for defending market positions. And it plays a critical role both in informing private sector managers about imminent strategic threats they face from competition and in helping public sector decision makers understand more clearly the potential implications of their policy decisions (such as trade negotiations).

Competitor analysis consists of a systematic collection and analysis of data on a company's competitors. For any company at any given time, different options exist with relation to its competitors: to take the *offensive* against the competitor, to *deter* the competitor from attacking, to *defend* against the competitor if already under attack, or to *ally* the company with one competitor against another. As Sun Tzu wrote around 550 B.C. in *The Art of War*:

> To win every battle by actual fighting is not the most desirable outcome . . . to conquer the enemy without resorting to war is the most desirable.
> The highest form of generalship is to conquer the enemy by strategy . . . the next highest . . . to conquer the enemy by alliance . . . the still next highest . . . to conquer the enemy by battles . . . the worst . . . to conquer the enemy by besieging walled cities.

Although we are not so bellicose as Sun Tzu, the quote well illustrates the scope of choices available to the strategist.

As discussed in previous chapters, the developing world often underrates its ability to compete in certain market segments. A mindset about the competition exists that is fundamentally *limiting* in nature. To develop a mindset that breaks out of those limitations, it is essential to master the fundamentals of competition: to "go micro." Part of the mandate of "going micro" is developing an understanding of what firms need to win in competition with one another. Because firms are competing for customers, we have spent time analyzing how to identify and meet customer needs. But competition is also *against* other firms, so it is important to develop the discipline of constantly analyzing and responding to competitor moves.

Competing industries in different countries have, broadly speaking, different sources of advantage—some passively inherited, some created by business leaders, and others created by public policy makers. Understanding how these sources of advantage affect competition today is critical; it will help leaders understand more clearly the terms in which they are competing. Understanding how these sources of advantage might evolve in the medium to long term, however, is even more important. Any static picture of the competitive environment will be obsolete as soon as it is developed. To think about competition, it is necessary to think systematically and dynamically. Government initiatives by other countries today may produce rich competitive environments in five or ten years. It is best to identify these conditions now in an ongoing way, so that there will be no unpleasant surprises in the future. "Benchmarking" competitor industries enables firms and industries to stay abreast of changing competitive dynamics and provides insight into the reasons for the success or failure of policy or strategy initiatives.

The Colombian Flower Industry Revisited

Our cost analysis of the Colombian flower industry showed that Colombia is currently more competitive than Mexico: it can produce certain flowers at a significantly lower cost than Mexico can. And in transportation costs, Colombia still maintains a slight advantage over Mexico in getting goods to their final destination, at least on the East Coast of the United States. While that is good news for the Colombian flower producer today, the situation is rapidly changing.

The main thrust of our work in the flower sector, therefore, was to help it identify future challenges and to prepare new strategies. The industry needed to better understand the evolving nature of distribution channels and changing customer preferences. Our hypothesis was that as macropressures such as revaluation mounted, the Colombians would need to develop a migratory strategy to change the basis of their competition, going from cheap labor in commodity flower markets to more specialized flowers less susceptible to macroeconomic fluctuations.

To address those challenges, we performed several analyses, including a cost analysis for red roses (the sample flower selected to estimate the overall cost position of the industry) and a competitor profile of the Mexican flower industry. Figure 9-7 shows that the Colombians maintained a strong cost advantage in the production of red roses. The Mexicans, however, have been accruing advantages across their competitive environment that could eventually make them a formidable competitor. The challenge for Colombian producers is to identify where Mexico's future sources of advantage will be and to begin configuring themselves now to mitigate risks to their success.

The first step in competitor analysis is to perform a *strategic audit* of one's own firm to make explicit one's own strategies and assumptions about the market. In the Colombian flower industry, there are many

Figure 9-7   Relative Cost Position for Rose Production:
Mexico versus Colombia, 1993

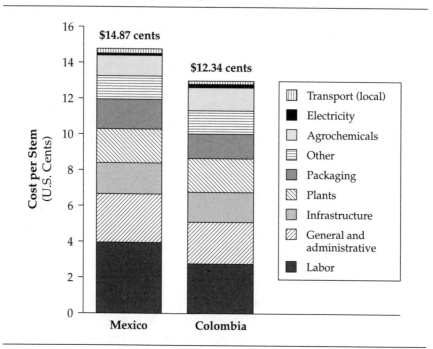

Sources: Interviews with Mexican and Colombian growers, Monitor analysis.

different firms pursuing numerous different strategies, but on the whole the industry shares common traits in its strategic approach.

The principal export market for Colombian flowers is the United States (90 percent of exports). The principal flowers exported are roses, chrysanthemums, pom-poms, and carnations. Almost all of the flowers are flown from Bogotá to Miami, where they are purchased on consignment by flower brokers. The Eastern seaboard accounts for approximately 40 percent of total flower consumption in the United States, with the Florida area making up 10 percent. Colombia's current distribution strategy is to ship all flowers directly to Miami, where flower brokers sell the flowers to U.S. wholesalers and charge the Colombians a standard box fee of U.S. $12, regardless of the selling price of the flower. The flowers are trucked to wholesalers from Miami to their respective destinations. This strategy, developed in the 1960s, has given Colombia a very strong market position in the areas where it competes in the United States.

The Colombians did not follow the Dutch model of creating an auction system; instead many of the large Colombian producers opened up brokerages in Miami. The question facing the Colombian flower producers (and their government, which benefits greatly from the foreign exchange earnings and employment generated by the flower industry) is: Will their current distribution strategy continue to be successful?

Having made explicit what the Colombian strategy is, it can be contrasted with the Mexican strategy to determine the nature of Mexico's threat. The cost analysis has already demonstrated that Colombia is more cost competitive than Mexico. The real challenge is to determine how long that advantage will last and how transportation costs to the final consumer will change that position. Our research shows that the real advantage Mexico brings to bear is its geographic location and a diverse growing climate. While not currently cost competitive, if it is able to achieve its plans, Mexico will be able to ship, by land, flowers to many locations in the United States less expensively than Colombia will be able to fly them to Miami and then ship them.

Perhaps more important, as discussed in chapter 3, the Mexican distribution strategy appears to be to remove the role of the flower broker and to focus on geographic segments that play to Mexico's geographic strengths. In other words, Mexico does not look poised to fight the Colombians for East Coast market share but rather to compete in the Midwest and western United States. Chicago, for example, consumes 21 percent of the flowers in the United States and is not now served directly by Colombia; Colombian flowers must clear customs in Miami and then be transported to Chicago.

It should be noted that Mexico has never been an export threat to Colombia, because the volume of its exports has been so small. In 1992, Mexico exported only $30 million to the United States, a figure dwarfed by Colombia's $350 million. Mexico, however, has managed to create (or respond to) a domestic demand for flowers that positions them very well. They now sell 90 percent of their flowers domestically, at prices sometimes actually higher than what they could get by exporting them. Colombia, by contrast, is selling less than 1 percent of its production domestically. It is generally acknowledged, however, that the Mexican producers create a lower quality flower because of poor flower production technology. In addition, the Mexican consumers, while willing to pay competitive prices for flowers, do not demand as high a quality product as do U.S. consumers. Therefore, while domestic demand is high, it is not the type of demand that anticipates international demand and is therefore not resulting in the upgrading of the Mexican flower industry.

With the passage of NAFTA, however, many industry observers believe that Mexican growers will increasingly target the U.S. market. It is also widely believed that many U.S. growers may move to Mexico to take advantage of cheaper labor rates. If that is true, flowers produced in Mexico could make substantial inroads into Colombia's traditionally dominant position.

This brief overview of the competitor analysis of the flower industry should make several points clear. The most fundamental rule in analyzing competitors is to begin with a strategic audit of one's own firm and industry; to make sense of competitor information, it is necessary to have a benchmark against which to compare it. In addition, it is critical to identify which competitors to analyze and to understand why they are being analyzed and what information can be gained from them. The purpose of performing a competitor analysis is to create a "competitor action profile" that will aid in the design and implementation of distinct strategies.

A competitor profile should address the following four fundamental questions:

1. Is the competitor satisfied with its current position?
2. What likely future moves or strategy shifts will the competitor make, and how dangerous are they?

3. Where is the competitor most vulnerable?

4. What will provoke the greatest and most damaging retaliation by the competitor?

The Competitor Action Profile: Integrating the Three C's

The competitor action profile should be the integrating tool for the three C's of competitor analysis, cost analysis, and customer analysis. In other words, by providing a snapshot of key competitors in critical segments, the competitor action profile can enable a firm to see how the fundamental strategic choices being made affect the competitive environment.

Strategy

A competitor's choices express themselves in its behavior. Strategy is what companies *do*, not what they say they do. Table 9-3 is an example of a competitor profile, with the strategy portion of the profile highlighted. This is a profile of Goya Foods, a firm described in chapter 4 as having decided to focus on serving the Hispanic food and beverage market in the United States. For Colombian fruit juice firms wishing to enter the U.S. market, it is essential to understand who the current players are and what strategies they are pursuing.

Goya's strategy is clearly defined and quite effective. Its historical success limits the options available for Colombian firms wishing to enter the fruit juice market in the United States. Goya's strategy to develop a broad product line, control distribution channels to Hispanic markets, and maintain a strong geographic focus has put up significant barriers to entry for new Colombian firms. While that should not stop aspiring Colombian firms from trying to enter the U.S. market, it should narrow their feasible options. Goya's consistent, focused strategy will more than likely remain so; there are no anticipated changes in market trends that would radically alter the competitive horizon.

That is in contrast to, say, the flower or printing industry, where the passing of NAFTA has created a much more unpredictable environment for Colombian firms vis-à-vis Mexico. Potential benefits of the agreement are difficult to measure; the alternative strategies that may result from it are equally difficult to anticipate. A dynamic and changing environment results in changing strategies. Consequently, past strategies might be less likely to reveal future strategies than one might hope. In this case, having a clear understanding of the relative strengths and

Table 9-3 Competitor Profile: Goya Foods, 1993

Strategy	Capabilities

• Differentiated food products company focusing on Hispanic consumers in the United States and Puerto Rico
• Proliferate product line (840 products) to leverage brand equity with target market
• Exploit widespread distribution infrastructure through direct store delivery
• Manufacture most products in Puerto Rico
• Focus on metropolitan areas with significant Hispanic population
• New focus on mainstream supermarkets and Mexicans, Central and South Americans
	Strengths
	• Excellent sales and distribution capabilities
	  – largest sales staff of any Hispanic company in the United States
	  – distribution centers in seven U.S. cities
	• Deep pockets
	  – largest Hispanic-owned company in the United States
	  – $453 million in sales (1992)
	• Excellent brand recognition
	• Strong in northeast United States (with 80 percent share of Hispanic foods) and with Hispanics of Caribbean descent
	
	Weaknesses
	• Minimal presence in western United States and with Mexicans and Central/South Americans

Goals	**Assumptions**
• Penetrate mainstream supermarkets and migrate to western United States • Shift product mix from 5 percent Mexican food to 20 percent in next five years • Hire more distributors who serve Mexican market • Begin to penetrate markets in Latin America through joint ventures • Currently targeting Mexico and Venezuela	• *"There is no Hispanic market, there are many markets."* —Frank Unanue, president, Goya Foods • Main competitors are U.S.-based firms, with strong Latin focus – Libby's, Hunt's, Campbell Soup

weaknesses of a rival firm's domestic competitive environment will help to anticipate future strategies.

In studying competitors, it helps to keep in mind that sources of competitive advantage tend to fall into one of the basic categories of advantage depicted in the matrix in figure 9-8. In the flower industry, for example, Colombian firms tend to consider themselves differentiated producers with a narrow product scope, while the Dutch would

Figure 9-8 Competitive Scope

		Low Cost	**Differentiation**
Competitive Scope	**Broad**	**Overall Cost Strategy**	**Differentiation**
	Narrow	**Cost-Based Focus**	**Differentiation-Based Focus**

Source: Michael E. Porter, *Competitive Strategy* (New York: Free Press, 1980).

be very broad in product scope with clearly differentiated products. As already mentioned, while the Colombian producers consider their product to be differentiated, their inability to charge a higher margin for their flowers actually means they are competing more on the basis of cost than differentiation. But the purpose of the matrix is not to indicate the relative merit of each corner, but rather to force firms to make an explicit choice about in which corner they wish to compete.

Understanding the concept of basic strategic choice is critical to understanding competitors. Again, what matters most about strategic choice is its explicitness. Each strategic option has its relative merits that can be debated, but once a strategy is chosen, it should be explicit. Because firms often choose conflicting strategies or fail to pursue those strategies which they do choose with focused determination, they make themselves vulnerable to competitors. Generally speaking, there is no *right* strategic choice; there are, however, characteristics of a right choice. When a competitor makes certain strategic choices, therefore, the rival firm can test those choices by answering the following questions:

1. Are the competitor's choices clear?
2. Are its choices consistent with one another and with the company's published strategy?

3. Are the choices consistent with the competitive environment in which it competes?

4. Are the choices clearly prioritized?

5. Are the choices supported by concrete policies and actions?

Mapping competitors' choices over time can reveal persistent tendencies and patterns of behavior. In addition, identifying key *functional* implications of competitors' strategic choices can help a firm or industry to focus on areas in which it could improve. Developing an integrated understanding of a competitor's choices and testing them for consistency can lead to the discovery of other patterns of competition. Finally, by testing a competitor's strategy against its own, a firm can develop a strategic agenda to improve its own competitive position.

An interesting case study in competitor analysis is the evolution of the Japanese automobile industry. In the early 1970s, Japanese firms made clear choices to serve a particular niche of the automobile industry: consumers who valued trustworthy, inexpensive cars. As a result, the Japanese pursued a strategy of producing limited product lines of inexpensive automobiles. Their strategic choice enabled them to innovate in the manufacturing process as well, because they were not, like their competitors in the United States, pursuing strategies of vertical integration but rather the development of a complex system of suppliers to their production process. Having achieved success with a narrow product scope, in the 1980s the Japanese firms began broadening that scope. They looked for ways to leverage their existing technology and manufacturing capabilities with entry into other segments of the market by pursuing a broader geographic scope of customers and by developing a more customer-oriented approach to competition while maintaining their focus on producing inexpensive cars. By the 1990s, firms like Toyota and Nissan had carved out for themselves part of the luxury car market with their Lexus and Infinity brands. They were able to develop a truly differentiated product, but did so based on the successes they had experienced in each of the previous decades.

Capabilities

Capabilities include those resources—physical, financial, informational, human—that a rival firm has converted to competitive advantage. Most traditional competitor analysis focuses on capabilities; specifically, on functional strengths and weaknesses. Most capability analyse are only marginally useful because they focus excessively on a few functions, such as product or financial data. Also, there tend to be limited data available, which results in an overreliance on conventional wisdom to interpret it.

It is important to *benchmark* all major functions of a competitor, to base one's analysis of that competitor on performance, not assertions, and to monitor its performance over time. Examples of the types of data that are useful include sales, market share, net income, return on assets, return on equity, leverage ratios, capital expenditures, and cash flow. If a competitor is pursuing a differentiated strategy, it can also help to contact its customers and attempt to gauge the degree of satisfaction they have along specific criteria.

When analyzing capabilities, it is a good idea to develop an *operations profile* of the competitor. That typically includes plants, equipment, home office configuration, and sales force configuration. It should also consider the organizational capability of the company.

Competitor capability analysis should also include *research on products*, which means it is essential to develop a basis for comparison. Again, a firm should know its own capabilities first. Ideally, that would include a "product profile" consisting of the following types of information over time: performance characteristics, price points and average net selling price, volume sold, channels of distribution, end-use segments, and internal profit and loss analyses. Ideally, this same information can then be gathered from relevant competitors and a comparison analysis performed. Getting such information from competitors is difficult, but there are ways to get it: by looking at price lists, talking to salespeople, visiting competitor stores, talking to company representatives, and collecting as much publicly available information as is possible.

The competitor capability analysis we performed in Colombia on R. R. Donnelley, a major competitor in Colombia's printing and publishing sector, was valuable to Colombian industry leaders because it revealed critical information about a new competitor. (See table 9-4.)

For a firm to understand its competitors' capabilities, it must develop a clear sense of its competitors' cost position relative to itself. And, if possible, it is helpful to develop an understanding of how well competitors are meeting customers' needs.

Table 9-4 Competitor Profile: R. R. Donnelley

Strategy	Capabilities
• Use Reynosa maquiladora plant to print short-run professional and juvenile books primarily for the U.S. market – however, trying to sell to domestic market as well • Become major player in the Mexican market with San Juan del Rio, Querataro, and Mexico City plants – in March of 1992 purchased Laboratorio LitoColor's operations in those two cities – plans to expand plant in San Juan del Rio from 9,000 square meters to 14,000 square meters by end of 1993 – new web press and perfect binding line	**Strengths** • Large financial base provides inexpensive financing and economies of scale in machinery and primary materials purchasing • Recently appointed president of Mexican operations, Jesus Ramos, is experienced and highly respected within Mexican market – provides needed market know-how **Weaknesses** • Pricing for children's books at Reynosa above most competitors in Mexico • Productivity at Mexico plant does not match U.S. plants • Underutilized assets (50 percent capacity utilization)

Goals	Assumptions
• To reach U.S. $4MM in domestic sales by 1994, U.S. $50MM in 1995, and U.S. $100MM by 1998 • To make Reynosa maquiladora plant • To begin phone directory production in the near future	• Internal Mexican market will grow, particularly if NAFTA is ratified – sees large opportunity in phone directories • New technologically advanced machinery will provide it with a competitive advantage over other local companies

Sources: Infotec interviews, Monitor interviews, *Graphic Arts Monthly*.

Goals and Assumptions

Many managers are reluctant to analyze "qualitative" issues such as goals and assumptions, which often determine strategic choice and help define the competitor's definition of victory. In that sense, it is important to determine all of the relevant goals: financial, nonfinancial, corporate, business unit, and personal.

Company goals are often driven by a combination of key constituent expectations, strategic history, and strategic architecture. In other words, a competitor's goals may be shaped largely by such things as shareholder pressure, government intervention, employee or union influence, managers, or customers. At the same time, the goals will be framed in part by the competitor's past experience in making strategic decisions; the horizon of options will be shaped by past failures or successes. A firm's strategic architecture might also play an important role in framing and developing company goals. Given certain constraints (human resources, leadership, structure, systems), goals might be necessarily limited.

Assumptions are the individual and collective rules of thumb that guide decision making. They stem from the same sources as a competitor's goals and are sometimes hardwired into the company. Though sometimes hard to articulate, knowledge of assumptions is essential to understanding the competition's mindset; whether right or wrong, they influence decision and action. In fact, obsolete or misleading assumptions are particularly significant in what they can tell us.

Knowledge of competitors' goals and assumptions allows the firm to avoid unnecessary battles and to exploit competitor weaknesses. Some goals are explicit and can be found in public statements, annual reports, or interviews. Others may be inferred from more creative investigation (of financial performance, organizational structure, and executive backgrounds).

Summing Up: Competitor Knowledge Learning Points

Competitor analysis is one aspect of the *three C's* of critical learning actions needed for creating sustainable strategies and is an important part of the mandate for firms to "go micro."

1. Competitor analysis consists of a systematic collection of data and analysis of the different *options* that exist with relation to

competitors: taking the offensive, deterring and defending against the competitors, or allying with one competitor against another.

2. Competitor analysis should aid in the *design and implementation* of distinct strategies that will enable firms to compete more effectively in the global marketplace.

3. Mapping competitor choices over time can reveal persistent tendencies and *patterns of behavior*, enabling firms to anticipate, rather than react to, competitor actions.

SUMMARY

As Cervantes knew, learning is not without its "inconveniences." He mentions "dizziness in the head" and "weakness in the stomach" among others. Our view is that it is more costly *not* to do the learning.

The types of learning we have discussed in this chapter—the three C's—inform the strategy choices that firms get to make. Such learning can be one of the great points of leverage in mitigating the problems inherent in the seven patterns and turning them into opportunities for growth.

Customer learning, for example, will help firms rely less on *factor conditions* as they learn that they are often competing from within a poor constituency of "five forces," with a lot of rivalry and little ability to influence customer behavior. Understanding costs and competitors has the effect of improving *relative position* by clarifying the sources of sustainable competitive advantages and the fundamental weaknesses that need to be worked on. The combination of all three C's allows firms to make a decision about their capacity and the desirability to *forward integrate* and provides the basis for *interfirm cooperation*.

Perhaps the most innovative use of this type of firm-level learning is to inform the government–private sector dialogue about the realities of the international competitive environment, which provides an opportunity to overcome *paternalistic* behavior. That does not mean that government should use that information to take an overtly interventionist role; however, at present so much of the dialogue between the government and the private sector is colored by poor information that the result is often negative attributions and *defensiveness*.

Improved, strategic-type learning will help to focus a country's leaders on creating sustainable, hard-to-imitate advantages that would position local firms closer to end-users. The benefits will include the formation of international alliances and the creation of high and rising value for increasingly sophisticated customers who are willing to pay more money for the unique value they perceive. Learning of this kind creates informed choice, which improves competitive positioning, and can help to turn the seven patterns into sources of advantage.

CHAPTER TEN

Steering Mechanisms

I have come to believe that it is more important for the government to be consistent *even* if they are consistently stupid.

—*Peruvian textile manager*

In earlier chapters we suggested that several factors have kept Andean firms from creating the seven opportunities for sustained growth and in the preceding chapter discussed in detail one of those factors, a lack of strategic focus. Another contributing factor that bears close examination is the limited long-term thinking and investment that can be the unintended consequence of institutional and organizational structures.

Why has the style of strategic thinking and learning presented in chapters 8 and 9 not been adopted by more firms in the Andes or Latin America as a whole? Partly because government and industrial institutions have failed to provide an environment where long-term thinking can flourish. The lack of government clarity about policies and institutions creates uncertainty and short-term thinking in the private sector. At the same time, industry associations come to believe that to be effective, their efforts are best spent on influencing government policy rather than educating industry leaders in strategy and management. This shift of focus from market realities to government policies contributes significantly to the patterns of uncompetitive behavior discussed in part 1.

We refer to organizational structures and policies as *steering mecha-nisms* and believe that they often play a large role in limiting the quality of learning that can occur in complex organizations—whether companies, industry associations, or governments. There are three types of steering mechanisms: (1) organizational, (2) legal and administrative, and (3) informal. Organizational mechanisms involve the design and formal flows of power, authority, and communication throughout an organization. Informal mechanisms involve the culture of a particular organization—modes of conduct that are not written down but that clearly influence the way things are done: what can be said, how people should behave, how people learn or work together. In a corporation, legal and administrative mechanisms involve the establishment of guidelines for concerns such as vacation and sick time, use of computers or photocopiers, or expense reimbursement. In the government, these mechanisms involve a wide variety of laws, regulations, decrees, and policies that have a dramatic impact upon a national economy.

This chapter will focus on the implications of legal and administrative mechanisms from the government perspective by examining in detail the case of the Bolivian government. The analysis demonstrates how the steering mechanisms developed in an organization over a period of time can constrain the strategic choices available to those working in or with that organization. We look at this process in the Bolivian government for a period of forty years. We do not intend to delve deeply into Bolivian history but rather to develop a sense for how policy actions, over time, create steering mechanisms that limit an organization's ability to capitalize on the seven opportunities for sustained growth discussed in the first part of this book.

CASE STUDY OF THE BOLIVIAN GOVERNMENT

A nation's portfolio of policy instruments, its steering mechanisms, affects the strategies adopted by its firms. It does that by:

- Influencing the balance between market competition and market regulation.
- Creating trade-offs between economic growth and redistribution of wealth.

Depending on which areas a given administration emphasizes, firms will alter their behavior to maximize their own gain in those systems. A great irony in the developing world is that, though many business managers tend to be rational, predictable people, they have developed strategies that often seem quite irrational. The irony lies in how effective these managers have been in creating successful firms in very difficult environments while at the same time finding it so difficult to adjust to the realities of global competition. When a government creates a complex set of mechanisms to manage the economy, such as tariffs, tax rebates, and preferential interest rates, businesspeople develop business strategies that leverage those artificial advantages. Understanding how government actions create organizational and administrative mechanisms that fundamentally alter the behavior of business leaders is a critical step in creating a process that will enable those leaders to change that behavior.

Throughout this chapter, the reader should keep in mind two questions:

- How do government policies affect the conditions in a nation's competitive environment?

- How do government policies influence the strategic choices available to a firm?

State Capitalism: 1952–1972

When President Paz Estenssoro took power in 1952, Bolivia was predominantly rural and underdeveloped, with agriculture and related industries employing 72 percent of the population, but contributing only 33 percent to GDP. The extensive *latifundia* system had created an ownership structure where 6 percent of the landowners controlled 92 percent of the cultivated land, and the imbalance of power and wealth between the privileged few and the majority of the population was widely recognized.

While agriculture accounted for the majority of employment at that time, it was the mining sector that created most of the economic rewards and foreign exchange earnings. In the 1930s, Bolivian mines were very productive and globally competitive, but with the approach of the 1950s, with key veins drying up and insufficient capital investment, Bolivian mining operations were no longer competitive on a global level.

In light of this environment, President Paz Estenssoro created a strategic agenda whereby the state would become the "master strategist" of the economy and intervene to correct aberrations in the market that had led to such a concentration of wealth and lack of equity in the population. He designed mechanisms to redistribute wealth to peasant groups through extensive agricultural reform and increased investment in rural education and services. He also nationalized the three largest mining companies and extended the state's scope in managing other state-owned enterprises. The "state capitalism" model he employed had the following features:

- The public sector took responsibility for most capital investments.

- The government had an active role in managing the microeconomy.

- Special relationships between government and favored segments of the private sector developed to promote economic activity and employment.

Part of Paz Estenssoro's economic strategy was to develop an import substitution model of economic development by erecting tariffs and subsidies to encourage industrialization in Bolivia. His hope was that the increased state investment, close cooperation with business, and protected environment would create the impetus for industrialization. To bankroll those efforts, he also needed to ask for significant assistance from the United States and to develop foreign investment codes that favored U.S. firms.

What kinds of institutional mechanisms were created as a result of that type of strategic choice and action by the government? In addition to the increasingly complex organizational structure needed to carry out the expanded activities of the state, there was a complex set of policy initiatives that had a profound impact on the way business was conducted in Bolivia. A sampling of these can be found in table 10-1.

Paz Estenssoro believed that the state had an important role to play both in pushing the industrialization process and in providing a social safety net. Those beliefs led him to create an enlarged role for the state that he hoped would create an environment that would foster innovation. Instead, he developed a complex mix of policies that created a legal and regulatory environment that actually inhibited innovation and national upgrading—the very goals he was trying to achieve. By creating multiple exchange rates, high tariffs, a devaluing currency, and increased state participation in natural resource extraction, the government created incentives for business leaders to become less competitive.

Table 10-1 Bolivian Economic Policies, 1952–1956

Policy Instruments \ Policy Areas	Monetary	Fiscal	Trade	Foreign Direct Investment	Incomes	Sectoral
Legal	• Multiple exchange rate regime	• Spending shifted from military to health, education	• Selective import restrictions issued	• Petroleum investment code rewritten to favor U.S. interests	• Agrarian Reform Decree • Pongueaje and pongo service for campesinos eliminated	• Export, sale of all minerals monopolized by state
Administrative	• Subsidized credit given to SOEs[1]	• Budget deficits allowed to increase	• Tariffs raised to increase government revenue	• Petroleum alliances with foreign private investors	• COB[2] launched • Food, other subsidies given to miners	• CBF[3] extended large subsidies to private sector
Direct Market	• Money printed to finance budget deficits	• 33 percent of 1958 budget paid for by U.S. funds	• Exchange rate allowed to devalue with rising inflation	• Foreign aid invested in modern road system	• Public Law 480 imported food from United States	• 67 percent of mines nationalized into COMIBOL[4]
Economic Results	• Accelerating inflation between 1952 and 1956	• Expanding budget deficits	• Trade controls unable to prevent rising trade deficits	• Increased foreign aid • Minimal private foreign investment	• Increased wages hurt by rising inflation	• Increased importance of natural resource exports for economy

Sources: Template adapted from James Austin, *Managing in Developing Countries* (New York: Free Press, 1990), 89; Herbert S. Klein, *Bolivia: The Evolution of a Multi-Ethnic Society* (New York: Oxford University Press, 1992); Jeffrey Sachs and Juan Antonio Morales, *Bolivia 1952–1986* (California: International Center for Economic Development, 1988); and Monitor interviews.

Notes: 1. SOE = State-owned enterprises
2. COB = Central Obrero Boliviana
3. CBF = Government Development Corporation of Bolivia
4. COMIBOL = Corporación Minera de Bolivia

There was little competition that would encourage innovation, and preferential policies let businesses earn relatively easy income. Furthermore, the activities he undertook led to a twenty-fold increase in the cost of living between 1952 and 1956, a real drop in GDP of 13 percent, and increased budget deficits.

The years 1956–1972 tell a similar story: many presidential administrations trying to develop a role for the state that would enhance the productivity of the economy and protect its citizens from economic hardship. Instead, government policies created an increasingly complex environment for firms to compete in; the changes in government approaches created uncertainty, which limited private sector investment, and the government continued to increase its involvement in industry. Moreover, there was a resurgence of economic nationalism in the early 1970s, including the nationalization of the Gulf Oil Company, the annulling of U.S. Steel contracts, and the expulsion of the U.S. Peace Corps.

The Banzer Years: 1972–1976

In 1972, Colonel Banzer took office and committed himself to developing more sophisticated advantages for Bolivian firms while maintaining Paz Estenssoro's focus on redistribution policies. He had the good fortune to be at the helm of leadership when Bolivian exports were earning record income for the nation, creating a positive environment for making significant investments in the national economy. Export income rose from $226 million in 1970 to $650 million in 1974 to give Bolivia its largest trade surplus ever. The principal driver of this success was a doubling of tin prices between 1973 and 1974.

Colonel Banzer used the wealth from rising mineral prices and easy foreign credit to fund ambitious investments in infrastructure, mining, and subsidies for industrial development. It was a classic case of the government trying very hard to do the right things and trying to create the types of advantages necessary for firms to compete successfully. But with the excess of funds came an increased amount of corruption, and the bloated administration was tremendously inefficient at completing projects. In fact, one example is the construction of the twenty-story building where the current Ministry of Economic Development is housed. It began in 1972 and was not finished until early 1990 because of the politics and inefficiencies associated with state-led development efforts.

Banzer's portfolio of policy initiatives, representative highlights of which are shown in table 10-2, created strong incentives for members of the private sector to position themselves not for the external markets, but to benefit from local government purchases and programs. Government steering mechanisms tend to distort real market signals, and limit the ability of firms to position themselves strategically.

In this environment of rising export earnings, easy credit, heavy investment, and increased corruption, the government did try to diversify the economy from its dependence on tin, moving into other minerals and petroleum. And it experienced modest success with regard to exporting those other goods, but they were not much more structurally attractive than tin. That is one reason why reliance on basic factor advantages and poor knowledge of customer needs have been consistent themes in Latin America: there is an abundance of natural resources, and governments tend to be poor judges of industry attractiveness.

The period following the Banzer regime witnessed a collapse of national consensus and a dramatic weakening of the economy. Both government leaders and the private sector began to focus again on basic sources of advantage, and business leaders exploited access to political leaders for personal gain. When Siles Zuazo took power in 1982, he faced demands from the population for higher wages and higher levels of employment that led him to increase social spending, protect industry from international competition, and increase government payrolls at SOEs (state-owned enterprises). He also approached stabilization through heterodox programs that tried to limit the social costs of fixing a weakening economy. As one Bolivian industry leader said, "Business was no longer about investment or strategy; it was about speculation and self-protection."

The Crisis Years and Beyond

In 1985, the Bolivian economy was in ruins. Inflation reached a peak of more than 24,000 percent per year (in August 1985), the extensive state mining system was devastated by the collapse of tin prices, and social pressures were intense. President Paz Estenssoro had returned to power and faced the reality that neither the International Monetary Fund (IMF) nor the World Bank were willing to support further efforts to buttress heterodox stabilization programs. The Byzantine economic

Table 10-2 Bolivian Economic Policies, 1972–1978

Policy Instruments \ Policy Areas	Monetary	Fiscal	Trade	Foreign Direct Investment	Incomes	Sectoral
Legal	• Exchange rate fixed after 40 percent devaluation in 1972	• Military expenditures increased	• Manufactured product tariffs raised	• Foreign investment code liberalized	• Wage freezes in public, private sectors	• Law of industrial incentives to promote nontraditional exports
Administrative	• Loose monetary policies to accommodate inflows of foreign funds	• Increased taxes on tin • Tax rebates for nontraditional exports	• Advanced deposit requirements on imports	• Guaranteeing of foreign loans to private sector	• Subsidization of food prices • Substantial allocation of land through agricultural reform	• YPFB, COMIBOL, ENAF[1] spending focused on capacity increases, limited exploration
Direct Market	• Industrial credit loaned from Central Bank	• Infrastructure, development projects take 48 percent of budget	• Natural gas treaty with Argentina	• Increase in borrowing from foreign, public, commercial sources	• Tax, other incentives to encourage firms to locate in outlying regions	• Subsidies for nontraditional exports
Economic Results	• Double-digit inflation	• Public sector debt financing consuming 30 percent of exports • Misspent investment money	• Exports grew from $200MM to $700MM	• Foreign debt grew by 200 percent	• Slow, steady increase in GDP/capita	• By late 1970s, excess smelting, refining capacity, falling raw material extraction

Sources: Template adapted from James Austin, *Managing in Developing Countries* (New York: Free Press, 1990), 89; Herbert S. Klein, *Bolivia: The Evolution of a Multi-Ethnic Society* (New York: Oxford University Press, 1992); Jeffrey Sachs and Juan Antonio Morales, *Bolivia 1952–1986* (California: International Center for Economic Development, 1988); and Monitor interviews.

Notes: 1. YPFB = Yacimientos Petrolíferras Fiscales de Bolivia
2. COMIBOL = Corporación Minera de Bolivia
3. ENAF = tin smelting company

structure erected over the preceding decades was fundamentally al-
tered. Exchange rates were stabilized, trade and capital accounts were
liberalized, government deficits and printing of money were curtailed,
and the entire tax regime was restructured. The policy portfolio looked
something like that in table 10-3.

After Paz Estenssoros' effective fight against hyperinflation, his suc-
cessors have had to address the dual challenge of maintaining macroeconomic stability and trying to find a way to ameliorate the widening
disparity in income. President Paz Zamora (1989–1993) began to dismantle the state's dominance in key sectors of the economy and developed policies to encourage greater private sector participation in exports by introducing new investment codes and trade policies, but
insisted on maintaining tight control of the fiscal environment.

President Sánchez de Lozada, since his election in 1992, has attempted to bridge the gap between economic growth and social equity
through an innovative capitalization program, whereby state assets
would be sold, but the benefits of the sales would go directly to the
people, through the development of a pension plan. His macroeconomic policies indicate a conviction that the state cannot be a competent economic strategist in the affairs of the nation, which clearly
distinguishes him from his predecessors of the past forty years. He
does, however, share his predecessors' desire to redistribute the nation's
wealth. And, having witnessed firsthand the many strikes, student
protests, and teachers' marches, we can understand why the political
leadership would find it difficult not to develop policies to address the
protesters' concerns with regard to the country's social needs.

The Impact of Steering Mechanisms over Time

Government policies and steering mechanisms can be plotted on a
matrix; it is not a scientific approach, but it is informative nonetheless.
In figure 10-1, the mapping for Bolivia is quite simple: it categorizes the
presidential administrations of the past 40 years on two dimensions:
identifying the focus of national economic objectives and policies and
identifying the principal economic strategist in the economy. The
findings are consistent with what we've previously stated: over time,
inconsistent policies and steering mechanisms create an unpredictable
and difficult-to-manage environment, where the private sector becomes
competent in lobbying, not in learning. Decades of state dominance in

Table 10-3 Bolivian Economic Policies, 1985–1989

Policy Instruments \ Policy Areas	Monetary	Fiscal	Trade
Legal	• Exchange rate unified • Interest rate ceilings removed • Foreign currency banking deposits legalized • Contracting in foreign currencies authorized	• Tax regime overhaul, introduction of 3.5 percent asset tax, regressive VAT, wealth tax • Sharp drop in fiscal spending	• Multiple tariffs replaced with 20 percent uniform tariff
Administrative	• State banks, subsidized credit eliminated • Development loans channeled through private banks	• Tax collection systems improved • Reduction of state bureaucracy	• Import quotas eliminated • Privatization of import valuation
Direct Market	• Reduction of money printing • Decision to remonetize slowly • Capital/debt ratios for private banks increased • Bank portfolio supervision by government increased	• Freeze on public sector salaries, investment	• Currency devalued heavily in 1985, then floated with progressively fewer interventions
Economic Results	• Inflation tamed within weeks • Liquidity problem for banks • High real interest rates; large gaps between lending and savings rates	• Budget deficits reduced but not eliminated	• Import surge

the economy created a culture of expectations concerning its role. The state had crowded out not only private sector money, but also private sector imagination, which could have helped to solve the collective problems of the country. In such an environment, businesspeople, if they want to succeed, have to be good at watching the government and at managing the changing structures, laws, policies, and organizations the government creates. Bolivia's business leaders did not have to become good at any of the fundamental business strategy disciplines. The Bolivian private sector developed, in a word, a paternalistic atti-

Table 10-3 (cont.)

Policy Instruments \ Policy Areas	Foreign Direct Investment	Incomes	Sectoral
Legal	• Restrictions on capital inflows, outflows lifted	• Wage indexing eliminated • Employment termination simplified	• Price controls eliminated in most markets • National Transportation Company assets transferred to municipalities
Administrative	• Tax amnesty for flight capital • Dollar deposits allowed without proof of origin	• Gasoline prices raised, indexed to exchange rate • Subsidies for social services	• COMIBOL[1] workforce reduced by 23,000 to 7,000 • YPFB[2] workforce reduced by 6,000 to 4,000
Direct Market	• Rapprochement with IMF, World Bank, Paris Club • Foreign debt payments halted temporarily • Repurchased loans on secondary market at 11¢ on dollar	• Public sector prices raised • Emergency Social Fund established for short-term work on infrastructural projects	• Public utility, fares for urban transportation decentralized to local governments • Holdings of CBF[3] ceded to regional development corporations
Economic Results	• Resumption of foreign lending to Bolivia • Repatriation of flight capital	• Unemployment soared with depression, collapse of mining	• Labor unions crushed by COMIBOL[1] reforms

Sources: Template adapted from James Austin, *Managing in Developing Countries* (New York: Free Press, 1990), 89; Herbert S. Klein, *Bolivia: The Evolution of a Multi-Ethnic Society* (New York: Oxford University Press, 1992); Jeffrey Sachs and Juan Antonio Morales, *Bolivia 1952–1986* (California: International Center for Economic Development, 1988); and Monitor interviews.

Notes: 1. COMIBOL = Corporación Minera de Bolivia
  2. YPFB = Yacimientos Petrolíferras Fiscales de Bolivia
  3. CBF = Government Development Corporation of Bolivia

tude toward development and competition. The strategic actions and steering mechanisms Bolivian leaders had devised insulated the private sector from the need to change. Now, with stability at hand, the greatest challenges Bolivia faces are how to grow and how to get the government and private sector to work together in a way that does not limit innovation and upgrading.

Figure 10-1   Bolivian Economic Policies over Time

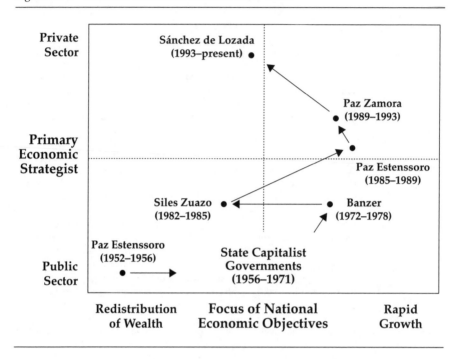

NATIONAL DEVELOPMENT STRATEGIES

What are the choices a government has in the trade-off between economic growth and social equity? As the preceding discussion should make clear, many specific decisions must be made, and each has real consequences—not just for the economy but for the signal it sends to the private sector. We would like to end this discussion with a brief overview of what broad national economic strategies are open to decision makers and how they relate to the discussion about equity versus growth.

We have observed six national strategies or archetypes of strategies. Rarely, have we found one nation that fits neatly into one strategy-archetype. Most national strategies can be better understood by dividing them into two traditional categories: *growth* strategies, which include monetarism, open trade, and industrialization; and *equity* strategies, which consist of agriculture-led, redistribution, and socialism.[1] Bolivia has migrated between many of these strategies over the past forty years, as has Peru over the past twenty-five years. Colombia moved aggressively from industrialization to open trade over a period of just fourteen months during President Gaviria's administration. Peru made the same move in only four months after Fujimori consolidated his power in 1991.[2]

Traditional Growth Strategies

The *monetarism* strategy emphasizes stabilizing markets, freeing prices, and developing markets to guide the allocation of an economy's resources. The private sector takes responsibility for generating wealth based on the emerging entrepreneurship, abundant freedom, and little government guidance. The role of the state is minimized. The underlying assumptions are that resources are allocated by the free markets and that the government should focus on simply providing a consistent and stable environment; if the government does that job well, the nation need only wait for the entrepreneurial class to emerge as the engine for economic growth. Chile exemplified this model between 1973 and 1983, as did Peru in the early part of this decade. It was also a prevailing model of thinking during the 1980s under Ronald Reagan in the United States and Margaret Thatcher in Great Britain.

Open trade strategy differs from monetarism by emphasizing the development of foreign trade and investment. It shares the monetarist reliance on market forces to allocate resources and prices, and it views international competition for trade and investment as the driver of growth. Companies are responsible for developing trade and investment links with the international economy, and there is an active role for the government in supporting those activities. The private sector in theory agrees to be responsible for export growth, but it continually accuses the government of being indifferent or incompetent when it comes to providing the necessary support. The government in turn often sees the private sector as greedy, inefficient, and eager for subsidies.

That is the current model in Peru and Colombia, and it was in effect in Japan between the 1960s and 1980s and in Germany between the 1970s and 1990s. In our observations of that model, the government takes significant responsibility for administrative and legal reform, and virtually none for creating positive conditions for microeconomic reform or firm-level assistance.

Industrialization is the import substitution strategy that seeks to achieve growth through the rapid expansion of the manufacturing sector. There is a focus on consumer goods for the domestic market, usually behind high tariff walls. There is heavy government intervention to increase production and manage the international economic links; that is, in the direction of investment capital, subsidies, and investment funds that promote capacity expansion.

Companies tend to depend on the government for monetary support and for strategic guidance, which may take the form of subsidized export production and exchange rate depreciation, discussed in the chapter on paternalism. The government is viewed as the source of advantage, and there is a production or supply-driven mentality as well as significant defensiveness on the part of the private sector against change. Industrialization approaches are less accepted than they have been in recent decades. Korea used the model in the 1950s, Brazil in the 1960s, and Colombia used it until the late 1980s.

Traditional Social Equity Strategies

We have chosen to place the generic *agriculture-led* strategy in the social equity section because of its inward or domestic orientation, its emphasis of improving income for the impoverished rural population, and its objective (for the government) of self-sufficiency. This strategy seeks to achieve economic growth through the rapid expansion of the agriculture sector and to free up resources so that they can be used to develop other sectors. For example, the manufacturing sector would be helped in three ways: low prices for agricultural products would limit inflation, which would create a more stable environment for manufacturers; improved agricultural efficiencies would release labor for other sectors to use; and finally, the expanded agricultural sector would itself create new manufacturing opportunities.

The government is primarily responsible for supporting an agriculture-led strategy, providing trade protection, and serving as a key purchaser of agricultural products and capital equipment. In this strategy, the concentration of land ownership determines the distribution of income. Both the public and the private sectors have an inward focus, and the government assumes responsibility for the growth and distribution effects.

This model was in effect during the postwar boom in the United

States and Canada, as well as in the Philippines and India. Proponents of this model held a lot of hope for improving the standard of living of the average citizen in Africa since independence began in the late 1950s.

Redistribution strategies seek to create a more even distribution of economic wealth and to maximize employment. This system assumes that there is no trade-off between income redistribution and generating growth, and it is often used as a complement to one of the four strategies already discussed. The government is central to this strategy, and its administration is often decentralized so as to improve its responsiveness to low-income groups. The strategy often involves four elements: an initial redistribution of assets, including land, financial, and productive assets; the creation of local institutions to support local employment initiatives; heavy investment in human capital; and government support of labor or employment-intensive strategies in companies. The bottom line is that the government assumes paternalistic responsibilities for ensuring a minimum standard of living for the general population. While the redistribution model is at least partially incorporated into the current thinking of many nations, a very strong example of it can be seen in Bolivia.

Socialism, in its classic form, deemphasizes the private sector and leaves the government in control of all economic assets. Ownership is by the state through collectives and usually accompanied by centralized planning. The allocation of resources is typically governed by quantitative targets and administrative prices. Income distribution tends to be even, and the formally planned market tends to be accompanied by a robust informal market to redress shortages and the marginal distribution of goods. The key idea is that the worker will take care of his or her job responsibilities and the government will take care of everything else. Of the twenty-six nations that have experimented with classic socialism, only two examples remain: North Korea and Cuba.

Countries have wealth creation and distribution strategies, too. Often these national development strategies are implicit and the result of the sum total of many policies and tools that no one group or organization understands or controls very well. As with the strategy of a firm or even an individual, good national development strategies are those that are explicit, informed, balance the past with the future, are an exercise in integration, create a menu of options, and enable specific choices.

When a nation, like a firm, fails these tests of a good strategy it often creates confusion and unanticipated results.

SUMMARY

The case of Bolivia represents what we have observed throughout the Andes and other developing nations—constantly changing development strategies and inconsistent public policies have over time created organizational and administrative steering mechanisms that reinforce— in fact, help to create—the seven patterns of uncompetitive behavior. Competition based on basic factors is reinforced when there is neither confidence in how the government will behave in the future nor a qualified human resource pool from which to draw. When faced with that dual problem, firms tend to mitigate their risk by choosing industry segments that have low barriers to entry and exit. They tend to maximize short-term gains because they have no confidence that any investment in the long-term will be fruitful. This creates a reinforcing pattern: firms actively encourage the government to ensure they are at least able to achieve short-term gains, which translates into strong lobbying efforts and often antagonism toward the government when it is not responsive to their needs. This breeds paternalism and defensiveness. Import substitution policies that limit competition make it less necessary for firms to understand their customers and their competitors. This in turn makes it difficult to choose good segments in which to compete and limits the need for knowledge about relative competitive position. Finally, import-substitution-oriented steering mechanisms have inhibited the development of strong clusters because firms do not need to cooperate in order to succeed in those highly regulated environments.

As we suggested earlier, there have been several contributing factors to the inability thus far of firms in the Andean region—and in developing countries in general—to turn the seven patterns of uncompetitive behavior into opportunities for sustained economic growth and social equity. We have attempted to make a case that a major reason has been the rapidly changing national development strategies and unpredictable steering mechanisms that limit long-term strategic thinking and investment in innovation.

If leaders of developing countries can begin to develop informed and explicit national development strategies and make steering mechanisms consistent and predictable, they will help create environments more conducive to long-term thinking and investment. This, in turn, will encourage better choices and a higher grade of learning at the firm level that will ultimately lead to the development of more productive firms.

CHAPTER ELEVEN

Mental Models

Everything is human relations.
—*Edward Gannon, S.J., professor of philosophy*

We have discovered that there are at least two ways to interpret results: first, we can look at the strategic actions and at the steering mechanisms—*the visible part of change*—that have caused the results. Second, we can try to comprehend the hidden aspect of results—*the invisible part of change*—or the "mental models." Mental models consist of *paradigms of knowledge,* which make up a kind of library that informs an individual's perspective, and *frames of reference.* Frames of reference include beliefs, inferences, and goals that inform an individual's perspective. There is a dynamic relationship between paradigms and frames, which we can demonstrate in a simple but useful model, shown in figure 11-1.

In this chapter we plan to walk the reader through four questions:

1. What are some of the basic beliefs that influence frames of reference?

2. What are the groups that we can describe according to their frames of reference—who is out there?

3. Where can we start in attempting to bring those groups to a shared vision?

4. What is the relationship between frames of reference and the "seven patterns of uncompetitive behavior"?

Figure 11-1 Mental Models

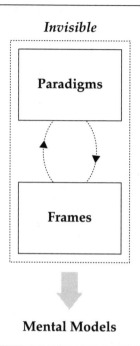

Our ultimate goal in exploring frames would be to identify leaders by belief systems regarding wealth creation and distribution, group them by like characteristics, and discuss ways in which the groups can think about moving toward a shared vision of how to compete in the future. We begin with a very comprehensive, data-driven view of the way Venezuela's leadership thinks about competitiveness. This example should be of interest to social scientists, economists, and Venezuelans, but may not be interesting to those with little appetite for numbers.

We then move to a more integrated view of how our research has helped us identify five archetypal frames of reference. An under-standing of these archetypes should help inform the debate about competitiveness and wealth creation. We have evidence that the five archetypal frames exist in many nations and hypothesize that, although the distribution in each country will be unique, every nation has leaders who fall into the five groups.

WHAT BELIEFS INFLUENCE FRAMES OF REFERENCE?

We have been surveying leaders and opinion makers for several years,[1] and in our work in Venezuela[2] we used a survey containing more than 200 questions and covering a wide variety of topics, including:

- The nature of wealth creation.
- The country's capacity to compete.
- Social context.
- Faith in government.
- Openness to free trade.
- Openness to international learning.
- Organizational effectiveness.
- Company-level strategy.
- The relationship between work and achievement.

We based our first analysis of the survey results on how respondents in traditional, demographic groups, such as the public sector, private sector, labor, press, and academia, answered the questions. We discuss these results below. We then apply the more sophisticated techniques of segmentation analysis (described in our chapter on customer learning), to the realm of mental models. This second technique allows us to group respondents according to their mental models of how to compete in the future as a first step toward building a shared vision among the groups.

The Nature of Wealth Creation

What is striking in our analysis is the high degree of agreement, not dissent, in the views of Venezuela's public and private sectors. In general, leaders of both sectors are well informed and have a positive outlook on issues related to wealth creation. Nine out of ten believe that a changing business environment is something to be welcomed and embraced. Fewer respondents (59 percent), although still a majority, agree that successful companies *create* markets for products and services rather than let the markets come to them. Similarly, 57 percent agree that wealth is a product of human initiative and effort and therefore can be infinite, and 56 percent agree that unrestrained competition is a force that promotes excellence and enriches a society. Although a small group (16 percent) states that unrestrained competition nurtures envy and threatens the stability and solidarity of a society, in general, respondents in Venezuela—and in most of the countries we have surveyed—have an optimistic attitude toward competition, innovation, and wealth creation.

Venezuela's Capacity to Compete

While respondents are optimistic about competition, innovation, and wealth creation in the abstract, they are less optimistic about Venezuela's capacity to compete. Half of the leaders believe that domestic companies cannot compete without government assistance, and the vast majority (73 percent government and 82 percent private) believe that the government should provide domestic companies with export credits. Similarly, half of all leaders surveyed feel that the nation's prosperity, which is today driven primarily by oil, will still be driven primarily by oil in thirty years. On a brighter note, a small majority of leaders (62 percent of government and 57 percent of private) agree that Venezuela has the potential to become world class in industries other than oil.

The Social Context

There is almost complete consensus in Venezuela that the social situation is dire and that the government should play a strong role in addressing social issues. Seven out of ten leaders in both the public and the private sectors believe that too many people are suffering from economic reform. Approximately nine out of ten leaders agree the government should do more to help the poor and that government policies should be designed to guarantee a minimum standard of living.

While there is agreement on the problem, there is less agreement about the causes of social suffering and what should be done about it. More than half of the Venezuelan leaders surveyed do not appear to link social suffering to the country's long-standing dependence on oil, stating instead that there is enough oil in the country so that no one should suffer. About half of the leaders in both the public and private sector agree that the government should regulate prices in some industries, while the other half emphatically disagree. Similarly, slightly less than half (38 percent private and 45 percent public) believe that price controls are necessary to protect the poor.

There is, however, a high level of consensus about some things the government should *not* do. Fewer than 20 percent in both the private and public sectors agree that public companies that continue to lose money—but employ many poor people—should continue to operate. Similarly, fewer than 20 percent of both the private and public leaders agree that government policies should subsidize outright the profitability of businesses.

Faith in Government

In a country like Venezuela, in which the government has historically played a powerful, interventionist role and is struggling to compete in the world's increasingly open economy, it was not surprising to discover an intense lack of faith in the competency and trustworthiness of the Venezuelan government. Not only does the vast majority (86 percent) of the private sector disagree that government officials in Venezuela know what is best for the country, but the vast majority of the public sector itself (74 percent) does not believe it knows what is best. Similarly, 84 percent of the public and 93 percent of the private sectors believe that the private sector can run business more effectively than the government. Furthermore, 76 percent of the respondents from the private sector state outright that elected officials cannot be trusted.

In addition to faith and trust in government, the survey also addressed general views on corruption. Here we found one of the few wide divergences between the public and the private sector. While 84 percent of the private sector believe that corruption is the main cause of poverty in the country, only 56 percent of the public sector does. However, a large percentage of both groups (60 percent private and 45 percent public) do admit that bribes are often the only way to get things done in Venezuela. With both the public and private sector engaging in, or at least witnessing, corrupt practices, it becomes difficult to label corruption as strictly an issue of government trust. As one Venezuelan minister pointed out when asked what he was planning to do to reduce corruption: "Corruption is not a problem that rests solely with the government; it pervades Venezuelan society."

Openness to Free Trade

While the Venezuelan leaders surveyed nominally endorse many "open trade" policies, they are reticent to give up the government supports they have grown accustomed to over the years. Almost all respondents, 88 percent private and 86 percent public, endorse a floating exchange rate, and nearly the same percentages, 84 percent and 75 percent, agree that the government should do more to promote foreign investment. However, more than half (62 percent public and 58 percent private) agree that industries need the protection of barriers and tariffs to be competitive. Similarly, 64 percent of private and 58 percent of public leaders continue to believe that the government should levy substantial tariffs on imports.

Openness to International Learning

In general, the Venezuelan leaders surveyed are open to learning and to international influences. They believe immigrants should have the same opportunities as Venezuelans, that foreign firms should be treated the same as domestic firms, and that Venezuela should maintain its access to international television programming. Furthermore, there appears to be wide acknowledgment, 77 percent public and 79 percent private, that Venezuelan firms are more likely to succeed if they enter into international alliances.

Organizational Effectiveness

With the striking exception of PDVSA, the government-owned oil producer, public sector organizations in Venezuela are viewed as ineffective, and received very low approval ratings from both the private and public sector leaders (see figure 11-2).

Interestingly, the biggest discrepancies between the private and public sectors occur in their evaluations of the head-of-state, foreign investors, and the industrial associations (*gremios*). The public sector appears to be less critical than the private sector in evaluating the influence these groups have in improving the competitiveness of industries. When it comes to evaluating the performance of the legal system, the national legislature, the education system, and the labor unions, there is virtual unanimity that the performance has been poor.

Company-Level Strategy

While almost all of the respondents appear to embrace the concept of innovation, their responses to specific questions suggest that the concept of innovation has not been internalized and applied at the company level. For example, there is complete consensus that well-trained workers make a company more competitive, that rational risk-taking is a good habit, and that a poor national economy is no excuse for a firm's poor performance (78 percent of both the public and private sectors). However, a significant minority, 42 percent private and 30 percent public, believe that many companies become successful simply by imitating their competitors. Similarly, 44 percent of private and 32 percent of public leaders believe that the reward for taking risks in business is too low. Interestingly, the patterns of responses and our own follow-up discussions suggest that leaders do believe companies are responsible for their own success, but, in our view, espouse passive, unoriginal strategies to achieve that success.

The Relationship between Work and Achievement

While Venezuelan leaders do not appear to openly and enthusiastically espouse innovative strategies at the company level, they do recognize the importance of human resources, the source of innovation. Respondents in both the private and public sectors believe that a company has an obligation to its workers that extends beyond pay. Most leaders (87 percent public and 82 percent private) agree that when a company is profitable, the owners should share the profits with workers by giving them higher wages. Additionally, they believe that the company has a special obligation to help workers who have been with the company for a long time. They overwhelmingly agree that age matters little in picking managers and that one worker's success does not diminish the success of other workers.

However, there appears to be a strong minority that is pessimistic about the Venezuelan workers' abilities. Six out of ten public sector leaders and four out of ten private sector leaders do not believe that most employees can be trusted to make independent decisions. Similarly, six out of ten public sector leaders and four out of ten private sector leaders believe that people who work hard get paid the same as

Figure 11-2   Rating of Venezuelan Organizational Effectiveness

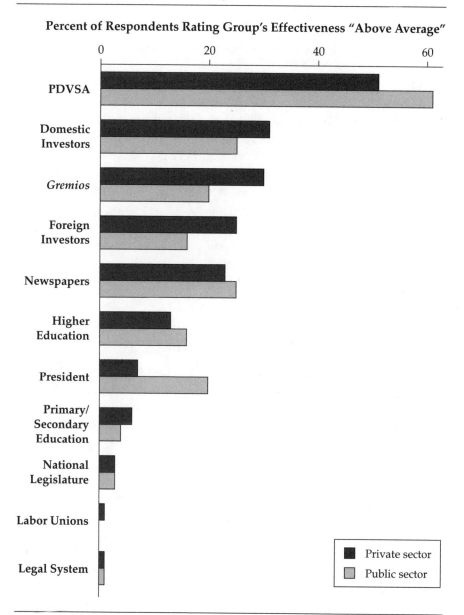

Percent of Respondents Rating Group's Effectiveness "Above Average"

Source: Monitor, Venezuelan National Competitiveness Survey, 1996.

those who do not work hard. In general, although the respondents believe that success is not a zero-sum game, many think that the rewards are often given to those who do not work, which can be a strong disincentive for others to innovate and work hard.

While examining the public and private sector views on work and achievement, on company-level strategy, on wealth creation, and the wide variety of other issues included in the survey yielded interesting and occasionally surprising results, the most surprising result was the similarities, rather than the differences, between these two key demographic groups. We were left wanting to know more. Was there really such a strong consensus among private and public sector leaders across all of these issues? To answer that question and to better understand the underlying belief systems operating in Venezuela, we needed to move beyond our simple demographic breakout of government and private sector views on the issues. We needed a more sophisticated approach, an approach that would help us understand "Who is really out there?"

WHO'S OUT THERE?

To discover "who is really out there" we applied segmentation analysis techniques to our survey results and grouped respondents on the basis of computer analysis of their response patterns, rather than their demographics. We hoped this help us understand not just *what* people think about the issues but *how* people think and why they hold certain views.[3]

We designed our survey to test sixty "attributes" or characteristics surrounding the issues outlined at the beginning of this chapter, including the nature of "wealth creation," "openness to learning," and "attitudes toward work and achievement." Using factor analysis, the sixty questions were grouped into fourteen "factors" based on the patterns of answers of the respondents across the sixty attributes. In other words, when respondents' questions tended to move together in a pattern, these attributes were grouped under a broad "factor heading." For example, respondents tended to have similar response patterns to the statements: "Firms in Venezuela should spend more on R&D" and "Educated employees make a company more competitive." The factor analysis identified the correlation between these two attributes and grouped them under a broad factor heading, which we called "Embraces Innovation." Table 11-1 lists all fourteen of the factors around which the sixty attributes were ultimately organized, as well as some of the more descriptive attributes associated with the factors.

Once we had reduced the responses to fourteen concepts, or factors, we were able to group the respondents based on their responses to those concepts. This "segmentation" is similar to the customer segmentation discussed in chapter 9, on strategic action. The results were striking. Our customer, in this case the leadership of Venezuela, is *not* the monolithic entity that one might think based on demographic analysis alone. Five distinct segments emerge, with each including representatives from the public sector, the private sector, and other groups such as labor, the press, and academia. Therefore, the major social cleavages in Venezuela may not be *among* traditional demographic groups, such as the private sector or public sector, but *within* each of these traditional groups.

Figures 11-3 and 11-4 illustrate the differences that emerge as a result of the segmentation analysis. By grouping sets of questions together, we created two indices that captured some of the key issues we were studying, and then measured where various groups fell along the indices. The first index, along the vertical axis, is the degree to which each segment views natural resources or innovation as the "source of advantage." The second index, along the horizontal axis, is the degree to which each segment views the government or the private sector as the "leader in industry." Figures 11-3 and 11-4 allow one to see immediately the different group views that emerge as a result of the segmentation; views that would have been missed had the results been analyzed solely on the basis of traditional demographic groups. In figure 11-3, the demographic groups are literally "on top of each other," while in figure 11-4 there are vastly different views about innovation and industry competitiveness among the five segments.

We can now think of Venezuela not as one country, but five. We named these five "countries," or segments, based on the profiles of each group suggested by the fourteen factors. In these names we attempted to capture the essence of the underlying beliefs of the groups: the Frustrated Partners, the Somewhat Satisfieds, those Looking for a Referee, the Go-It-Alones, and the Open Traders. We have summarized

Table 11-1 Frames and Paradigms: Fourteen Issues Separating Venezuelan Leaders

Factor	Individual Concepts	Factor	Individual Concepts
Government Economic Intervention	• Government should regulate prices • Government should subsidize the profitability of business • Government sould protect industries through tariffs and trade barriers • Government should not allow exchange rate fluctuation	Smart Means "Steady"	• Average citizens know what is best for Venezuela, and have an influence on affairs • Companies can find success through invitation or by sticking with a winning product • Risk taking is a bad habit • Working from Caracas, the government can meet the needs of Venezuela
Government as Social Provider	• Government should guarantee minimum standard of living and improve distribution of wealth • Too many people are suffering owing to economic reform • Government should directly own/control businesses • I expect the government to help me prosper • There is enough oil in Venezuela so that no one should go hungry	Sees Bureaucracy	• Workers are rewarded whether they work hard or not • People don't get what they deserve • Employees can't be trusted to make good decisions • A poor national economy is an excuse for a firm's bad performance
Government as Catalyst for Private Sector	• The government should supply the private sector with information, technical assistance, and export financing	"Hands Off"	• The poor are responsible for their own plight • Legal immigrants deserve the same rights as citizens • The government should treat foreign and domestic firms the same way • Firms benefit from international alliances
Government as Protector of Private Sector	• The government should impose barriers to trade • Firms in Venezuela need government help to compete in the world market • The reward for risk taking in Venezuela is too low	Citizenship Means Participation	• Society's rules must be followed • It is my duty to vote and pay taxes • I make sacrifices for the future
Trusts the Government	• You can trust elected officials • The government does a better job running business than the private sector • Corruption isn't the main cause of poverty in Venezuela	Enough Cooperation	• There is enough cooperation between companies, and between companies and universities
Embraces External Interaction	• Despite international price fluctuations, Venezuela has the power to control its economy • The government should attract foreign investment • Venezuela should not reduce the percent of internationally produced television shown	Open to Change	• Venezuela can diversify its economy • Venezuelans can change the way they think • Managers need not be older than their subordinates • Not many things depend on fate • It is not enough for only a few to be educated
Embraces Innovation	• Firms in Venezuela should spend more on R&D • Educated employees make a company more competitive	Relationship Viewpoint	• Companies are obligated to share profits with workers and look after long-term employees • Often, bribes are the only way to get things done • Daily family life comes before work • Taxes should be higher for the rich

Figure 11-3 Views on Innovation and Leadership Based on Traditional Demographic Segmentation of Leaders

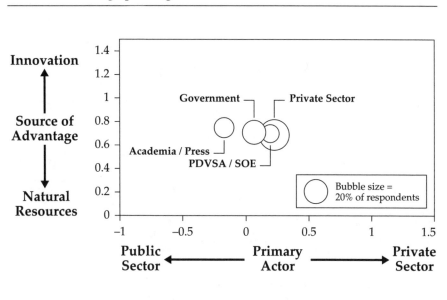

Source: Monitor, Venezuelan National Competitiveness Survey, 1996.
Note: Results represent indices of two to five questions related to source of national advantage and primary actor in the economy.

their profiles, based on the key descriptive factors that "define" their segment, in table 11-2, and describe each segment in more detail in the sections that follow.

Frustrated Partners

The Frustrated Partners were so-named because of their simultaneous belief in a strong partnership between government and private sector and their extreme lack of trust and belief in the government's ability to play its part. Respondents in this group recognize Venezuela's potential but are frustrated because they feel that the government is not doing its part to help the private sector achieve this potential.

The Frustrated Partners have relatively progressive thoughts on competitiveness and innovation. They are more likely to view wealth as infinite and the product of human initiative and to believe that competition promotes excellence. Additionally, they do not expect the govern-

Figure 11-4 Views on Innovation and Leadership Based on Segmentation of
Leaders by Mental Model

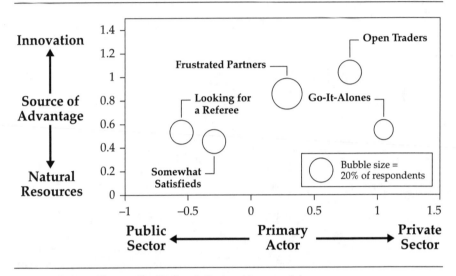

Source: Monitor, Venezuelan National Competitiveness Survey.
Note: Results represent indices of two to five questions related to source of national
advantage and primary actor in the economy.

ment to protect industries or directly intervene in the economy. Instead
they view the government as a catalyst, whose role is to set a stable
platform on which industry can compete. They view the diversification
of Venezuela's export base as critical.

In terms of company competitiveness, the Frustrated Partners believe
that successful companies try to *create*, rather than *react to*, markets for
their products. According to this group, companies should invest in,
and share profits with, their employees, and spend more money on
R&D. They are nonhierarchical in their view that young managers can
be effective. However, they are more likely to be dissatisfied with their
organizations' current level of competitiveness.

Frustrated Partners strongly believe that political reform in Venezuela
has not gone far enough, and they are pessimistic in their outlook on
the competitiveness of Venezuelan industry and the performance of the
domestic economy over the next five years. Furthermore, they are
highly likely to state that bribes are often the only way to get things
done in Venezuela, suggesting a certain fatalism about the country's

Table 11-2 Segment Description: The "Five Venezuelas"

Segment	Size (Percent)	Key Descriptive Factors
Frustrated Partners	29	• Most strongly views government as role catalyst • Does not feel government should intervene economically • Trusts the government the least • Does not feel there is enough cooperation among companies • Values relationships strongly (open to bribes) • Is open to change
Somewhat Satisfieds	20	• Is least likely to embrace innovation • Is least open to change • Strongly views government as protecting the private sector • Is content with the status quo • Strongly supports government economic intervention • Is satisfied with level of cooperation
Looking for a Referee	20	• Most strongly views government as social provider • Is least likely to embrace external interaction • Most strongly views government as protector of private sector • Most strongly endorses government economic intervention
Go-It-Alones	13	• Does not view the government as catalyst • Is highly unlikely to view government as protecting the private sector
Open Traders	18	• Strongly embraces innovation • Least likely to view government as social provider • Is the most open to change • Is most likely to embrace external interaction • Is highly unlikely to view government as protecting the private sector • Does not endorse government economic intervention • Is most likely to trust the government

ability to change. These leaders want a stronger partnership between the government and the private sector in terms of providing information, technical assistance, and export financing. They would even be willing to offer more support for universities, technical institutes, and other companies if only they might receive some support from the government as well. The Frustrated Partners appear to be trapped between their belief in the role of the government as catalyst and their complete lack of faith in the government's ability to play that role.

Members of this group are strongly represented by the private sector. The segment comprises 29 percent of total respondents, 33 percent of the private sector, and 17 percent of the public sector. It also represents 26 percent of the managers of the state-owned enterprises (SOEs), the press, and academics. The attitude of the Frustrated Partners might be summed up in the expression, *"No hay salida"*—There's no way out.

Somewhat Satisfieds

The second segment that emerged from the analysis we called the Somewhat Satisfieds because they appear to be *somewhat* content with the status quo in Venezuela. These leaders are not thrilled with the current situation, but they have few strong opinions about what is necessary to change it. Any views they do have tend to be more traditional than innovative.

Taking the Frustrated Partners' position a step further, the Somewhat Satisfieds think that the government should be the lead actor, not just a partner, in the economic realm as well as in the social realm. For example, they believe that the government should intervene in the economy with regulated prices and subsidies as a means of addressing social issues. Since the Venezuelan government has a long history of active intervention in the national economy, it is not surprising to discover that the Somewhat Satisfieds are relatively content with the conventional mix of government policies and are not looking for anything new or innovative.

The group is content with the current level of cooperation that exists between companies and other institutions. They are traditionally hierarchical in the sense that they think that managers need to be older than their subordinates. Additionally, they do not believe that employees can be trusted to make sound decisions or that hard work gets rewarded in big institutions. Ironically, despite these negative views on how firms in Venezuela currently operate, the Somewhat Satisfieds do not agree that the firms are responsible for improving the situation, agreeing instead that the poor national environment is a good excuse for a firm's bad performance. In fact, among all five segments, the Somewhat Satisfieds are the most satisfied with firms' efforts to improve their current level of competitiveness.

The Somewhat Satisfieds are, however, only *somewhat* satisfied with the current situation in Venezuela. They doubt the country will be able to diversify its economy over time, and they believe that it is difficult to change the way people think. They are also slightly pessimistic in their outlook on the competitiveness of the country and the improvement in the domestic economy over the next five years. Although they believe that economic reform in Venezuela did not go far enough, they appear to be less critical of the government than other segments. Leaders in this segment do not think the current situation in Venezuela is ideal, yet do not have strong views on how to effect change.

The Somewhat Satisfieds make up 20 percent of the total respondents, 20 percent of the private sector, 17 percent of the public sector, 19 percent of managers of the SOEs, and 16 percent of the academics and the press. Members of this group are less fatalistic than they are passive.

Looking for a Referee

Those respondents who fall into the Looking for a Referee segment come closest to being traditional "protectionists." The group name reflects the fact that they are looking for someone—that is, the government—to establish and monitor the "rules of the game" in the national economy. These leaders seek a "level playing field" for citizens and companies. They strongly support government protection through tariffs and trade barriers and do not believe the exchange rate should fluctuate freely. They are most likely to believe that the government should guarantee a minimum standard of living to the average citizen and that it is all right for the government to control businesses and to help industrialists prosper. They are among those who believe that if the government does its job, there should be enough oil in the country to make sure that no one goes hungry.

Those leaders in the Looking for a Referee segment are somewhat isolationist. They agree that the government should give preferential treatment to domestic firms and that little or no benefit will be gained from international alliances. Furthermore, they believe that foreign organizations such as multilateral funding institutions have too much power in Venezuela.

A greater percentage of this segment than the other four believes that wealth is finite and that nations, rather than firms, must struggle to create it and to redistribute it. Its members are highly unlikely to believe that competition is a force that promotes excellence and enriches society or that successful companies try to *create* new markets for their products and services.

Those Looking for a Referee are not optimistic about the economy or the competitiveness of Venezuelan firms in international markets. More than other segments, this group sees the world through a bureaucratic lens and attributes Venezuelan firms' lack of competitiveness to the country's poor performance. They concur that too many people are suffering from economic reform but that political and economic reform has not gone far enough, although they have less hope in such reform than most of the other four groups do. They are the least satisfied with efforts to become more competitive and with the current level of competitiveness.

This group of leaders makes up 20 percent of the total respondents, 16 percent of the private sector, 37 percent of the public sector, 11 percent of the state-owned enterprises, and 29 percent of the press and academics. If we had to sum them up in one sentence, we would say they believe that the government should play a lead role in industry performance and that they expect special treatment for Venezuelan firms.

Go-It-Alones

Polar opposites to those Looking for a Referee, the fourth segment, labeled the Go-It-Alones, reject government intervention of almost any kind. These leaders are strongly opposed to a government that supports the private sector with regulated prices, subsidies, export financing, and protection from import competition. They even reject technical assistance from the government. They want no special treatment from the government, believing quite strongly that foreign firms should be treated similarly to domestic firms. Interestingly, even this relatively antigovernment group believes in a strong role for the government on social issues, suggesting that there are no "pure monetarists," no "Chicago Boys" in Venezuela.

The Go-It-Alones are a pessimistic group. Seventy-eight percent of them believe that the government has too much power, and 92 percent believe that the economic and political reform has not gone far enough. Half of them believe that in five years local businesses will be less competitive and the domestic economy will not improve.

Despite their dramatic rejection of the status quo, the Go-It-Alones do not appear to be progressive in their views on competition and wealth creation. Only half of them believe that wealth is infinite and the product of human initiative, while a full 42 percent believe it is finite and that a nation must struggle to redistribute it to the people. Sixty-seven percent believe that competition is a force that promotes excellence and enriches society, and only 56 percent believe that successful companies try to create markets for their products and services. More than any other group (79 percent) the Go-It-Alones feel satisfied with both their efforts to increase competitiveness and their current level of organizational competitiveness.

The smallest of the five segments at only 13 percent, the Go-It-Alones comprise 15 percent of the private sector, 10 percent of the public, 15 percent of the managers of SOEs, and 6 percent of the press and academics. In sum, this segment is basically saying to the government, "Just lower my taxes and leave me in peace."

Open Traders

The Open Traders, our fifth and final segment, are the group most open to change and most likely to embrace innovation. They are "open" in their opposition to regulated prices, subsidies, tariff protection, and exchange rate manipulation. They strongly favor risk taking and innovative business strategies. They are "traders" in their support for interaction with foreigners in the form of international alliances, education programs, and media and in the importance they place on export diversification.

The Open Traders are the most optimistic of the five segments about the government, the competitiveness of industry, and the improvement of the domestic economy. They do not trust the government, but they trust it more than three of the other groups. While they, like the other segments, believe that economic reform has not gone far enough, this group of leaders is most optimistic that Venezuela can diversify its economy and change the way the country thinks. They are less fatalistic than any other segment. These leaders advocate increased spending in R&D and investment in employees. They are the only one of the five groups to support diversification of the export base as a national objective.

Of the five segments, Open Traders have the most progressive views on wealth creation and competition. More than any other group (69 percent), they feel that wealth is infinite and the result of human initiative and effort. More than any other group (77 percent), they also believe that competition is a force for positive change in a society. They would like to see more involvement of companies and foreign organizations in Venezuela. Sixty percent believe that private sector companies do not have enough influence in national affairs. Forty-four percent believe that even foreign organizations should have more influence in national affairs.

Interestingly, the Open Traders include a disproportionately large number of state-owned enterprise managers. The Open Traders make up 18 percent of our total leadership respondents, 16 percent of the private sector, 20 percent of the public sector, a full 30 percent of SOE managers, and 23 percent of the press and academics.

In summary, the Open Traders believe in competing by investing in people.

Demographic Summaries of the Five Dominant Frames

While the five segments are distinguished from one another by their views and beliefs rather than demographics, there are some notable demographic tendencies, as we hinted at above. The Frustrated Partners are overwhelmingly represented in the private sector, focused on natural resource production, and come from the midwestern part of the country. The Somewhat Satisfieds are spread evenly throughout the organizations, are underrepresented in natural resource businesses, and are found mostly in the eastern part of the country. Those Looking for a Referee tend to be in the government and in the western part of the country. The Go-It-Alones tend to be managers in both state-owned enterprises and the private sector, specifically in manufacturing, and tend to be found in Venezuela's interior regions. The Open Traders also tend to be Caracas-based managers, mainly in state-owned enterprises operating in natural resource and manufacturing industries.

Given all of the data on views and beliefs of the five segments, as well as demographic clues about who and where these segments are, how can we think about beginning to bring these groups together?

How Can We Bring These Groups Together?

Although there are extreme differences within this "country of countries," there are also some important views shared that could form a basis for bringing these groups together. We were surprised to find that all five segments, despite vast differences on many critical issues, actually share very similar views on government priorities. All five segments see the following as top priorities for their government: improving primary and secondary education, reducing corruption, attracting foreign investment, improving health care, reducing government spending, and creating a stable environment for business.

Additionally, on many individual issues, there are shared views. For example, all respondents agree that Venezuela's persistent focus on raw petroleum is not a positive thing for the country and that diversifying into tourism, manufactured goods, and agriculture is vital to the nation's future. All segments believe that the government has too much power, feel that economic and political reform has not gone far enough, and support some level of innovation in both business practices and government regulatory improvements. None of the segments trusts the government, yet all believe that the government has an important social role to fulfill. Still, as the significant differences between the segments suggest, there is more variance in the responses than might be healthy for a country attempting to make some complex decisions over the next five years.

When thinking about bringing the groups together, we wanted to understand not only what is already shared among the groups but also what divided them. To better understand these differences, we sorted our original fourteen factors based on "size of the differences," or the variance within each factor, as shown in figure 11-5. The length of each bar equals the "size of the differences" among the five segments' responses on that factor.

We learned that the most divisive factor of all fourteen is the one that

Figure 11-5 Range of Factor Scores in Decreasing Order of Impact

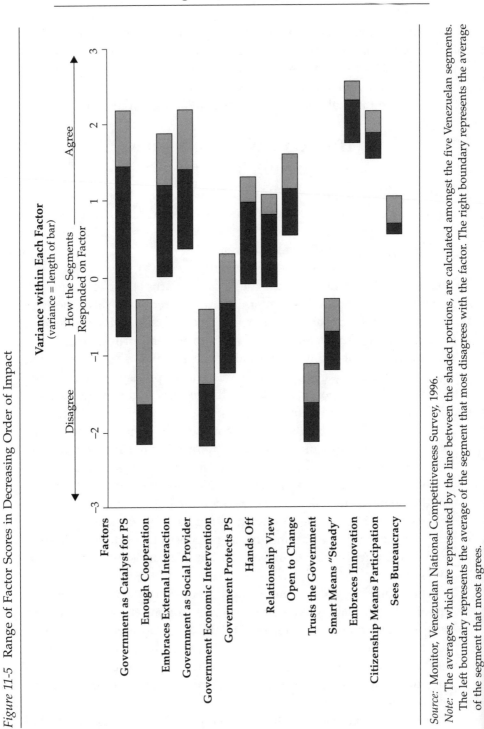

Source: Monitor, Venezuelan National Competitiveness Survey, 1996.
Note: The averages, which are represented by the line between the shaded portions, are calculated amongst the five Venezuelan segments. The left boundary represents the average of the segment that most disagrees with the factor. The right boundary represents the average of the segment that most agrees.

sees the government as a catalyst for the private sector. Not only does it produce the greatest range of responses but it is one of the few factors that crosses over the "zero mark" in figure 11-5. The "zero mark" represents the line between agreement and disagreement on that factor. What this means is that some segments agree and others disagree that the government should be the catalyst for the private sector. As you can see in the figure, on most other factors, while there is considerable variance in the responses of the five segments, all segments tend to come down on the same side of the issue. That is to say, few of the bars cross the "zero mark."

The most divisive factor, government as a catalyst for the private sector, is defined as the need for the government to supply the private sector with information, technical assistance, and export financing. We believe that if we could get more agreement on this one factor, we might get more leverage than from any other factor. If the country can resolve its differences on this one factor, it might move dramatically toward a shared vision of competitiveness, wealth creation, and distribution.

We studied the segment groups on this factor to learn that the average response was 1.47 on a scale of –3 to +3 in the direction of agreement and that the biggest difference exists between the Frustrated Partners, at 2.18 (indicating strong agreement that the government should act as catalyst), and the Go-It-Alones, who answered –0.76 in the direction of disagreement (government should not play the role of catalyst). Thus the gap between the two, or the "size of the difference," on this issue is a whopping 2.94 points on a scale whose length totals only six units (2.94 refers to the length of the top bar in figure 11-5). Relative to the "gaps," or bar lengths, on the other issues, this 2.94 gap on government as catalyst is a particularly wide one to bridge.

From what we know about the Frustrated Partners, we might make a few inferences about the rationale behind their views on the government as catalyst issue. At 29 percent of the total, Frustrated Partners are the largest of the five segments. They tend to be overrepresented by the private sector, to be affiliated with natural resource industries, and to be least satisfied with their industries' current competitiveness. From this we might infer that they feel a need for export assistance in the form of technical assistance, market information, and export financing to help them find better markets or to ride out the downward part of a cyclical industry.

The Go-It-Alones, on the other hand, are the smallest segment group at only 13 percent of total respondents. They are half the size of the Frustrated Partners. They tend to be managers of state-owned enterprises and private companies in manufacturing industries. Polar opposites of the Frustrated Partners, the Go-It-Alones are the most satisfied with their current efforts at competitiveness.

The difference might be summed up as follows: Frustrated Partners are a big group in raw materials industries that are not competing well, while the Go-It-Alones are a small group in manufacturing segments that are competing more effectively. These are two groups in vastly different situations, sending vastly different messages to the government concerning the country's economic needs. It might take a very discerning ear high in the government to segment the messages from such different groups.

The "Five Venezuelas"

As the discussion of "gaps" above reinforces, Venezuela is not one country. It is a country of countries. And Venezuela is not one economy. It is an economy of economies. Attributing certain behaviors, intentions, beliefs, goals, and learning to something called the private sector, or to something called the public sector, is no easy task. The fact is, we have never found anywhere in our work in any country something that we might refer to as the "private sector view," or the "government perspective." They do not exist. Only frames of reference exist; yet the judgment is often made that such assigned views do exist, leading directly to the pattern of defensiveness we discussed in part 1 of this book. We have just discussed five frames that exist in the world, and we have used the case of Venezuela to point out that it is a nation's unique distribution of those frames of reference that either offers or impedes the chance to create complex decisions, which are required for an innovation-based economy.

In the next section we discuss the relation between frames of reference and the original seven patterns of uncompetitive behavior. Our thesis will be that one can understand the reasoning behind those patterns better now as a result of improved awareness of "who is really out there."

What's the Connection Between Frames of Reference and the "Seven Patterns"?

The evidence is growing that it is the attitudes of a country's leaders, or more specifically, their frames of reference, that inform the creation of the organizational structures and strategic actions that dictate the patterns of wealth creation and distribution found in uncertain environments.

This section is devoted to identifying linkages, through storytelling and hypothesis generation, between how decision makers think—that is, their "mental models"—and the actions and results that we observe.

Reliance on Basic Factors

Thirty-eight percent of all of our respondents and 52 percent of those Looking for a Referee believe that wealth is finite and that nations must struggle to redistribute it. The Looking for a Referee segment appears to be less confident in the future of the economy than the other groups and fears that the country is more likely to become weaker in the next five years in terms of competitiveness. Perhaps because of that attitude, this group is more likely to think that the government should be the lead actor in the economy and that government protection, in the form of tariffs and subsidies, is necessary.

Although not technically in the Looking for a Referee segment, one Colombian businessman we know—whose identity we have disguised—typifies the group. This man was very successful in the import substitution era and built huge plants with mighty capacity that dominated the local markets for a long time. He made a fortune and came to be regarded as "ten years ahead of his time" by at least one government leader.

Our view is less charitable. This was a man who learned to influence the government and to secure contracts that no one else could get. A man of considerable charm, he argues persuasively that he "did not want subsidies and protection"; all he wanted was "a level playing field."

After all, he protested, if the country's electric utilities and transportation system were inefficient, no one in the nation could compete on a price basis. Furthermore, his argument went, if the government was afraid of massive unemployment, the last thing it should have done was let imports into the country that would destroy the local producers. This industrialist told us once that his joy was "building plants." And soon after he built that last one, the government of Colombia, under the leadership of President Gaviria, opened the economy to import competition and his businesses started losing more than a million dollars a month, by his own reckoning.

In all the decades that this man competed, he never built a plant that did much more than light processing. He was part of the Looking for a Referee segment who, in the course of time, was disappointed by the government and never saw the possibilities in producing more complex products. For all of his belief in comparative advantages, and his frame of reference through which he saw that influencing the government was his real advantage, he decided to move out of Colombia and invest his money in the U.S. stock market, where he claims that he gets higher returns than he ever did "building plants."

The factor-driven imagination might still be alive in the Looking for a Referee segment and in others who remain in the developing world. This is the group in greatest danger not of having committed to the wrong strategy but having committed to the right strategy for too long.

Understanding of Customers

Approximately two-thirds of our respondents think that a good strategy for a business is to find a winning product and "stick with it." Almost one-third believe that successful companies offer products that they already know customers will buy. This view is especially apparent in the Looking for a Referee segment, with almost half of the respondents in agreement.

Unfortunately, when one believes in comparative advantages and has a production orientation like "building plants" in a small, protected environment, one is unlikely to come to value customer learning. And that is what we have found in the Andes and in most developing nations. In fact, 45 percent of all of our respondents in Venezuela believe that many companies become successful simply by imitating their competitors.

As discussed elsewhere in the book, when companies imitate their competitors by adopting the same strategies, producing the same products, and so on, a kind of "strategic convergence" develops that leads to unhealthy rivalry, transfers leverage from the producers to the consumers, and drives down profits.

In many of our studies, we have found that producers sell their products at cross purposes with the consumer. One example is the Peruvian asparagus industry, which stops selling to the U.S. consumer every year during the season when all competition subsides, despite the fact that U.S. consumers would eat asparagus year-round. Another example is the Colombian leather producer who tried to sell to the U.S. consumer through magazine ads but had no U.S.-based showroom, despite the fact that the most attractive leather-purchasing segments in the United States do not usually buy through magazines but through showrooms. Without a good understanding of customer needs and buying patterns, even the best products will fail.

Interfirm Cooperation

Almost 80 percent of the respondents state that their firms would be more likely to succeed if they entered into international alliances. Overall, our respondents also suggest that there is not enough cooperation between companies, or between companies and universities. Only the Somewhat Satisfieds suggest that the current level of cooperation is adequate. The segments feeling most strongly about the need for greater cooperation are the Frustrated Partners, followed by those Looking for a Referee and the Open Traders.

This may suggest that given a small, protected environment, where customers were not demanding and exports won according to how cheap they were, it is not surprising to think that businesses and universities never felt the pressure to increase cooperation. There was no perceived need to get better at creating and structuring processes for shared learning and upgrading that would build complexity and the ability to serve more demanding consumers. What businesses really became good at, as we have pointed out, is "blaming the cow." It remains to be determined whether the cow is the head of state, a cabinet member, a supplier, or in fact really just a cow.

In one country we introduced the idea of a national job data bank that would match qualified personnel with the appropriate job. The rationale was to raise the overall quality of the recruits by introducing an element of competition. Companies would compete to recruit the best candidates, identified for all companies to see, in the national job bank. Similarly, job candidates would compete to improve their skills relative to other candidates in the job bank in hopes of being recruited. One leader who we might describe as a Somewhat Satisfied did not view this system as beneficial to him. He told us that the idea was uninteresting to him because his advantage was in his ability to recruit the best people; he did not want other firms that might one day be his competition to have access to a high and rising standard of human resources. "Why should I help other firms in this country get excellent resources?" was his succinct response. With the question phrased in that way, this leader's viewpoint is rational. However, rephrasing the question might have changed his mind: "Why should I help myself get better resources than I am getting now?"

Understanding of Relative Position

The essence of relative position is the ability of the Andean firm to want to learn about the competition, not just to imitate successful strategies (a strong tendency throughout the region) but to understand the essential dynamic between the most attractive customers, the competitors that attempt to please them, and the firm in question. As we have stated, most Venezuelan firms believe that finding a successful product and "sticking with it," often by observing competitors and imitating them, is the way to succeed.

The Somewhat Satisfieds appear to typify this thinking more than the other segments. This group, which embraces traditional solutions, seems uninterested in learning how to improve. In Bolivia, we worked with members of the flower sector, who insisted they could compete in the competitive U.S. market. They further insisted that they were making a lot of money, especially on Valentine's Day and Mother's Day. We did an analysis of their relative cost position against the Colombians and learned that the transportation costs alone were three times the Colombians' costs and that they were losing money throughout the year and making money on only those two days. We advised them to give up the U.S. market for now except for those two days. The reason was that the Miami brokers, who, interestingly, are mostly Colombian, were using the Bolivian flowers merely as swing capacity at peak times. One senior exporter in the Bolivian flower industry said that before seeing the data he thought the Bolivians were good flower exporters; afterward, he said, he felt that "most of us are really just gardeners."

We advised the Bolivian flower producers to compete for the growing markets in Santiago, Buenos Aires, and other regional capitals. They would then have some relative transportation advantages and could begin to build more complex advantages in flower quality and product scope before attacking the Colombians in Miami again.

The best attitude toward relative position is, not surprisingly, from the Open Traders who embrace innovation and openness to change and are generally the most outward-oriented of the five segment groups.

Opportunities to Forward Integrate

We tested the proposition that firms benefit from international alliances and observed an increasingly familiar pattern: the Frustrated Partners, Open Traders, and Go-It-Alones are big supporters of international alliances, while the Somewhat Satisfieds and Looking for a Referee are less interested.

In industries like flowers, fruit juices, and traditional agriculture products, the real wealth that has been created has been captured offshore. The brokers, or middlemen, who are capturing the wealth insist that the quality, consistency, and specialized service required for producers to develop more sophisticated relations with the brokers are simply not there. This may be because the key segment groups do not espouse innovation and interfirm cooperation, do not appear to be outward-oriented, and view the real wealth potential they possess as their fertile ground and sunshine rather than their ability to satisfy the customer—in this case both the middlemen and the end-consumer.

In the flower industry throughout the Andes we see a lot of Looking for a Referee types who believe that if the government would just devalue the currency and provide some export incentives, exports would fly away from the shore and everyone would get wealthier. The fact that they tend to be huge employers of marginalized people, who might retreat into the hills and grow and export things less benign than flowers, gives them a very powerful political and social argument. So the trade-off becomes the short-term political and social argument of those Looking for a Referee versus the argument for long-term economic growth put forward by the Open Traders. In the meantime, there remains little activity in the forward integration of firms in the region.

Defensiveness

Our intuition, as well as our research based on surveys, focus groups, and thousands of discussions with business and government leaders around the world, leads us to believe that economic development is not about macroeconomic policy; it is about human relations. The writer Francis Fukuyama, in his recent book *Trust*, suggests that "the most important lessons we can learn from an examination of economic life is that a nation's well-being, as well as its ability to compete, is conditioned by a single, pervasive cultural characteristic: the level of trust inherent in the society."[4]

Defensive reasoning destroys trust. Defensive reasoning is that which we depicted in the introduction and chapter 7, in our description of the dynamic between the cabinet member in Colombia and the head of the flower producers' association. In the new language of this chapter, the cabinet member would be the Open Trader, the president of Aso-colflores a member of those Looking for a Referee. If you recall, the cabinet member suggested that the flower growers would disappear in the next five years because they were competing on basic advantages such as sunshine and cheap labor and were not actively upgrading their transportation logistics systems into the U.S. market. The flower association agreed that its industry would disappear in the next five years because it had an inefficient airport, expensive electricity, and an overvalued currency, all of which are problems for the government to solve.

Both the flower association chief and the cabinet member were correct in their depiction of the disadvantages. What they lacked was a shared vision: a larger and more robust picture of competitiveness that could have informed a more productive discussion of how to compete. And without that shared vision, they began to make inferences about each other's behavior and intentions that led to the aggressive behavior suggested by the letters they published in the newspaper, reprinted in the introduction. That aggressive behavior shut down learning and impeded their ability to make the kinds of sophisticated choices they needed to make to upgrade the industry—that is, how to fix the airport, provide competitively priced energy, improve transportation logistics to the end-user, find attractive segments, and compete with the rising threats of low-cost flowers from Mexico and rising quality in Ecuador.

Since that time, there is a new Minister of Foreign Trade, a new president of Asocolflores, the airport has been improved a bit, and exports are up in nominal value, which many in the country point to as a victory. But profit margins for the individual firms continue to be squeezed by increased competition. Many flower producers have failed and gone out of business, and many *campesinos* have lost their jobs.

The irony of this story is that the Open Trader and the segment Looking for a Referee are from the same country—the same town, in fact. They have no personal rivalry between them and they both want what is best for the country. But because of their different frames of reference, they have chosen to bicker and to advocate strongly, choosing to defend a position that can be described somewhat as their traditional position rather than to strive to inquire, to learn, and to gain a shared perspective. All of that has been exacerbated by a lack of trust.

And those frames of reference, much as we depicted in the chapter on defensive reasoning, have informed the paradigms both the minister and the association head have chosen for wealth creation: comparative advantage. The combination of their frames of reference and paradigms, which we call their mental model, or the invisible part of change, has informed the way they have structured their organizations—not to learn and inquire and build shared vision but to advocate continually and to defend their positions. Those organizations have created strategies that are beginning to unravel when it comes to satisfying customer needs, and the results they are achieving in terms of wealth creation and distribution are not positive. And the countries are poorer. In light of these results, people tend to look for help wherever they can get it, and that leads us to the last of the seven patterns.

Paternalism

The pervasive paternalism in the Andes is perhaps most apparent in Venezuela. When it comes to the nation's ability to compete, leaders of all kinds believe that the government should provide export credits, and many (44 percent) believe that without government assistance, industries in the country cannot compete. Eighty-four percent of the private sector leaders state that the government needs to do more to attract investors, and 29 percent think that industries need government protection.

On the social side, nine out of ten leaders think the government has to do more to redistribute wealth and protect the minimum standard of living of all citizens, and a large number (54 percent public and 38 percent private) believe in regulating prices for the average person. Seventy-six percent of the private sector leaders in our study believe that elected officials cannot be trusted, and 84 percent believe that corruption is the main cause of poverty in the country.

We infer from our research that if you ask the average private sector leader in Venezuela what is the crisis in the country, he or she will say that it is a crisis of confidence; they don't believe their leaders will do what they need to do to improve their country. It may, in fact, be a crisis of paternalism as well as a crisis of confidence. In simple terms, private sector expectations for the public sector may be too high. In the new world of global competitiveness, no government could handle all of the economic and social tasks the Venezuelan government has taken on—even though that is what some Venezuelans have come to expect.

Those Looking for a Referee expect the most from the public sector. They insist that the government intervene in pricing, subsidies, and protection, with a view toward guaranteeing a minimum standard of living for workers. After all, they reason, theirs is a rich country and no one should ever go hungry. The Open Traders are so completely opposed to these views that it is fair to say they are polar opposites to those Looking for a Referee.

The demographics also suggest that these two groups are polar opposites. Those Looking for a Referee, which make up one-fifth of total respondents, tend to be government-based, service-oriented people in the western and interior parts of the country, while the Open Traders tend to be the state-owned enterprise managers of natural resource firms based in Caracas.

One practical example of paternalism and the high expectations people have for the government in Venezuela is in the labor union movement. The major union's position papers provide a clear vision of objectives in terms of economic development, social well-being, and quality of life. Union leaders strongly suggest, however, that this quality of life has to come through a redistribution of wealth through government intervention rather than as the natural result of better business strategies and the increased competitiveness of industry in general. They feel strongly that the government should take the leading role in what they call "essential industries" such as petroleum and mining.

The unions recognize the current crisis in Venezuela; however, its leaders do not appear to accept a great deal of responsibility. As their reasoning goes, they blame the current crisis on "erroneous neoliberal macroeconomic policies," notably of ex-president Andres Perez in 1989. Also to blame is the "lamentable shift in power from the state" and state-controlled industries of the 1970s to the "elitist neoliberals," whose capital flight caused the debt to skyrocket and started the downward spiral in which the country now finds itself.

Unfortunately, because of labor's strong opinion that the government should lead the country out of the current crisis and that the current government is ill-equipped to do so, the views of the labor group may be dooming the country to more, not less, defensiveness, further impeding the country's ability to work itself out of such a complex dilemma.

SUMMARY

In this chapter we have approached the complex problem of understanding some of the prevailing beliefs about wealth creation and distribution of income. First, we used the example of Venezuela, which because it is a country with a great amount of uncertainty is also a rich environment for learning. Second, we introduced a methodology for determining how to know a little better "who is out there" through our discussion of the five very different segment groups identified in Venezuela—groups we believe exist in many other countries. We described these groups and the attitudes and "mental models" they hold with a view toward learning what it is that may unify them behind a shared vision. Finally, we reintroduced the seven patterns of uncompetitive behavior described in the first part of this book and examined the frames of reference that may be driving these patterns and inhibiting creation and equitable distribution of wealth.

We have seen that creating wealth is no longer about macroeconomics and the advantages with which countries are born. It is more complex, involving a wide array of steps, such as building integrated frameworks based on cutting-edge concepts of measuring results, categorizing the scope of strategy choices, understanding institutional dynamics, making paradigms explicit, and understanding how and when paradigms become obsolete. Most important, creating wealth in the future will involve pulling the integrated frameworks referred to above together with the fundamental understanding of "who is out there," what they believe, and how one structures a process to move towards shared understanding. As the quote with which we began this chapter suggests, everything (including wealth creation) is human relations.

CHAPTER TWELVE

The Hidden Sources of Growth

The people . . . spread the news of the good quality of the soil and its privileged
position with respect to the swamp.
—*Reference to the mythical town of Macondo in* One Hundred Years of Solitude
by Gabriel García Márquez

We have now discussed in detail three broad themes: firm strategy,
government steering mechanisms, and divisiveness among leaders that
have kept developing countries from pursuing the seven opportunities
for sustained economic growth identified in the first half of the book.
A fourth theme addresses a much more fundamental question: How
does the leadership in the developing world view wealth creation and
distribution? In the final analysis, the institutions and strategies that
leaders design reflect their fundamental beliefs about how the world
works. This chapter aims to explore some of these beliefs and their
relationship to the seven patterns of uncompetitive behavior and the
opportunities they hold.

We begin with a brief review of what several thinkers have thought
about wealth and productivity. We then consider how changes in the
global economy present the possibility that wealth creation in the
twenty-first century will be about total global competition rather than
administered local or regional competition. Finally, this chapter will
review a "new way" of thinking about wealth and productivity.

THE OLD WAY OF THINKING

Adam Smith, the Scottish political economist and philosopher whose
Wealth of Nations (1776) laid the foundations of classical free-market

economic theory, also spoke of international trade and is credited with the notion of "absolute advantage." His theory of absolute advantage states that the world's low-cost producer of an item is the nation that should export that item. This theory made sense as long as domestic and international markets were relatively undeveloped. It does not, however, make allowances for the impact of the global integration of trade and investment. Today his assumptions are tested by new phenomena: the dominance of global trade and the mobility of capital and skilled labor, as well as the role of technology in lowering costs and increasing quality. Smith's ideas became the basis for much learning and led the way for other economic thinkers of the time, such as David Ricardo.

As domestic markets became more efficient, a new theory evolved stating that nations should focus on those areas in which they could produce goods more efficiently than other nations, and to import goods they could not efficiently produce. That new idea was David Ricardo's theory of comparative advantage.

In Ricardo's theory, trade is based on the relative labor productivity of nations and on the differences in the general environments of nations that appear to provide some advantages to some nations in specific industries. Another version of the theory, called the Heckscher-Ohlin Theory, put forth by Swedish economists Eli Heckscher and Bertil Ohlin,[1] was based on the idea that all nations differ in their endowments of production factors, such as land, labor, natural resources, and capital. Nations gain advantage, the theory goes, by processing those factors intensively and more efficiently than other nations. Comparative advantage rests upon the productivity with which firms and nations can mobilize and use their stock of natural endowments. Over time, this has led government leaders to focus many of their economic growth strategies on improving a nation's ability to compete on these basic factors, which results in an overdependence on natural resources, among other things. This practice has actually thwarted the ability of nations to rapidly upgrade their competitive environments or to develop sophisticated mixes of inputs that would lead to higher degrees of productivity or open the doors for innovation.

Because of this style of thinking, many governments have come to the belief that one of their most important roles is to help improve the cost structures of businesses by manipulating the cost of inputs; in effect, to improve and sustain the "comparative" advantages of firms through protection and subsidies. For example, we observed in Venezuela that almost half of the public and private sector leadership surveyed believe that wealth is a finite resource; that in thirty years the prosperity of Venezuela will still be almost completely dependent on oil; and that without the direct support of the government, their industries could not compete in the world market. These perspectives reveal a way of thinking about wealth creation that will actually limit leaders' ability to create more complex and sustainable sources of wealth.

Our awareness of "the old way," or comparative advantage thinking, helps us to understand why the seven patterns outlined in the first half of the book exist. First, as mentioned above, when a country's leaders believe that wealth lies in that nation's natural advantages, they spend their efforts exploiting natural advantages, which can be broadly defined to include the exploitation of low-cost labor (some would say the degradation of human capital). Second, knowledge of customers' specific preferences is not regarded as an advantage when the product for sale is so basic and possesses only rudimentary features. Third, any knowledge that exists about relative position tends to be focused on what the government should do to lower the cost structure of firms (energy, transportation, raw materials, exchange rates, labor rates), and not on what firms can do to position themselves for more sustained, competitive growth. Fourth, forward integration is not viewed as a source of advantage, because knowledge of outbound distribution logistics and end-user preferences does not affect what leaders see as the country's "true advantage"—its natural wealth. Fifth, interfirm cooperation is not a source of advantage either, because complexity in the product is not required if forward integration and customer knowledge are not valued and because most of the firms are rivals in the quest for access to their country's raw materials. Sixth, defensiveness occurs between the government and the private sector (and within the private sector) when the government is viewed as the allocator of benefits. And seventh, paternalism is rampant because wealth is viewed as access to raw materials, which is almost always controlled or strongly influenced by the government.

The old way of thinking outlined briefly above, combined with the firm-level strategies and government steering mechanisms it engenders, has not resulted in greater rates of wealth creation and distribution in the developing world. As the trend toward economic liberalization continues and global competitive pressures mount, this old way of thinking will become even less adequate to improve the quality of life for the majority of people in the developing world. In an "era of total competition,"[2] the rules of the game are changing and firms throughout the world must prepare themselves to compete differently. This is both a great threat and a tremendous opportunity for firms in the developing world.

In this era of total competition there are two interlocking processes that are creating a virtuous cycle of change. The first is that transportation and communication costs have been dropping at a dizzying pace.[3] Second, governments are increasingly coming to view their role as facilitating the exchange of products, services, and learning rather than as using their "good offices" to obstruct trade and to protect domestic corporate interests.[4] A result is that total competition is allowing customers to become more demanding and is reducing the power of suppliers—especially those that offer basic, uncomplicated goods and services.

Because traditional boundaries and borders are disappearing, or at least becoming so permeable that their traditional integrity is transformed from something that keeps things separate to something that facilitates exchange, knowledge will play an increasingly important role in determining the winners and losers of global trade.[5] The two processes mentioned above will compel government and business leaders in the twenty-first century to think quite differently about development strategies and competition.

As mentioned earlier, our research has confirmed that those nations which export manufactured goods are wealthier than those which export simple materials; the market pays a premium for the knowledge imbedded in manufactured goods.[6] And the borderless world will enable knowledge to flow with increasing speed and frequency to areas where it can best be deployed. For the leaders in the developing world who have grown up being taught that they had an abundance of natural wealth, like oil, tin, or favorable growing conditions, this will pose a unique challenge. It should no longer be a source of national and personal pride that developed countries seek ways to access these natural resources but rather a unique challenge to be overcome: how to embrace globalization and convert comparative advantages into sustainable, knowledge-based competitive advantages. (Table 12-1 compares and contrasts representative aspects of the "old way of thinking"

Table 12-1 Old and New Ways of Thinking

	The Old Way of Thinking	Thinking in "The Era of Total Competition"
Context	Fragmented industries, labor intensity, low skills, trade based on growing conditions, natural resources, and cost of capital	Cheap computing and communications power, buyer needs vary, factor inputs are lesser percentage of product costs, global access to raw materials is improving
Beliefs Assumptions Attitudes	Static and reductionist thinking toward advantage, which is defined as abundance of raw materials; cheap supply inputs is key to advantage; nations compete; government behavior is the advantage	Dynamic and integrative thinking: competitiveness is high productivity, nation is platform with dynamic between trade and investment, firms compete. Social capital: trust, justice, and sophisticated human resources are sources of advantage
Public and Private Perspectives	Government sees its duty as lowering firms' costs for trade; private sector believes it should inform and influence government	Private sector focused on markets and innovation, government focused on its role in the innovation process
Tools	Monetary and trade policies: government uses tariffs, quotas, subsidies; private sector uses licensing for technology inputs and lobbying	Government tools include education, developing specialized infrastructure, predictable environment; private sector uses strategic planning process—specifically, market segmentation techniques
Strategic Actions	Big companies using economies of scale (linear efficiency) to sell cheap labor and competing on price with low investments in machinery and learning; government lowers interest rates, devalues currency, administers subsidies, and provides export incentives	Focus on finding attractive industry segments based on customer preferences, then operational excellence, high quality interfirm cooperation, and differentiated products
Results	Inadequate foreign direct investment for upgrading, exporting commodities at low prices; low wealth creation and poor income distribution; defensiveness between government and private sector; paternalism; poor interfirm cooperation; linear growth at best	High-quality firms are attracted to countries to develop core processes and products, exports are high-productive products in attractive industry segments, wealth is created at high rates and distributed to most productive workers, in whom the government and the private sector continually invest

inherited from Smith and Ricardo with thinking in our contemporary "era of total competition.")

A New Way of Thinking

If, as we have argued thus far, the seven patterns of underdevelopment persist because of poor strategy, weak institutions, divisive behavior, and comparative advantage thinking, what can be done to reverse them? As should be clear by now, we think that a renewed emphasis on microeconomic learning should inform the decisions that firm and government leaders make. To improve the standard of living for average citizens throughout the developing world, economic growth is going to have to be high and sustainable. Growth will occur if one of two things happen: increased resources are mobilized to push growth or productivity is enhanced. It is important not to confuse the two. For example, according to Paul Krugman, Singapore's success in achieving 8.5 percent growth between 1966 and 1990 and 6.6 percent improvement in per capita income is not sustainable.[7] He argues that Singapore's success is based on the one-time mobilization of massive resources to stimulate growth, and he argues that there were few corresponding productivity gains.

As we pointed out in chapter 8, on strategy, productivity is defined as the amount of output that can be generated by a given amount of input. Economists refer to two different types of productivity improving approaches: x-efficiency and allocative efficiency.[8] *X-efficiency* refers to efforts to utilize more efficiently each of the individual components of productivity (for example, worker training to improve labor productivity or more efficient machinery to lower electricity consumption). *Allocative efficiency* is concerned with improving the mix of inputs so that the right trade-offs are being made between the deployment of specific resources to a given task. For allocative efficiency, it is important not only to use the resources being deployed efficiently but also to determine how certain resources can substitute for other resources—in other words, how the mix of resources used can be reallocated to improve overall output. For example, firms might ask: How can we use more equipment to substitute for labor and/or materials? or How can we substitute knowledge for hard work? Regional or national leaders might ask: How can we take the revenues from the export of raw materials and invest in sophisticated human capital?

For the leader in the developing world, the challenge is to create the conditions where both operational productivity and better choices about the allocation of resources can be made. Knowledge is the key ingredient in improving allocative efficiency. The goal is to rely less on basic raw materials and the hard work of inexpensive human capital, and to rely more on superior forms of capital, such as how efficiently the institution learns and disseminates knowledge.

Why knowledge? Research has shown that even for a company with many plants in the same country, using the same equipment, making the same products, and selling to the same customers, the productivity of the most efficient plant can be three times that of the least efficient.[9] Even when differences in plant ages, transportation logistics, accounting treatments, production runs, product scope, and extraordinary items are discounted, the productivity differences can be of the order of two-to-one. What, then, explains the difference in productivity at these plants? The difference is simply knowledge of how to do things. In fact, one explanation of Japanese growth in productivity does not include such things as manufacturing prowess, access to cheap capital, or the sense of security and loyalty that comes from the seniority system or lifetime employment. According to this research, Japanese companies have grown because of their skills at "organizational knowledge creation."[10]

Increasing productivity growth does not occur often in the developing world because of an overemphasis on keeping down labor rates and the cost of purchased materials and a tendency to believe that big purchases of capital equipment for its own sake will improve productivity.[11] All of this is exacerbated by the fact that incentive systems rarely compensate managers for teaching each other; in fact, these systems often produce the opposite, deleterious effect of encouraging them to compete with each other. Therefore, managers do not often share information on the right mix of inputs of energy, materials, capital and labor.[12] Examples abound.

One way to look at the problem of the Colombian leather industry, whose managers "blame the cow," is that the sector continues to try to improve its throughput of low-quality leather, harsh chemicals, and cheap labor (x-efficiency) instead of working together to gain access to marketing guidance and design knowledge (allocative). Likewise in Bolivian soy, managers think they should concentrate on putting more land under cultivation instead of upgrading and coordinating their plants with a view toward producing more complex products like mayonnaise and health foods. In both industries, firms prefer working hard to mobilize more of the same kinds of resources rather than working together to gain new knowledge that enables original choices and new "mixes" of inputs into their own productivity equation.

Productivity at the Regional Level

Another question that surfaces is the role that regions within nations play in enabling damaging patterns to persist. Developing countries must create the type of environment that will support and encourage firms to achieve and sustain strategic advantages. Michael Porter has identified four broad attributes of a nation or region that, individually and as a system, constitute the "diamond" of regional productivity.[13] The diamond provides a critical missing link in the effort to create an environment in which firms in developing countries can make better choices. (See figure 12-1).

First: Factor conditions refer to the presence of advanced and specialized human resources, technical infrastructure, and other factors of production needed in industry. The question is not about what a coun-

Figure 12-1 The Diamond

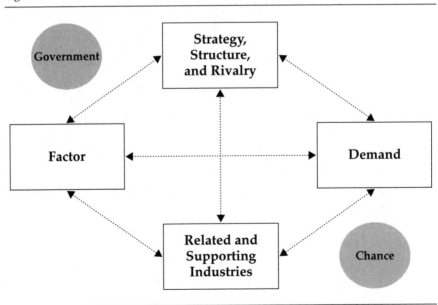

try is born with but about how it has upgraded those conditions. For example, it is good to have smart, literate people, but does the country have enough engineers? It is good to have a natural deep-water port, but are the containers moved efficiently at the port facility?

Factor conditions can be upgraded, depending on the sector that they best serve. For example, the flower sector in Colombia needs to upgrade specific elements of the airport infrastructure, such as the refrigerated bodegas, loading docks, and inspection facilities. In global competition, where Costa Rica has sophisticated airport logistics, Mexico the best access to the United States, and Ecuador cheaper labor, Colombia's sunshine will not be a competitive advantage.

Second: Demand conditions refer to the sophisticated local customer base demanding the latest innovations and the highest quality standards. It is important for local demand to anticipate global demand so that the signals that the producers receive help them learn, adjust, and ultimately upgrade to compete for the world's most sophisticated demand.

For example, flower demand in Colombia is low and unsophisticated compared with Mexico, where the people have a 2,000-year-old tradition of purchasing flowers, or with the Netherlands, which boasts the highest per capita consumption of flowers in the world. Similarly, Colombian consumption of textiles is low, partly because the country doesn't experience a change of seasons and therefore has no need for seasonal fashions. In addition, Colombian consumption of paper is low and unsophisticated because the country is primarily a rural society that does not purchase a variety of printed materials.

Third: Related and supporting businesses are strong local suppliers and distributors who can contribute to the process of innovation, and related businesses that reinforce skills in the same product and process technologies or marketing channels. Trust among buyer and supplier does not exist in an inward-looking economy, where the market pie is small and people are used to carving it up among themselves. In this situation we have found that strategies are not shared and that cost information is jealously protected, which inhibits learning, planning, and sharing objectives for cost reduction and opportunities for differentiation in the marketplace.

Fourth: Firm strategy, structure, and rivalry is about choice, positioning, and the presence of capable, committed, and fiercely competing local rivals. The degree of rivalry in some innovation-driven economies is astonishingly high. In Japan there are 9 major auto manufacturers, 19 fax machine manufacturers, 35 audio equipment makers, and 113 producers of machine tools. Rivalry has forced those firms to improve to the point where they can successfully compete with anybody. In an investment-driven environment like Korea there are 3 auto manufacturers, 18 motor vehicle audio manufacturers, and 200 companies that produce printed circuit boards. A quick review of Japan and Korea's trade data confirms that when there is strong rivalry in the local economy, firms compete favorably in the global marketplace.

In the Andean region, however, rivalry is generally low because the market has been kept small, capital markets are insufficient to prompt new business formation, and government and private sector leaders view rivalry as leading to unnecessarily duplicative efforts in producing similar products for the same consumers. The rivalry that does exist often is driven by personality differences and family loyalties.

Productivity is a system made up of intensely localized phenomena. In nations or regions with internationally competitive industries, the determinants of the "diamond" tend to operate as a system, with each determinant reinforcing the others, leading to constant upgrading and change throughout the system. Because of the interrelated nature of the diamond, nations are rarely home to just one competitive industry; rather, an environment is created that leads to the development of clusters of mutually supportive industries. Those clusters are linked together as a system through *vertical* (buyer-seller) and *horizontal* (common customers, technology, channels) relationships.

Because of the mutually supportive nature of industries within a cluster, there tends to be a clear concentration of internationally competitive industries in a number of clusters in any nation. Thus, identifying strong or potentially strong clusters and understanding the nature and strength of the linkages within those clusters is critical to understanding and enhancing the international competitiveness of a region.

Colombia has some remarkably concentrated geographic-based clusters: textiles in Medellín and Bogotá, tourism and petrochemicals on the northern coast, and paper and printing in Cali. These geographically-based clusters are a function of both incipient competitive advantages and the fact that Colombia is a rugged country with poor road and telecommunications systems that tend to keep some parts geographically separated. What's more, much new business formation is family-driven, not unlike the way it is in the Italian textile and apparel clusters mentioned earlier in the book.

Our research has shown that much of the variability in national wealth is determined by very specific and identifiable regions within a nation—that the conditions for enabling firms to compete and be productive are local.[14] Creating rapid growth in productivity at the regional level is based on getting the four determinants of the diamond working together as a system. For example, a region will obtain only minimal productivity growth if the basic factors are improved. This is the case of Peru and tourism. The leadership has stabilized the environment and built some very basic infrastructure to improve its tourist industry, but it has not built a culture of trust, innovation, or cooperation. From a strategic perspective, Peruvian tourism is analogous to the soy or fishmeal industries discussed in chapter 1—tremendous natural resources (such as Machu Picchu), but little investment in higher-order, intangible assets such as customer learning. In fact if Peru achieves President Fujimori's goal of having 1 million tourists by the year 2000 without making significant changes in current strategy practices, Peru may do great damage to one of its greatest potential industries.

Without improved strategies to appeal to more sophisticated and demanding tourists, an improved cluster of related and supporting firms, and the development of specialized and advanced factors, Peru can only hope to attract greater numbers of the type of tourist it has attracted all along. It will then run the risk of damaging the pristine environment with large numbers of undemanding tourists rather than upgrading the pristine environment with smaller numbers of the more highly-demanding tourist mentioned in the example of the Peruvian hotel outlined in chapter 2. For their inability to make more complex choices, they risk enjoying linear growth until the numbers reach that point of inflection that begins to destroy the very environment that they are selling.

High-Productivity and the Hidden Sources of Growth

Exploiting comparative advantages, the "old way of thinking," represents a style of reductionist thinking that looks for easy answers and keeps countries from seizing opportunities for sustained economic growth. Comparative advantage thinking creates rigid steering mechanisms, simple and often uninformed strategic actions, and subsequently, poor results when it comes to wealth generation and distribution.

How can we use the "new way of thinking" with its focus on knowledge, productivity growth, and particularly "allocative efficiency," to understand the seven patterns and to develop strategies that break these patterns and unlock the inherent "hidden" sources of growth in the developing world?

Leaders who really understand productivity at the company and regional level will adapt different frames of reference, organize their institutions differently so as to be nimble and learning oriented, and execute informed and focused strategies that provide more positive, sustainable results in wealth creation. The seven patterns become the imperatives of this integrative, "high-productivity" thinking which would unlock the hidden sources of growth include the following:

- Export complex products.
- Invest in knowledge of more demanding and sophisticated customers.
- Understand and improve relative competitive position.
- Study the opportunities for forward integration.
- Improve interfirm cooperation.
- Engage in productive reasoning.
- Avoid paternalism.

Export Complex Products

A nation's international trading performance is a key indicator of productivity. Trade provides a tremendous opportunity for improving wealth because it allows countries to focus on exporting goods and services they can produce more productively while importing goods where their advantage is weak.

World Bank research indicates that rapid growth in exports, together with improved human capital, is why the East Asian countries have enjoyed so much economic success.[15] The research suggests strongly that specific advantages arising from trade includes such things as new equipment acquisition, increased foreign direct investment (FDI), technology licensing, and the transfer of nonproprietary technology and customer learning—all of these, in turn, can improve productivity.[16]

Our own research indicates the capacity of a nation to export complex products and services is correlated with its ability to create wealth for its average citizen—that the overdependence on the export of natural capital is limiting the ability of natural resource-dependent nations to develop high and rising standards of living.

Our studies of more than twenty-five oil-exporting countries show that while the average citizen of the smaller nations enjoy increases in wealth, in the more populous nations like Mexico, Venezuela, and Indonesia, purchasing power per capita remains low.[17] In fact, among all the oil exporters, there is only a small positive correlation between rises in oil exports and rises in the standard of living.[18]

On the other hand, there is an increase in wealth per capita when a nation is able to export successfully from the most innovation-based areas of its economy.[19] Clearly, looking for ways to compete by exporting complex products to sophisticated and demanding customers improves the wealth of nations. Which brings us to the second hidden source of growth.

Invest in Knowledge of More
Demanding and Sophisticated Customers

Knowledge of customer preferences is perhaps the key input into high productivity. As previously mentioned, in the Colombian leather sector we uncovered five segments of handbag purchasers in the United States and one in which Colombians had a chance of winning. This was a segment of retailers that wanted to purchase in showrooms, not the magazines where the Colombians were advertising. This segment demanded a threshold level of craftsmanship but valued relationships with the producers and the ability to return products for refunds with little hassle. As producers that have long competed on price, which was supported by a devalued currency, it is only recently that the Colombian leather manufacturers have come to other ways of thinking about competition.

Another example is the Peruvian fishmeal producers. They have little or no understanding of the lucrative Japanese markets in edible fish, so they give way to the Korean and Japanese boats, which pay the Peruvian government a fee to take the best quality fish out of the Humboldt current off the coast. Similarly, the Peruvian and Venezuelan tour operators resist changing their transportation schedules to meet the needs of the high-paying foreign tourist seeking comfort.

Companies in developing countries need to do two key things to uncover the source of hidden growth in customer learning. First, acknowledge that customers have many different preferences and that there exist segments of customers that are attractive to serve and segments that are unattractive to serve. Second, acknowledge that it is increasingly important to design knowledge capture mechanisms inside the company that improve the process of deciding which customers to serve. Making sound choices, understanding how the customer defines value, and executing efficiently against that vision helps to improve productivity—and is the second hidden opportunity for growth.

Understand and Improve Relative Competitive Position

Knowledge is also the key factor in improving relative position. The Colombian polypropylene producer needed to understand its competitive position relative to its rivals in Venezuela, Mexico, and the gulf coast in Texas and Louisiana. They needed to understand their relative costs in electricity, transportation, and especially raw materials. And they needed to know this so they could have an informed discussion with the Colombian government and make sound strategy decisions at the firm level.

The textile producers in northern Peru needed to understand who else in the world was making fabrics based on cottons that could substitute for their high-quality Pima cotton. So they learned about cottons from Malta, Egypt and the Philippines along such dimensions as the length of the cotton strand and its ability to absorb dyes.

They learned the fundamental distinction between uniqueness and substitutability. Even though Pima cotton is grown only in northern Peru and is therefore unique, it is highly substitutable by other high-quality cottons in the world along the dimensions for which customers are willing to pay. The Peruvians thought they were highly differentiated, but with profit margins declining, they had to recognize that their relative position was affected by the substitutes.

Similarly, the Bolivian flower sector tried to compete with the Colombians in the huge U.S. market by sending their flowers through the brokers in Miami. They reckoned that if the Colombians could win there, then they could win because they also had sunshine, cheap fertile ground, and even lower labor costs. What they came to learn was that their transportation costs were three times the costs of the Colombians and that they could not compete there except in the capacity as the swing producer in times of excess demand—like on Valentine's Day. Now they are looking at regional capitals like Santiago, Chile, and Buenos Aries, Argentina where they have the transportation advantage over the Colombians.

Companies in developing countries need to engage in knowledge-based activities to uncover the sources of hidden growth in relative competitive positioning. As we have stated, this means changing the values of the company, its steering mechanisms, and its strategies. Knowledge of relative positioning is the third opportunity for "high productivity."

Study the Opportunities for Forward Integration

Knowledge of when and how to forward integrate represents one of the most important hidden opportunities for growth. Opportunities for forward integration are plentiful in developing countries and need to be studied carefully. In the case of the fruit juice sector in Colombia, we learned that to move forward in the "production chain" would be costly in terms of buying space in the grocery markets and delivering the required quality and consistency standards. We recommended against forward integration at the time.

In the case of agroindustry in Peru, however, we found that the opportunity to sell asparagus to the growing U.S. market could be leveraged much more effectively by moving closer to the U.S. consumer, who was willing to pay higher prices for quality asparagus during times of the year that asparagus is "out of season." The middle-men in the United States significantly reduced their purchases of the asparagus on the belief that the consumers never bought it at those times of the year. Our consumer research indicated that asparagus buyers would be enthusiastic year-round buyers and that they were surprised to learn they might be able to obtain asparagus throughout the year.

The Colombian polypropylene producer was unaware of the existence of at least forty customer segments in the United States for plastic made from its product, and it has yet to take advantage of those opportunities. We learned that downstream from basic polypropylene there are many attractive opportunities to make plastic moldings for such things as car bumpers. Similarly, in the flower industry, especially in basic flowers like carnations and roses, much of the real value is captured further downstream by the Miami-based brokers, the truck delivery services, and the retailers—including both the traditional flower shops and the grocery markets where most impulse flower buying occurs.

Understanding where most of the value in a production chain is created is critical to future growth in developing countries. Traditionally, economic forces and government polices have conspired to limit the imagination of exporters attempting to learn and improve their access to end-users. Forward integration, therefore, is the fourth hidden source of growth.

Improve Interfirm Cooperation

The fifth source of hidden growth is improving the relationships of related and supporting institutions. These relationships enable firms to compete by helping them to lower their cost structure or improve their ability to add unique value for a customer who is willing to pay for it.

Returning to our "blame the cow" example, the tanneries in Colombia could provide higher quality and more consistent hides for the manufacturers, the slaughterhouses could take more care not to damage the hides when they separate the meat, and the ranchers could find better ways to secure the cows than overbranding them. The cows (we do not want to blame everyone *but* the cow) will need to learn to stay away from the barbed-wire fences.

The flower producers in Bolivia, Ecuador, and Colombia would benefit from more research and development that could be shared in their sector—especially in fighting plant diseases; the nineteen government organizations that regulate the Peruvian tourism sector limit the ability of firms to make complex choices; the Venezuelan oil sector could provide some of the advantages of their scale-efficiencies to the petrochemical exporters; and the state-owned cotton producer in Bolivia could find ways of improving the consistency and pricing for the local textile exporters. Chambers of commerce and industry associations need to focus on training executives and gently reorienting governments instead of lobbying and influencing government officials.[20] Moreover, it should be noted that the lesson of interfirm cooperation, like most of the other lessons covered in this chapter, applies to countries outside the developing world.[21]

Interfirm cooperation is the fifth hidden source of growth and productivity, and it is based to a great extent on cultural attitudes about trust and cooperation, outward orientation, long time horizons, and integrative thinking. Which brings us to the sixth source of advantage.

Engage in Productive Reasoning

Few of the previous advantages can be developed without productive reasoning and learning—between and among—owners, partners, strategic alliance members, suppliers, employees, and so forth. As we have argued elsewhere in the book, in the case of the Colombian flower sector, the defensive reasoning by the government and the industry association over the devaluation of the peso has impeded the industry's progress. And in the case of Peruvian textiles, the Pima cotton producers at first blamed all of their problems on the government's opening of the economy to competition from imports. The Bolivian soy bean producers in Santa Cruz believe the government in La Paz is corrupt and incompetent, and the government says that the soy producers are greedy. The largest purchaser of machinery goods in Colombia does not even have regular meetings with the members of the industry association that represents that sector. And in Ecuador, one leader told us: "The national sport of Ecuador is having the trade unions attempt to impeach cabinet members."

If we begin with obsolete paradigms, make inferences that are not grounded in sound data and valid reasoning, the only result possible is to create defensiveness that impedes useful discussion and learning. It is in finding means of productive—that is, nondefensive—learning that the sixth hidden source of growth resides.

Avoid Paternalism

Our surveys conducted in Latin America suggest that the Latins' capacity to trust their governments is small. In Venezuela, 76 percent believe that you cannot trust elected public officials, and 85 percent believe that government officials are incompetent.[22] However, as we have demonstrated, many of the advantages that the business sector seeks in developing countries are based on functions the government provides: the provision of subsidies, protection, devaluation, inside information. The paradox of paternalism is that in most developing countries, the private sector perceives the government as the source of most of their advantages, yet is mistrustful and critical of that same government.

That was the case in Bolivia, where the soy producers consistently criticized the government and were shocked to learn that the *main* source of their advantage was not their fertile soil, sunshine, or farm productivity, but rather the price protection that the government provides them in the form of the Andean Pact trade agreements.

We have not measured in a scientific way how much time senior businesspeople spend trying to influence government officials, but our informal polling strongly suggests that businesspeople consider it the biggest use of their time. As we have demonstrated, industry associations and chambers of commerce are better configured to lobby than to learn, and in studying the government rather than consumers they take their eyes off of the real prize in the era of total competition.

The seventh hidden source of advantage, therefore, is to convert the time spent on trying to influence the government into time spent learning about customers, costs, and competitors.

SUMMARY

In this chapter, we explored the beliefs and views that leaders have about wealth creation and distribution, and the relationship these views have to the seven patterns of uncompetitive behavior. We reviewed historical ways of thinking about wealth creation based on models of comparative and absolute advantage and discussed how this "old way of thinking" can prevent countries from seizing opportunities for sustained growth.

In contrast, the "new way of thinking" we presented, based on knowledge and productivity, can result in exponential growth levels in countries which realize productivity increases not just through increased operational productivity, but in better "allocative" efficiencies focused on investments in knowledge and human capital.

Finally, we revisited the seven patterns of uncompetitive behavior that we discussed in earlier chapters to illustrate how the "new way of thinking" can turn these patterns into valuable opportunities for growth.

But there is yet another challenge: How can these components of exponential productivity growth fit together into an overarching framework for positive change? We leave that for the final chapter.

PART THREE

INTEGRATING THE PIECES

In this book, we have argued that there are familiar patterns of economic behavior in the developing world that have become less and less productive. We have also argued that these patterns are rooted in deeply held ways of thinking that must be changed if the patterns of behavior are going to change. The first part of this book was an exploration of the familiar patterns, the second part an explanation of their underpinnings. This third part aims to establish an overarching framework that brings all of the disparate themes discussed thus far into a somewhat manageable form that can help leaders break these persistent patterns.

CHAPTER THIRTEEN

A Framework for Action

Paul Krugman says that "broad insights that are not expressed in *model form* may temporarily attract attention, and even win converts, but they do not endure unless codified in a reproducible, and even teachable, form." He clarifies what he means by a "good model" when he says it represents an "improved insight into why the vastly more complex real system behaves the way it does." Krugman also says, however, that "during the process of model building, there is a narrowing of vision imposed by the limitations of one's framework and tools, a narrowing that can only be ended definitely by making those tools good enough to transcend those limitations." He suggests that this "narrowing" is difficult for broad minds to accept.[1]

What follows is a model based on an integration of the previous sections of this book viewed from a slightly different perspective. The seven patterns, the firm-level strategies, the institutions, the belief systems—all are parts of a dynamic system created by leaders. If the patterns are to be broken it is critical to learn where the points of leverage in this system are—where leaders can insert themselves, their ideas, and their policies—to have the greatest impact. We call the model we have developed from all of the component pieces discussed in this book a "framework for action." This framework enables one to take immensely complex problems and break them down into more manageable parts. Krugman suggests that "we all think in simplified models all the time. The sophisticated thing to do is not to pretend to stop, but to be self-conscious—to be aware that your models are maps rather than reality."[2] We begin the third and last part of the book with that in mind.

RESULTS, STRATEGIES, AND STEERING MECHANISMS: THE VISIBLE PART OF COMPETITIVENESS

We consider the visible part of competitiveness to be that which is relatively easy to observe and measure—results, strategies, and steering mechanisms. We begin our discussion of the "visible" with results.

Results

If there is to be change, there has to be consensus about what must be changed. The effects of the attempt to change are identified as results, positive or negative. By almost any measure of prosperity, Latin America has had poor results over the past decades. Whether viewed in terms of the seven patterns of uncompetitive behavior, export performance, the standard of living, the provision of healthcare, income distribution, or economic growth, Latin America as a whole has been struggling. And there is no single variable that can explain this. It is not the Spanish colonizers' fault, it is not the governments' fault, it is not the cow's fault. There are a thousand reasons that explain why the results achieved have been so poor.

While gains in macroeconomic indicators have been quite remarkable throughout Latin America in recent years, the underlying structure of the microeconomy does not appear to be changing at the required pace. Macroeconomic stability is necessary but insufficient for creating sustainable growth. Social pressures are mounting as leaders have a hard time justifying austere macroeconomic policies without the benefits of growth and employment they are supposed to engender. And, as witnessed by Ecuadorian elections in 1996, voters are losing patience with the long-promised but seldom delivered benefits of macroeconomic stability.[3]

Latin American nations have been withdrawing from the global community for the past twenty-five years, capturing less and less world market share in the segments in which they compete. This is not necessarily because they are shipping less volume but because countries are earning less money despite their increased export volume. (See figure 13-1.)

From an industry-attractiveness perspective, most of Latin America's exports tend to be in natural resource–dependent industries, and almost without exception, prices in those principal export segments have been

Figure 13-1   Trade Statistics Analysis, World Export Share by Nation, 1970–1992

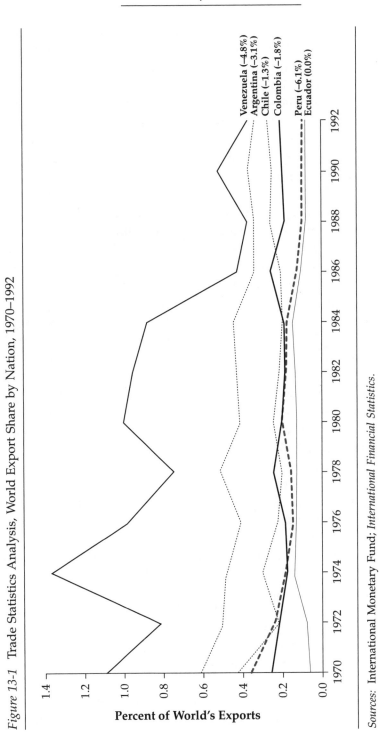

Sources: International Monetary Fund; *International Financial Statistics.*

Note: Colombian data for 1992 not reported.

dropping. In spite of the unattractive nature of these segments, firms continue to increase their dependency on basic factor exports. Our research in Latin America, for example, demonstrates that dependence on natural resource-based exports has been increasing, not decreasing.[4] The resulting economic structures are vulnerable to import pressures and price competition, and preclude movement toward more sophisticated or attractive segments of the global economy. When the structure of an economy is geared toward exporting natural resources, there is very little corresponding investment in the competitive environment that might yield more success in complex industries.

The results are not surprising: measures such as gross domestic product per capita, purchasing power parity per capita, and income distribution are getting worse. In fact, recent unpublished research by the International Bank for Reconstruction and Development reports that the gap between rich and poor is widening faster in Latin America than anyplace else in the world.

What are some of the microeconomic results that are of concern?[5] Firms that compete on basic factors, unless they have real monopolistic access to both raw materials and to markets, are seeing their profit margins squeezed by worldwide trends that are lowering prices in many commodities. To become more efficient, firms are investing in technology upgrades, which is often difficult to do with in-country debt financing, thereby forcing the financing in foreign currency, with consequent financial risks if the firms are not sourcing that foreign currency with a large percentage of their export sales.

Many firms are hoarding inventory in the hope that prices will improve, but meanwhile financing that inventory with expensive short-term debt and tying up money that might be better spent on innovation in the form of R&D and worker training.

There is also a trend of increased inventories in companies that fear supply will dwindle, be it from inefficient local suppliers or erratic government behavior that might devalue a currency, make the import of supplies more expensive, or, indeed, close the border to international suppliers because of political pressure. When inventory supplies increase, profitability declines, since firms need to finance those increases with the inefficient, uncompetitive, and overly protected capital markets.

While companies are reporting increased marketing expenses, there is not a corresponding upgrading in customer learning or evolution in the types of customers being served. Relative position is not improving at the level of the firm. If the products were truly differentiated, revenues would be improving—relative to assets deployed, or employees, or capital. If the firm were a cost leader, the impact would be in ratios of administrative expenses to sales, operating costs to sales, and other income-statement items almost as quickly as the advantages were created. Cash flows would show investment in specific machinery and plants, and we would see the general efficiency of the companies improve by the sales turnover and plant age ratios. On the whole, that is not happening.

Systems thinkers have told us that *bad results are the only results possible from a system perfectly designed to achieve them.* If that is truly the case, then it will be worthwhile to develop a deeper understanding of what the rest of that system looks like.

Strategic Actions

Chapters 8 and 9 were dedicated to the proposition that the seven patterns exist partly because firms are not making the right strategic choices. If one chooses an unattractive segment in which to compete, the results will likely be poor. This problem is compounded when the industry itself is also unattractive and the resources necessary to compete well (for example, skilled labor, efficient infrastructure, inexpensive capital) cannot be mobilized. Many of the strategic decisions made by business leaders in the past were actually the right decisions at the time but, in light of the pressures of globalization, need now to be revisited. See figure 13-2 for a diagram of strategic action.

The dramatic changes that firms experienced with the end of protected economies led to tremendous competitive pressures, and firm-level performance for many industries suffered. The results were poor. In light of those results, leaders had choices to make: to embrace the changes, or to resist them. Or, to state it another way, to learn or to lobby. Many business leaders—especially those pertaining to the "level playing field" frame of mind—opted for lobbying. This is actually an understandable response, given how difficult real learning is in some of these environments, and given that governments have previously shown no real ability to stick with an economic plan.

We have argued that to break the seven patterns discussed earlier in the book, improvement will have to occur on two dimensions: better

Figure 13-2 Stategic Action

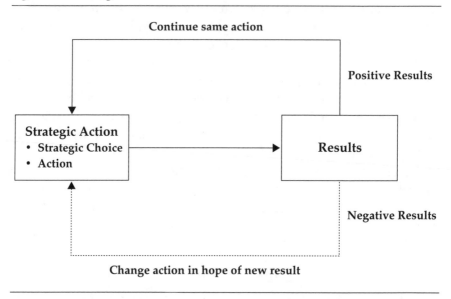

Continue same action

Positive Results

Strategic Action
- **Strategic Choice**
- **Action**

Results

Negative Results

Change action in hope of new result

strategy and improved productivity. This is not a revolutionary insight, but it is one that bears deeper reflection. Firms have not been able to pursue forward-thinking approaches in either strategy or productivity because the environments in which they operate have constrained the realm of possible options. Thus the possibility of creating differentiated products, or working closely together with the cluster of industries, has been severely constrained.

Steering Mechanisms

When the strategies or actions taken by an organization yield positive results, an instinct develops to solidify those particular actions into formulas for success. As organizations institutionalize those formulas for success, they become *steering mechanisms:* the laws, administrative policies, market mechanisms, and informal customs intended to ensure that the formulas for success continue to be followed. Thus companies develop mechanisms to ensure certain sales or production targets consistent with past successes. Or, governments develop a series of administrative institutions designed to achieve specific results.

Steering mechanisms can play a critical part in ensuring the success of a specific organization at a specific point in time. The risk, however, is that these very mechanisms can actually distort signals from the market and inhibit the ability of organizations to adapt to changing competitive realities. For example, when the Colombian textile manufacturers asked the Minister of Economic Development to institute price floors in Colombia for imported textile goods, they believed that these measures would eliminate fierce and possibly illegal competition and provide a level playing field on which to compete. While this measure may have improved the short-term results of the textile companies and kept employment levels high, mechanisms such as price controls can actually insulate firms from the competitive pressures they must feel if they are going to be able to become competitive themselves. (See figure 13-3.)

Mechanisms that distort market signals impede the development of a competitive economy. Firms will become more competent at managing government relations than customer expectations and will develop tremendously complex steering mechanisms to ensure that they have continued preferential access to markets. The goal is to remove mechanisms, even those originally designed to help firms, which in practice inhibit their incentives to learn and improve.

As the case study of policy development in Bolivia demonstrated in chapter 10, governments must make hard choices about where they will intervene in an economy and what the appropriate mix of policies and mechanisms will be. The choices governments throughout Latin Amer-

Figure 13-3 Steering Mechanisms

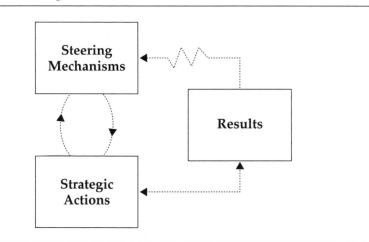

ica have made to pursue open-economy reforms in the first half of the 1990s have met with some success. Those choices, while difficult to make, have been relatively easy to execute. They are, according to former Venezuelan Finance Minister Moisés Naím, "Stage 1" reforms. For now, it is sufficient to point out that while Latin America has had much success in dramatically changing the activities of the state, these activities have been about what the state should *stop* doing, more than about what it *should* do. That observation has led Naím to write, "The discovery of the market will soon force Latin American countries to rediscover the state."[6]

That is precisely the challenge for government leaders going forward. Understanding what the government can and cannot do well is a fundamental lesson that must be learned if the seven patterns of uncompetitive behavior are to be transformed into opportunities for growth.

MENTAL MODELS: THE INVISIBLE PART OF COMPETITIVENESS

Fixing the "visible" part of competitiveness is a tremendously difficult, time-consuming, and daunting task to which thousands of people have dedicated themselves. There is another dimension to competitiveness, however, which is rarely touched on and yet holds perhaps the most promise in creating lasting change. There is a common perception in Latin America that results are a function of the context where people live and work—the visible structures and practices that they have little ability to change. We believe, on the other hand, that the results tend to be a function of the way people think the world works, which informs the way they frame their problems and relationships, which in turn affects the way they act. And it is these actions that yield the results we have been discussing. The way people think—their mental models—constitutes the invisible part of competitiveness—and this is where the point of leverage for creating lasting change lies.

Definitions

The world is complex, and each of us over time develops mental models to help us come to terms with that complexity. The concept of a mental model was introduced in 1943 by Kenneth Craik when he proposed that thinking is the internal manipulation of representations of how the world works. He suggested that we are not intelligent enough to hold actual reality in our imaginations, so we make do with simplified models of the world. As people receive new data, they interpret, or "frame," that data according to models that they have in their heads. If one were to change a personal mental model, he or she would interpret reality in new ways, even if given the same data.

One key aspect of mental models is the paradigms that are at play, which enable us to have an internally consistent perspective of the world. Paradigms provide our mental models with a unifying quality. Thomas Kuhn, a philosopher of science at Princeton who passed away in 1996, was the first to popularize the concept of a paradigm shift when in 1962 he said that a dominant new theory usually explains about 80 percent of things that have never been explained before.[7] The other 20 percent remains unexplained—anomalies. Over time, those anomalies begin to undermine the theory, until they force observers to reshape and redefine the problem, which requires that another new theory be developed to explain 80 percent of the remaining 20 percent. Kuhn suggests that these anomalies, this "20 percent," should not be swept aside blithely, but rather should be held up and venerated as a source of future insight. John Maynard Keynes said, "The difficulty lies, not in the new ideas, but in escaping from the old ones, which ramify, for those brought up as most of us have been, into every corner of our minds."[8] In the situations we have observed in the developing world, the anomaly is the fact that wealth is not being created and distributed at a sufficient rate, given the astounding natural and human resources that these countries possess.

The other key area of mental models is frames. A *frame* is a point of reference—the goals, attributions, beliefs, or perspectives through which an individual sees the world. Frames are concrete, first person, and specific. In chapter 11 we examined how dramatically different frames of reference can be, even within similar contexts. Frames are informed by the paradigms available to the individual, and individuals can be grouped according to sets of shared, or "like," characteristics. Frames indicate how individuals see themselves in relationship to their surroundings and other actors in their environment. In the case of Latin America, a common "private-sector" frame views the government as inconsistent, untrustworthy, and unconcerned with private sector problems. At the same time, there is increasingly a "public-sector" frame that says the private sector has grown accustomed to state-favoritism and handouts, and that says the way to improve competitiveness is simply for business leaders to *ponerse las pilas*—"put the batteries in." Those frames are at the root of the defensiveness and divisiveness inhibiting the development of more productive working relationships among firms and between the business and government leadership.

Frames of Reference

In the framework for action we propose, the invisible part of competitiveness is portrayed to the left of the visible, as shown in figure 13-4. Every leader has paradigms and frames of reference, but they remain largely implicit and not widely understood. Yet the influence these mental models have on the performance of business and government leaders is profound. Previous chapters established the existence of unproductive frames of reference and outdated paradigms. The following sections seek to provide an example of how these might be changed so as to encourage the development of more complex forms of competition in the developing world.

Figure 13-4 The Action Framework: Invisible and Visible Aspects of Change

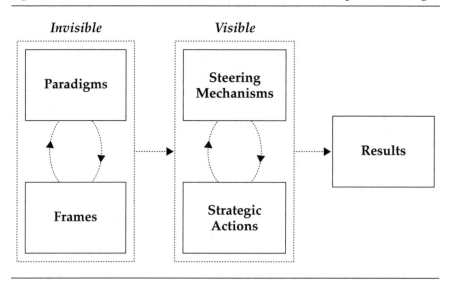

The Government Frame

The critical government frame will be to do everything for the private sector that it can possibly manage to do, except to impede competition. Thinking "micro," the government has the opportunity to develop specialized infrastructure, provide world class primary education, and create incentives for the private sector to develop university and technical education together with fostering an environment for government-to-private-sector and private-sector-to-academic alliances for training. The government can also foster an environment where domestic and international alliances take place—again, as long as it does not impede competition. On the demand side, the government can stimulate market learning opportunities and create antitrust legislation that fosters competition and attractive industry structures. At the end of the day, governments have to create an environment that is learning-based, that stimulates cluster formation, and enables an outward orientation.

Specifically, government ministers should seek to:

- Create environments that encourage sophisticated exports, understanding that such environments are critical to wealth creation and distribution.

- Create an environment for direct foreign investment that not only discourages simple exploitation of natural resources, but also encourages strategic investments in improving the competitive environment.

- Foster an environment where the government and the private sector make their vision of complex exports and their relation to foreign investment correct, explicit, and shared.

- Create advanced and specialized advantages for the private sector, based on that sector's learned and explicit strategic vision.

- Create a stable and predictable macroeconomic environment, with a particular emphasis on the creation of a stable and predictable exchange rate.

- Work on the country's ability to create incentives for improved productivity through taxes and spending.

Once agreement on these general objectives are reached, the hard work of developing specific strategies for realizing these objectives begins.

The government's frame of reference allows it to see the integrated aspects of trade, investment, and wealth creation and to begin to view its job not just as a watchdog over the "corrupt and ambitious" private sector, but also as a source for creating advantages that are not easily imitated by other countries. Working from this frame of reference, government officials would also try to help businesses compete by doing everything in their power short of impeding domestic competition or sheltering businesses from external pressure.

The Private Sector Frame

Working from their frame of reference, business leaders will improve their capacity to add unique value to their products and services for the sake of sophisticated and demanding consumers, who will be willing to reward them with higher profit margins. The private sector is increasingly amorphous, and frames of reference will vary among the participants. What follows is a breakout that fairly represents some of the constituencies with whom we routinely work.

"QUASI-PRIVATE" INSTITUTIONS

In the twenty-first century, it will be critical for industry associations, chambers of commerce, academic institutions, and labor unions to develop a frame of reference through which they view their roles as champions of business leaders in a new way: Not to revert to endless lobbying and criticism of the government, but to develop processes and programs to educate, train, and inspire leaders in the private sector to develop more competitive strategies. Through their frames of reference they should encourage dialogue between government and business but should not be paralyzed by the potential lack of dialogue; with global borders shrinking, there is no time to wait for the government before making changes.

Specifically, industry associations and chambers of commerce need to create more executive education programs focused not only on improving the operational efficiencies of businesses but also teaching business owners and public officials to occasionally redirect their view over the horizon of possibilities. Programs in organizational learning and behavior may be more critical than seminars on core competency theory, reengineering, and total quality, although those would also be of value.

Academics have to get their hands dirty; they need to help create value for the private sector now. They need to change the mental model that assumes that work in the private sector means sacrificing academic freedom or, as the Irish poet W. B. Yeats has described it, putting their hands in "the greasy till" of commerce. They need to get involved.

PRIVATE FIRMS AND ENTREPRENEURS

Private firms and entrepreneurs tend to think in the short term; they avoid risks and embarrassment, and they insist that all they are looking for is a level playing field with their competitors in other countries. Private firms and entrepreneurs often work in concert with the associations and other groups to lobby the government for "advantages" when they could instead be focusing on what they can do: engaging in customer learning, alliance building, and making explicit and shared agreements with one another on complex strategies. The opportunity cost of simply advocating one's personal views, rather than inquiring into and understanding the views of others is a huge hidden cost of doing business in developing countries and a force that runs counter to upgrading the competitive environment.

How should the private sector frame its position? Its goal has to be to upgrade the competitive environment and to find ways to learn about sophisticated consumers so that it might provide them with unique value. At the same time, the private sector needs to help build trust inside the country, both within the private sector and between the private sector and the government; to work with the government to build an efficient system of justice that protects investments in innovation and tangible and intangible property; and, finally and perhaps most important, to develop learning mechanisms that continually test and replenish frames of reference so that the country develops rules of behavior consistent with worldwide consumer and competitor trends.

Paradigms

We think of paradigms as the systematic ways in which individuals or institutions think about the world—economic theories, political theories, beliefs about justice or equity, to name a few. The predominant paradigm governing Latin American economies has been a vision of wealth creation through *comparative* advantages such as natural resource endowments. It is clear that the import-substitution policies (strategic actions and steering mechanisms) stemming from that paradigm are no longer effective.

With globalization comes an imperative for firms and governments to develop a *borderless imagination*—something quite different from the imagination that has developed in protected economies dependent on natural resources. Table 13-1 summarizes some of the paradigms at work in the developing world and suggests how they might change in the future. This list is not intended to be comprehensive nor authoritative but rather to illustrate what is meant by the need to develop different paradigms to help break the patterns and management practices mentioned above.

The Action Framework as an Integrated Whole

Having reviewed each component of the action framework in detail, we need to talk about how they work together. Paradigms and frames together are called *mental models* and represent the invisible part of change. Mental models inform the development and implementation of steering mechanisms and strategies. These work as a system, and the results of this system are determined long before they are apparent to most decision makers.

We have observed three fundamental ways in which leaders respond to bad results: reacting, redesigning, and reorienting. *Reactive* leaders realize that different strategic actions are required to improve results, and they develop new approaches to alter the bad results. The new strategies, however, are often continuations of the same set of activities—but the goal is to work at them harder. *Redesign,* on the other hand, stems from a leader's desire to get the structure of an organization more aligned with its goals and to improve operating efficiency. Finally, *reorientation* represents a fundamental shift in patterns of thought and behavior. Reorientation means wholesale change in mental models. We believe that this is the primary type of change that is needed throughout the developing world.

As shown in figure 13-5, all of the components of our framework work together. We do not believe it is possible to create sustainable change without addressing each component or category. For example, to improve the context of a country, change needs to begin with paradigms and frames; these new ways of thinking should engender different strategic actions, which should in turn lead to the development and implementation of a different set of steering mechanisms, which should lead to better results. These better results will lead to an improved economic and social environment.

The action framework is integrative and systemic in nature. First, the

Table 13-1 Representative Paradigms—Old and New

Paradigm Category	Specific Paradigm	The Old Way of Thinking	A New Way of Thinking
Wealth Creation	Comparative advantage thinking versus Competitive advantage thinking	• Comparative advantage • Wealth is finite and must be divided • Competition inhibits wealth creation • Nations compete • Natural resource driven • Simple products, mass produced	• Competitive advantage • Wealth can be infinite and must be shared • Competition helps wealth creation • Firms compete, not nations • Customer driven • Complex products
Social Capital	Human relations	Centralized power and authority • Paternalistic • Hierarchical organizations • Success is individual oriented	• Trust oriented • Interdependent • Meritocratic • Team oriented
	Human capital	• Labor and managers are fungible • Viewed as input costs • General education	• Source of competitive advantage • Source of infinite return on investment • Education as specialized, expensive
	Learning	• Linear thinking, *results* inform strategy choices and organizational design (single-loop learning) • Reductionist strategies • Technical and compartmentalized	• Systems thinking, results inform mental models (double-loop learning) • Integrative, interdisciplinary approaches • Team oriented
	Justice and social equity	• Redistribute finite wealth • Laws as constraints • Informal producers are marginalized	• Create wealth through innovation and distribute to most productive people • Laws as enabling investment in innovation • Informal producers increasingly integrated
Action Orientation	Organizational design	• Centralized, large, complex • Purpose is to allocate resources	• Decentralized, flat structure flexible, transparent • Dedicated to learning
	Change creation	• Macroeconomics drives decisions • Government is master strategist, prime mover • "Reactive, redesign"	• Microeconomics and business strategy drive decisions • Firm level, private sector • Cooperative, shared vision, explicit moral purpose • Integrated actions • "Reorientation"

Figure 13-5 The Action Framework: How Do You Change the Mind of a Nation?

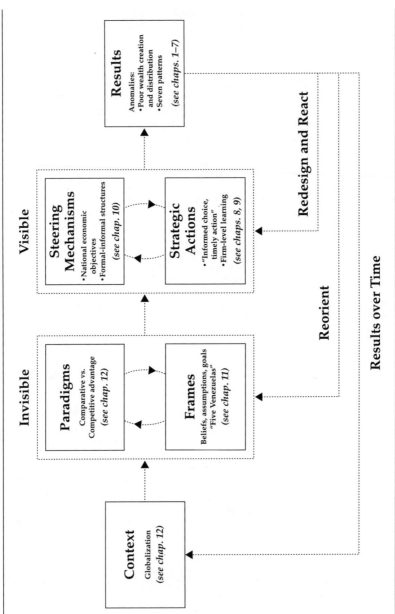

framework is born of *observations* made at the sectoral level. The more we understood the depth and intricacy of a particular sector problem—in the Colombian flower sector, for example—the more we found those same issues reflected in other sectors in other countries. The problems in the Colombian flower industry can therefore be considered a "fractal" of the nation's—and, indeed, the developing world's—problems and opportunities.

Second, the framework consists of *six categories* that are comprehensive and mutually exclusive. They make it possible to distill highly complex problems and dynamics into a group of categories that is easier to understand.

Third, the action framework is *integrative* in the sense that these categories have an impact on each other in a certain order; this points to a kind of causality at work here, a sense of forward motion.

Fourth, it is a *dynamic system,* in that it provides some notion of feedback. It is a closed system, because everything that we learned fits somewhere on the framework and is related to everything else.

Fifth, the framework makes it possible to discuss useful *points of intervention* and insertion. Because it has all of the above-mentioned characteristics, we can discuss where and how on the framework we would like to begin making changes. For example, do we start with strategy actions, or in the design of a steering mechanism? Or is this a reorientation problem?

Sixth, this is an exercise in *generative learning.* We began by studying other models of competitiveness, government instruments, and organizational learning. We practiced those models and fine-tuned the analytics before setting out to build our own models and then ultimately this framework, which is the result of our internalization of so many other people's work and our observations from the field.

Seventh, it is informed by the notion of *double-loop learning,* meaning that the real point of leverage on this framework is in the reorientation of the mental models of a country's leaders. This includes their capacity to deepen, change, inform, and replenish that invisible aspect of change that consists of their paradigms and frames of reference. In fact, reorientation, specifically, development of leaders' capacity to reframe their perspectives—is the goal of our work in general, and of this book.

Thomas Kuhn described how an anomaly can indicate the need for a paradigm shift. We think of the seven patterns of uncompetitive behavior as anomalies, a group of bad results. Their very existence indicates that leaders' current way of thinking about wealth creation and income distribution does not work, that we need a more robust theory of change to describe what is happening. Paternalism and defensiveness, the lack of customer orientation, poor relative positioning, and the other patterns are the anomalies or clues or even a growing body of evidence that point directly to the need for change.

We have three ways to interpret the evidence provided by these anomalies. We can interpret them as strategies that have gone awry. We can interpret them as institutions that need to be rebuilt. Or we can interpret them as mental models about wealth creation that are no longer sufficient.

PRECONDITIONS FOR CHANGE

This book has been about change. It has been about trying to understand why things have not changed positively for the majority of people in the developing world. It has been about trying to change the prevailing economic paradigms and views about wealth creation and distribution. It is one thing to identify what needs to be changed, however, and quite another to change it. Over time, we have developed a list of five questions we like to ask before becoming involved in any change effort. We offer them to the reader to help reflect on the possibility for change in developing countries. The questions are these:

1. Is there sufficient *tension* to motivate people to change?
2. Are people *receptive* to new ways of doing things?
3. Is the *knowledge* necessary to change available?
4. Does the leadership have a clear and compelling *moral purpose*?
5. Is the *leadership* capable of facilitating change?

The five preconditions for change are the points of greatest leverage in unlocking a nation's or an organization's ability to "move leftward" through the boxes in the framework for action.

Historian James Rudolph calls what Peru experienced prior to President Fujimori's administration a "multifaceted crisis": economic, social, and political crises. In 1992 he wrote

> *Economically,* a decade and a half of persistent recession had recently worsened into Peru's deepest depression of the twentieth century, with GDP declining 14 percent in 1989 alone; at the same time hyperinflation, measured at nearly 3,000 percent in 1989, so ravished Peru's currency, the

inti, that it was scheduled to be replaced in 1991, only five years after it had been created.

. . . The *social crisis* was most evident in a growth of poverty to levels that could appropriately be termed obscene: by 1990, it was estimated that a third or more of Peru's population was unable to supply its basic nutritional needs. The immense power of the apparently limitless profits from narcotics trafficking to corrupt an even broader segment of the population—a power that only grew with the deepening of the economic crisis—led many Peruvians to talk about a society-wide moral crisis as well.

. . . A rapidly growing insurgency—spearheaded by the Sendero Luminoso, or Shining Path—was the most visible aspect of a crisis so pervasive that it increasingly questioned the very legitimacy of Peru's *political and governmental structures.* State institutions had deteriorated to the point that they were routinely unable to provide electrical, water, sanitary, educational, health, police and judicial services.[9]

Political scientists Williamson and Haggard suggest that crisis has the "effect of shocking countries out of traditional policy patterns, disorganizing the interest groups that typically veto policy reform, and generating pressure for politicians to change policies that can be seen to have failed."[10]

As Anders Aslund, a close economic advisor to the Russian Federation during the beginning of its transition to market reform says, "Politically, it is easier to have a big package of radical measures accepted early on, when a deep sense of crisis prevails and various interest groups can not yet fully evaluate what they may gain or lose."[11]

The first part of this book, focusing on the seven prevailing patterns of uncompetitive behavior in the Andes, was written to cause some *tension* in the reader. The story of the Colombian flower growers is an allegory inasmuch as it is a specific story, with universal applicability, about a nation or a region or a group of decision makers who have relied too much on their comparative advantages to produce wealth. Those strategies worked for a while—for thirty years or so—and not very well, in fact. And as we hope we have illustrated, they will never work again.

When that story is finally said and done, the flower sector's attitudes, organizations, and strategies may be regarded as a mechanism through which much of Colombia's wealth was exported to other countries, mostly to the United States. The wealth was exported away because Colombia gave the United States its earth, its sunshine, and its beauty at subsidized rates because of an undervalued exchange rate and artificially suppressed wages; and because when the money was paid, it was paid to very few owners who declined to, or felt unable to, invest back into Colombia, into the productivity of their fellow human beings.

Profits were kept offshore due to political and economic instability; profits diminished because Colombia competed in highly competitive segments with easy-to-imitate strategies, and no one thought to invest in people; the concomitant rise in salaries would have destroyed the cost structure and therefore the pricing in such a commodity. The tension the reader should feel is that this net export of wealth has been occurring in most *"un-developing"* countries. And it is not just that "the world has changed"; it is not that we have made bad choices or that the governments do not work. It is that most leaders think—incorrectly—about how to create a high and rising standard of living for the average person in their countries.

The political base of cabinet members, senior civil servants, and legislators must be committed to an innovation-based economy: to innovation as the core of their strategy. The only way to even get close to such an ideal is through a process of building shared vision so powerful, so persuasive, so skillfully facilitated that the world has yet to see anything like it.

The inventory of hard and soft technologies required to build not just compromise or even consensus, but a robust model of cooperation and shared vision does not reside in any one person, and perhaps not in any group. But developing that capacity for change and learning will be the advantage of all intellectual communities and of nations going forward.

Reorientation and the change of moral purpose in a society occurs top-down, and the social consensus will not be built without *leadership* that is broad, explicit, and action oriented. People will have to begin to choose leaders by whom they are willing to be led. And the electorate has to upgrade its view of seeing leaders simply as people who can get them things—a danger that Kenichi Ohmae describes as a "civil minimum," whereby the leadership of a nation is hacked to death by the constraints of the requests put to it.[12]

The *knowledge* that leaders will require in order to upgrade and improve nations will include, but probably not be limited to, the following: the development of explicit action frameworks, the clarification of mental models, productive reasoning techniques, organizational design and behavior, moral philosophy, microeconomics, systems thinking, business strategy, and simulation technology. Finally, there will be a requirement for the knowledge of what Peter Senge calls "personal mastery." That is the capacity of leaders to, among other things, "focus on ultimate intrinsic values."[13]

As we have tried to illustrate repeatedly, one primary precondition for change that is shifting is that economic growth and social equity have the chance of being reconciled, given the other preconditions for change. Simply, investment in social equity will become viewed as critical for competitive advantage, and that competitive advantage will in fact not be achieved without the development of social equity. And as we have pointed out, when most leaders talk about social equity, they mean the distribution of a living wage to the majority of the population. In our mental model we talk about an upgraded conception of social equity to mean what we refer to as advanced and specialized social capital: improvements in trust, justice, human skills, and the capacity of a people to constantly replenish and upgrade their frames of references.

We hypothesize that in a world of what Adam Smith calls "absolute advantages" and David Ricardo calls "comparative advantages," where wealth was finite, we have created a "zero-sum" mentality that has bluntly influenced our politics.

Now things are different. Nobel laureate Gary Becker states that human capital is the only investment with the potential for unlimited returns, for exponential growth. This can mean that the dominant theory of "comparative advantages" and the related paradigms and frames no longer have to drive the development of our institutional mechanisms, our choices, and most important, our results. To frame it differently: comparative advantage does not have to drive our politics, our sense of justice, the sum of those notions that determines the relationship between communities and individuals.

Politics can be about building robust models of understanding that facilitate learning to make the increasingly complex decisions required to create wealth in an increasingly competitive world. Winners in politics will be those leaders who create and facilitate new models of wealth creation and social justice, which increasingly will be viewed not as antithetical but as two rapidly converging objectives. That problem will "dissolve."[14]

The emerging *moral purpose* will be to invest in the average citizen's productivity through education, health care, and specialized infrastructure, such as the provision of computing and communications power.

Leaders need to think about how to create the capacity for innovation; making leaps forward in an individual's or firm's or region's capacity to create value in the form of a product or service, for which foreign consumers will be willing to pay more money. And that money will be distributed to the average citizen in return for his or her contribution to the new value proposition.

The risk of failure will be high, and there will be many failures along the way; leaders should be forgiven for trying and sometimes failing to reorient mental models. The leaders chosen will have to be less brittle. We will require leaders who derive much of their self-esteem from learning and creating change rather than from being liked, being viewed as invulnerable, avoiding embarrassment, or always being in control.

There will be roles for all types of leaders: authoritarians like Fujimori, expert technicians like former President Gaviria of Colombia, and visionaries—well, there is plenty of room for them. The authoritarian will always be required to settle crises, the technician to redesign administrative, legal, and market mechanisms, and the visionary—occasionally—to change the mind of the community. We need leaders with the capacity to migrate from one role to the other as their environments change, as the explicit framework for action is upgraded, as their moral authority evolves.

The moral authority in an innovation-based environment will come from the wisdom of the leader to manage the other preconditions for change: electrifying and then clarifying for the electorate the new moral purpose of an innovation-based, upgrading economy girded by the high and rising standard of value created by the average citizen. This leader will facilitate the development and use of hard and soft technologies for change and learning. He or she will create a broad degree of real and sustained *receptivity* for change—in the political base, the opposition, and the increasingly complex populace.

With this book, we have argued that there is much reason for hope in the developing world—that patterns of behavior which have resulted in such poor economic and social results can be broken. We have also argued that there is a systemic way to think about these patterns—how wealth can be created in a way that is not only consistent with, but promotes, social equity. Our view is that all of the preconditions for change now exist. It remains for each of us interested in creating prosperity for the average citizen to nurture the hidden sources of growth.

Notes

All charts in this book are used from previously published materials with the knowledge of the clients and do not reflect the current competitive position of those clients.

Preface

1. *World Bank Development Report 1995;* research with 1993 data.
2. Paul Krugman, "The Fall and Rise of Development Economics," in *Rethinking the Development Experience,* edited by Lloyd Rodwin and Donald Schon, (Washington, D.C.: Brookings Institution, 1994), 50.

Introduction

1. According to the *Microsoft Bookshelf: Multimedia Reference Library* (1995), El Dorado is "a vaguely defined historical region and city of the New World, often thought to be in northern South America. Fabled for its great wealth of gold and precious jewels, it was eagerly sought after by 16th- and 17th-century explorers, including Sir Walter Raleigh."
2. Nontraditional exports were defined as those other than the traditional Colombian exports such as oil, minerals, or coffee.
3. We estimate that approximately 70 percent of the Colombian growers are not forward integrated. The majority of the flowers shipped through Miami are bought on consignment from these growers.
4. In numerous interviews with the Colombian flower growers and members of the Colombian flower association in 1993, it became evident that Asocolflores had made a strategic decision against involvement in any of the market challenges to focus its efforts on maintaining a favorable exporting environment. The purpose of the Colombian Flower Council, which was partially funded by Asocolflores and by special levies to the growers, was to challenge dumping charges. The Colombian Flower Council was also

charged with marketing Colombian goods and chose to pursue a strategy of mass-advertising with the objective of increasing overall flower consumption in the U.S. market.

5. The Colombian Flower Council remained active in its legal efforts to counter U.S. growers' charges throughout this period, as well.

6. ATPA is the Andean Trade Preferences Agreement, a trade agreement with the United States that gives preferential trade to Bolivia, Colombia, Peru, and Ecuador in an attempt to provide them with legitimate trade alternatives to cocaine.

7. Speech by Minister of Foreign Trade, June 1993.

8. This and the Minister's response appeared in *Asocolflores' Magazine*, June 1993.

9. This argument, which we will expound on in subsequent chapters, has also been supported in recent work by Jeffrey Sachs and Andrew Warner at Harvard University.

10. To illustrate the difference between a comparative advantage and a competitive advantage, we refer you to the Dutch versus the Colombian flower industry. Colombia has a comparative advantage in fertile soil, cheap land, and inexpensive labor—yet it is the number two exporter of cut flowers in the world. The number one exporter, Holland, has few comparative advantages—no cheap land, inexpensive labor, or great growing conditions—but it does have well-developed research and development techniques, sophisticated production and distribution technology, strong local demand; in short, they have many factors at play that are hard to imitate and that actually create superior cut flowers for which consumers are willing to pay a premium. That is competitive advantage.

11. The term *fractal*, which comes from the study of geometry and was coined by Benoit Mandlebrot, a Polish-born, French mathematician, means that irregular patterns are made of parts that are in some way similar to the whole; for example twigs and tree branches demonstrate the fractal property of self-similarity or self-symmetry. The concept of fractals has been adopted into chemistry, economics, analysis of the stock market, and meteorology.

Chapter 1

1. Factor advantages are one of the four determinants of competitive advantage of nations, according to the Porter theory. These advantages, together with demand; strategy, structure, and rivalry; and cluster advantages when working in a system allow a nation or a region to upgrade and innovate in order to create a better platform for the creation of firm-level strategy. See Michael Porter, *The Competitive Advantage of Nations* (New York: Free Press, 1990), 73–85.

2. Purchasing power parity is standard in this book because it is an estimation of exchange rate changes based on keeping prices of goods in different countries fairly similar by offsetting inflation differentials with changes in the currency exchange rates. It is coming increasingly into favor by economists in place of GDP per capita ratios for the comparison and distribution of wealth between countries.

3. For further research confirming the inverse relationship between natural resources exports and wealth creation, see Jeffrey D. Sachs and Andrew M. Warner, "Natural Resource Abundance and Economic Growth," National Bureau of Economic Research, Cambridge, Mass., December 1995, working paper 5398.

4. Bolivia's per capita income is officially $670, but is probably higher owing to the informal market. Haiti is poorer with an official per capita income of $340.

5. Percentages are 1992 figures and do not include fresh fish. While the figures need to be updated, the fresh fish segment will not change the story much. (Almost all fresh fish is consumed locally.)

Chapter 3

1. Polypropylene is a lightweight plastic used to make things like packing material, textiles, luggage, and ropes that float. In our research on this project we found at least forty specific downstream industrial segments.

2. The survey measured Bolivian leaders' assessment of how much prestige Bolivia has relative to their assessment of how much prestige they attribute to other nations.

3. *Brady bonds* are bonds issued by foreign governments (such as Mexico and Venezuela) under a program designed by Treasury Secretary Nicholas Brady in 1989 to help developing countries refinance their debt. Their principal is guaranteed by zero-coupon U.S. Treasury bonds.

4. Kenichi Ohmae, in *The Borderless World: Power and Strategy in the Interlinked Economy* (New York: Harper Perennial, 1990), 33.

Chapter 5

1. Porter, *Competitive Advantage of Nations,* 101–102. For those interested in further reading on the concept of the cluster, we recommend the following discussions: D. Audretsch and M. Feldman, "Innovative Clusters and Industry Life Cycle," Centre for Economic Policy Research, London, 1995, discussion paper; C. Debresson, "Breeding Innovation Clusters: A Source of Dynamic Development," *World Development* 17, no. 1 (1989); Paul Krugman, *Geography and Trade* (Cambridge, Mass.: MIT Press, 1992); Carl Dahlman, "The New Elements of International Competitiveness: Toward

More Integrated Policies for Latin America," OECD, Paris, 1994; Brian Levy, "Successful Small and Medium Enterprises and Their Support Systems: A Competitive Analysis of Four Country Studies," conference proceedings, World Bank Policy Research Department, Washington, D.C., 1994; Alfred Marshall, *Industry and Trade*, 3d ed. (London: Macmillan, 1927).

2. Arequipa, city (population 620,471 in 1993). Founded in 1540 on an Inca site, it produces leather goods, alpaca wool textiles, and foodstuffs.

3. Because of inflows of U.S. dollars for investment, privatization purchase, repatriation of savings to capture high interest rates set by tight monetary policy, and, in the Peruvian case, exacerbated by enormous inflows of coca leaf money.

4. Depending on whether measured versus purchasing power parity or relative to continued inflation (the exchange rate has held steady even though inflation remains in the teens, rendering a set dollar price worth less and less in real *sol* terms).

Chapter 6

1. Chris Argyris, *Overcoming Organizational Defenses: Facilitating Organizational Learning* (Boston: Allyn and Bacon, 1990), 10, emphasis added.

2. Ibid., 88.

3. Ibid.

Chapter 7

1. *Microsoft Bookshelf: Multimedia Reference Library,* 1995.

2. We have had this discussion many times with Michael Porter and have read Krugman and others on the topic. Our conclusion is that macroeconomists often see devaluation as a "correction" and microeconomists often see it as a subsidy for exporters.

3. Author interview with President Fujimori, April 1995.

4. Author interviews with World Bank officials and soy producers.

5. Complex trade is determined by analyzing the mix of approximately 3,000 products according to UN SITC Trade Statistics. These 3,000 products are then grouped according to industry, upstream products, related and supporting industries, and downstream products. This analysis was done for the Minister of Industry, La Paz, Bolivia, March 1996.

6. Bill Gates, *The Road Ahead* (New York: Viking, 1995).

Part Two

1. See James Austin's *Managing in Developing Countries* (New York: Free Press, 1990), for a very useful treatment of how these four variables interact.

Chapter 8

1. While most government economists equate productivity with labor productivity, our view is that productivity is best captured using multifactor productivity variables: capital, labor, energy, and raw materials. While, roughly speaking, knowledge is part of a firm's labor capital, it is increasingly important to think of knowledge as a specialized asset that must be captured, managed, and deployed in a discrete way, so we have listed it as separate from both capital and labor.

2. There is currently an engaging debate amongst leading strategy thinkers as to whether this bimodal thinking—either low-cost or differentiated—is still warranted. Some argue that there are world class examples of firms that have achieved a low-cost and highly differentiated position at the same time. We believe that if this is true, it is enabled by a robust competitive platform that a region or nation has developed, which supports such strong innovation.

   Our experience, however, is more clear: that in developing nations, the quality of the competitive platform rarely supports innovation on two such separate dimensions. We have suggested to leaders, therefore, in developing countries to choose one of the two dimensions on which to focus and succeed before attempting to innovate on the other.

   We anticipate this will be a bigger issue over the next few years and are hopeful that we will provide more research for scholars.

3. Michael Porter, *Competitive Advantage* (New York: Free Press, 1995), 120.

4. For an interesting discussion on cost accounting, see H. Thomas Johnson and Robert S. Kaplan, *Relevance Lost: The Rise and Fall of Management Accounting* (Boston: Harvard Business School Press, 1987).

5. The World Bank has published a compelling analysis of Southeast Asia's economic success that we recommend to those interested in national economic strategies. See *The East Asian Miracle: Economic Growth and Public Policy* (Washington, D.C.: World Bank, 1993). See also chapter 10 of this book for a more detailed discussion of national strategies.

6. Monitor Company's leadership surveys on wealth creation, productivity, and innovation.

7. Porter, *Competitive Advantage*, 199.

Chapter 9

1. Michael Porter, *Competitive Strategy* (New York: Free Press, 1980).

Chapter 10

1. For a very helpful treatment, see Keith Griffin, *Alternative Strategies for Economic Development* (New York: St. Martin's Press, 1989).

2. See *Monitor National Studies: Colombia 1993,* available at Ministry of Devel-

opment and IFI in Bogotá; *Peru 1995,* Ministry of Trade and Industry and PromPeru in Lima; and *Bolivia 1996,* available at the Ministry of Industry in La Paz.

Chapter 11

1. Our surveys have been taken for four years in seven countries on four continents and routinely question 250 to 500 public and/or private sector leaders in a one- to three-hour session on topics ranging from wealth creation, firm-level competitiveness, human capital, leadership, and change. The surveys are administered under controlled conditions and are kept to a standard of precision and comfort as measured by Monitor's team of statistical experts and specialists.

2. The survey respondents were chosen from lists of some of the most influential individuals in the public and private sector. The lists were generated in cooperation with the Government of Venezuela and various private sector chambers of commerce agencies, and they reflect a broad spectrum of industries and organizations. The surveys in Venezuela were administered to groups of ten to fifty respondents, with a trained team of Monitor employees present to brief and debrief respondents, as well as answer questions. Respondents were encouraged to be honest and were assured that their responses would be kept confidential. To limit response bias, throughout the invitation and administration process, the team did not mention that this was a study of openness and innovation; instead, the survey was labeled simply "national economic opinion survey." With only a few exceptions, the survey questions were closed-end; most were presented as seven-point scales.

3. The segmentation process was twofold: First, sixty individual questions were factor analyzed using principal components methodology and Varimax rotation/extraction. The handful of questions not already in seven-point format were transformed to match that format before being added to the analysis. Fourteen factors were chosen a priori to best compromise between parsimony and preciseness, and the mix of variables was pared down in an iterative process to avoid confounds and multiple loadings. The resulting fourteen-factor solution explained 50 percent of the total variance in the model—an acceptable level in the social sciences and certainly understandable given the diverse set of topics addressed in the survey. In the final analysis, each variable was assigned to the factor that it had weighed most upon, and the mean of each variable in the factor became the raw factor score. In the second stage, respondents were grouped based on their (normalized) responses to the fourteen factors using a hierarchical cluster analysis. We examined the resulting four-, five-, and six-cluster solutions and determined the five-cluster solution to be the most explanatory and striking.

4. Francis Fukuyama, *Trust: The Social Virtues and the Creation of Prosperity* (New York: Free Press, 1995).

Chapter 12

1. Eli Heckscher, Swedish economy professor of Bertil Ohlin, 1889–1979, Swedish economist and political leader. Ohlin taught (1924–1929) at the University of Copenhagen and later at the Stockholm School of Economics. He also led Sweden's Liberal party (1944–1967) and was Minister of Commerce (1944–1945). He shared the 1977 Nobel Prize in economics for his pioneering studies of international trade.
2. This phrase is taken from a speech by Mark Fuller, Chairman and CEO of the Monitor Company.
3. Moore's law, named after one of the cofounders of Intel, who in 1965 predicted that computing power per unit of price would double every two years into the near future. He was almost right. As it turns out, it has happened almost every eighteen months over the past thirty years.
4. There are six trade arrangements in the Western Hemisphere, and Colombia, for example, belongs to three. President Bush announced at the end of his administration that in the near future we would see NAFTA extended from "Alaska to Tierra Del Fuego." The participants at the Miami summit for the Western Hemispheric nations in 1995 agreed to eliminate all tariff and protection barriers in Latin America by the year 2007.
5. Ohmae, *Borderless World*.
6. In the last one hundred years manufactured trade has risen from 20 percent of trade to 80 percent. See Jeffrey Sachs and Andrew Warner's "Natural Resource Abundance and Economic Growth," National Bureau of Economic Research, Cambridge, Mass., working paper 5398, December 1995.
7. Paul Krugman, *"The Myth of Asia's Miracle:" Pop Internationalism* (Cambridge, Mass.: MIT Press, 1996), 175.
8. For background on productivity, see Kenneth Button and Thomas Weyman-Jones, "X-efficiency and Technical Efficiency," *Public Choice* 80, no. 83–104 (1994) (Kluwer Academic Publishers, Netherlands); Harvey Liebenstein "Allocative Efficiency vs. X-efficiency," University of California at Berkeley; and Richard Nelson, "Research of Productivity Growth and Productivity Difference: Deadends and New Departures," *Journal of Economic Literature* 20 (September 1981): 1029–1064.
9. This discussion benefited from conversations with Bruce Chew. For a look at the paper that alerted us to this dynamic, please see Bruce Chew, Kim B. Clark, and Steven C. Wheelright, *Dynamic Manufacturing: Creating the Learning Organization* (New York: Free Press, 1988).
10. Ikujiro Nonoaka and Hirotaka Takeuchi, *The Knowledge Creating Company: How Japanese Companies Create the Dynamics of Innovation* (Oxford: Oxford Press, 1995).

11. Monitor surveys of leaders show that technology is often regarded as a silver bullet that will make everything better and that tacit knowledge of how to do simpler, more routine tasks is often undervalued.

12. Cobb-Douglas formula.

13. For the complete treatment of the competitive diamond, please see Porter, *Competitive Advantage of Nations*.

14. Monitor research in Europe as part of our region-based studies.

15. See *The Asian Miracle* and *Enterprise Training in Developing Countries: Overview of Incidence, Determinants, and Productivity Outcomes* (Washington D.C.: World Bank).

16. See Wilson Peres and Ludovico Alcorta, "Innovation Systems and Technological Specialization in Latin America and the Caribbean," ECLAC/UNDP, New York, at the United Nations University, 1996, for good primary data and an excellent bibliography.

17. Countries profiled include all types of economies, sizes, and trade profiles: Argentina, Bolivia, Brazil, Canada, Chile, China, Colombia, Costa Rica, Ecuador, France, Germany, India, Indonesia, Italy, Japan, Korea, Malaysia, Mexico, Pakistan, Russia, Singapore, Spain, Sweden, Switzerland, Turkey, United Kingdom, United States, and Venezuela.

18. The correlation coefficient is +0.29.

19. This correlation is +.88 overall and is highest in the power generation, multibusiness, transport, and defense clusters, followed by telecom and office equipment. Again, see Sachs and Warner's "Natural Resource Abundance and Economic Growth."

20. See Robert D. Putnam, *Making Democracy Work, Civic Traditions in Italy* (Princeton: Princeton University Press, 1993), on the effects of civic culture on wealth generation.

21. The U.S. automobile industry is notorious for destroying this type of trust, unlike Japan's *keiretsu*, which have developed a greater degree of trust (and equity stakes in) supplier relations. For a fascinating discussion of Chrysler's efforts to develop its own *keiretsu*, see Jeffrey H. Dyer, "How Chrysler Created an American *Keiretsu*," *Harvard Business Review*, June/July 1996, 42.

22. Monitor's national survey of almost five hundred Venezuelan business, government, and academic leaders, undertaken in mid-1996. This survey was the basis of the discussion in chapter 11.

Chapter 13

1. Paul Krugman, "The Fall and Rise of Development Economics," *in Rethinking the Development Experience*, edited by Lloyd Rodwin and Donald Schon (Washington, D.C: Brookings Institution, 1994) 50.

2. Ibid., 51.

3. See Diana Sean Schemo, "Ecaudor Vote Narrows Race to Privatizer and Populist," *New York Times*, May 20, 1996.

4. See Monitor Company, "Creating the Competitive Advantage of Venezuela, Phase I," Ministry of Industry and Commerce, Caracas, Venezuela, Summer 1996.

5. We looked specifically at the DuPont equation, a detailed cash flow model, and a sources and uses diagram, all of which we built into one model of firm-level performance. Our financial statement analysis has been performed on scores of companies in approximately twenty sectors in half a dozen underdeveloped countries.

6. Moisés Naim, "Latin America's Journey to the Market: From Macroeconomic Shocks to Institutional Therapy," International Center for Economic Growth, San Francisco, 1995, occasional paper 62.

7. The word paradigm is open to many interpretations. Critics of Thomas S. Kuhn have found 22 distinct meanings for paradigm in his book, *The Structure of Scientific Revolutions* (Chicago: Chicago University Press, 1962).

8. John Maynard Keynes, British economist and author of *The General Theory of Employment, Interest, and Money* (Munchen: Duncker and Humbolt, 1936); quote is from the book's preface.

9. James Rudolph, *Peru: The Evolution of Crisis* (Westport, Conn.: Praeger Publishers,1992), 1–2 (emphasis added).

10. John Williamson and Stephen Haggard, "The Political Conditions for Economic Reform," in *The Political Economy of Policy Reform*, edited by John Williamson (Washington, D.C.: Institute for International Economics, 1994), 562.

11. Anders Aslund, *How Russia Became a Market Economy* (Washington, D.C.: Brookings Institution, 1995).

12. Kenichi Ohmae, *The End of the Nation State* (New York: Free Press,1995).

13. Peter Senge, *Fifth Discipline* (New York: Doubleday Currency, 1994), 147.

14. The philosopher Wittgenstein says that problems are not solved but dissolved. A strategist friend says that great strategy is reconciling what other people think are opposites.

Index

About the Authors

Michael Fairbanks is the coleader of the country competitive practice at Monitor Company. For more than a decade he has advised government and private sector officials throughout Africa, the Middle East, and South America. His clients have included heads of state, cabinet members, and chief executive officers. Fairbanks has also advised officials at the most senior levels of the World Bank as well as at development banks in Africa and South America.

He holds a degree in philosophy from Scranton University and a degree in African Politics from Columbia University. Before joining Monitor he worked for the U.S. Peace Corps as a teacher in Kenya; for the Department of State; and for the international divisions of Chase Manhattan Bank and the Hong Kong Shanghai Bank, specializing in financial advice to emerging nations.

His most recent activities include advising the Minister of Development in Venezuela and advising the Minister of Economic Development and the National Chambers of Commerce of Colombia as well as the African National Congress in South Africa, the President of the Republic of Tatarstan in the former Soviet Union, and the Mayor of Bogota, Colombia, on regional and national competitiveness strategy, human capital development, and company-level strategy.

Fairbanks has managed projects in more than 20 industrial sectors in 35 countries, including defense conversion for the State of California, petrochemicals and leather in Colombia, agro-industry and textiles in Peru, tourism in Ireland, telecommunications in Egypt, banking and

finance in Nigeria, defense conversion and the small business environment in the former Soviet Union, and forest products in Bolivia.

Fairbanks has given numerous competitiveness strategy seminars to
university audiences and public and private sector decision makers in
Western and Eastern Europe, South Africa, and South America as well
as recent speeches to the United Nations Conference Against Apartheid,
at the London School of Business; the Institute for the Americas, at the
University of California at San Diego; the Program on the Northern
Ireland Peace Process, at Harvard's Kennedy School of Government;
and the Distinguished Speakers Program, at Harvard Business School.

Stace Lindsay is the coleader of Monitor Company's Country Competitiveness practice in Latin America and the Caribbean. He is an adviser
to senior government officials, including several heads of state, and
chief executive officers throughout the region on international trade
performance, the impact of government policies on a nation's competitive environment, strategic options for industries facing increased
global competition, and firm-level strategic positioning.

He has lived and worked in Central America as a grass-roots development worker, and he holds degrees in International Relations from
Georgetown University and Oxford University, where he was a Rhodes
Scholar specializing in Latin American studies, with a focus on the
politics of humanitarian aid.

His recent activities include advising the Ministers of Economic Development in Colombia and Bolivia; the Minister of Industry, Tourism,
and International Trade in Peru; and the Ministers of Finance and
Economic Development in El Salvador. He initiated the National Competitiveness Seminar for senior government and business leaders in
Colombia, Peru, and Bolivia and is actively involved in training business leaders in firm-level strategy throughout the region. He is also an
adviser to a leading microfinance organization working to provide
access to capital for microentrepreneurs.

Lindsay has managed complex, multinational teams of professionals
in analyzing approximately 20 sectors in many countries including
tourism, clothing and agro-industry in Peru; flowers, textiles, and capital goods in Colombia; and the small business environment and the soy
industry in Bolivia.

He is often quoted in the international and regional press and has
written articles for trade journals on strategy and competitiveness. He

is a regular speaker at annual meetings and special events of regional chambers of commerce, industry associations, and universities. He has also been a featured speaker at the Harvard Business School and the Kennedy School of Government's Conference on International Economic Development.

Monitor Company is an international strategy consulting firm founded in 1983 by Harvard Business School professor Mark Fuller, the current president and CEO, and a group of colleagues. The company began with the mission of applying concepts developed by members of the Harvard Business School's business strategy area with the goal of ensuring that clients take the actions necessary to build sustainable competitiveness. Monitor Company has traditionally worked with individual companies to answer their most pressing strategic questions: how to penetrate new markets, what businesses to enter, how to anticipate and exploit changes in the competitive environment. Since 1990, Monitor has extended its network of clients to include regions and nations around the world. Monitor has worked with governments and businesses to enhance the international competitiveness of industries and regions. Today the firm, with 700 consultants in 14 offices on 5 continents, draws on a wide array of intellectual and industry resources to serve the global needs of its clients.